Employment and Industrial Relati

The European Foundation for the Improvement of Living and Working Conditions is an autonomous body of the European Union, created to assist the formulation of future policy on social and work-related matters. Further information can be found at the Foundation web site: http://www.eurofound.ie/

Employment and Industrial Relations in Europe

Volume I

Edited by

Michael Gold

and

Manfred Weiss

European Foundation

for the Improvement of Living and Working Conditions

1999

Kluwer Law International

The Hague / London / Boston

Library of Congress Cataloging-in-Publication Data

ISBN 92-828-5386-1 (OPOCE)
ISBN 90-411-1205-7 (KLI)

Published by Kluwer Law International,
P.O. Box 85889, 2508 CN The Hague, The Netherlands.

Sold and distributed in North, Central and South America
by Kluwer Law International,
675 Massachusetts Avenue, Cambridge, MA 02139, U.S.A.

In all other countries, sold and distributed
by Kluwer Law International, Distribution Centre,
P.O. Box 322, 3300 AH Dordrecht, The Netherlands.

This publication is developed from the series
European Employment and Industrial Relations Glossaries,
copublished for the Foundation by the Office for Official Publications
of the European Communities and Sweet & Maxwell.

Printed on acid-free paper

Printed in the Netherlands.

Foreword

European economic, monetary and social integration have seen substantial progress in the last 15 years. Developments in regulations and practices, and increased social dialogue on employment and industrial relations, have all contributed to this process. The Foundation believes that social dialogue at the international level can both enhance and benefit from a better understanding of the different national contexts in which dialogue takes place. An essential prerequisite for such improved understanding is an awareness of the principal aspects of the national industrial relations systems. This publication, covering eight EU countries, and its companion volume, which will cover the remaining seven, set out the key elements and concepts of industrial relations in the different Member States, from a comparative perspective.

The Foundation hopes that this publication will be useful to a variety of users and will be seen as a suitable complement to its other activities in the field of industrial relations, such as the EIRO database, and the series of *European Employment and Industrial Relations Glossaries.*

Clive Purkiss   Eric Verborgh
Director   Deputy Director

Contents

Notes on Contributors

Editors

Michael Gold: Royal Holloway College, University of London (European business and employee relations). He is also consultant editor of the European Industrial Relations Observatory based at the Foundation in Dublin.

Manfred Weiss: J.W. Goethe University in Frankfurt am Main (labour and civil law). He has held numerous visiting professorships overseas and has acted as consultant for many years to the European Commission, the ILO and various governments, particularly in Eastern Europe.

Belgium

Roger Blanpain: Catholic University of Leuven (comparative labour law and industrial relations). Amongst many other positions, he has been editor-in-chief of the *International Encyclopaedia for Labour Law and Industrial Relations* since 1975.

Nancy Luyten: admitted to the Brussels Bar in 1992. She has wide experience of international labour and social security law, and has worked at the Catholic University of Leuven (labour law) since 1994.

Denmark

Ole Hasselbalch: Aarhus School of Business (labour law). He has worked as a lawyer and research director for the Danish Employers' Confederation and currently edits *Arbejdsretlig Orientering*. He also founded and runs a data retrieval system on labour law, *Arbejdsretsorientering*.

Germany

Manfred Weiss: J.W. Goethe University in Frankfurt am Main (labour and civil law). He has held numerous visiting professorships overseas and has acted as consultant for many years to the European Commission, the ILO and various governments, particularly in Eastern Europe.

Greece

Yota Kravaritou: Aristotle University of Thessaloniki and European University Institute in Florence (law). She has also worked at the Institut d'Études Européenes at the Free University of Brussels. Her specialist area is equal opportunities.

Italy

Serafino Negrelli: University of Brescia (industrial relations). His interests focus on the motor, telecommunications and banking sectors. He also sits on the executive committee of the Associazione Italiana di Studio delle Relazioni Industriali.

Tiziano Treu: Catholic University of Milan (labour law). He is president of the International Industrial Relations Association and became Minister for Labour and Social Security in the Italian Government in 1995.

The Netherlands

Paul van der Heijden: University of Amsterdam (labour law) and director of the Hugo Sinzheimer Institute since 1989. He has also worked in the Dutch Ministry of Justice and as a judge in the Court of Law, Amsterdam.

Portugal

Pedro Furtado Martins: Catholic University of Portugal (law) and Labour Research Centre. He contributes to the European Industrial Relations Observatory, and specializes in the areas of employment contracts and dismissals.

António Nunes de Carvalho: Catholic University of Portugal (law) and Labour Research Centre. He is also a member of the Portuguese team contributing to the European Industrial Relations Observatory.

Mário Pinto: Catholic University of Portugal (labour law) and director of its Labour Research Centre. Amongst other publications, he has contributed the section on Portugal for the *International Encyclopaedia for Labour Law and Industrial Relations.*

Spain

Antonio Martín Valverde: judge in the Social Chamber of the Spanish Supreme Court. He has also taught and published widely, and was formerly director of the Department of Labour Law and Social Security at the University of Seville.

Introduction

Michael Gold and Manfred Weiss

The idea for this volume, which contains analyses of the industrial relations systems in eight Member States of the European Union, arose out of a long-standing project of the Foundation: the publication of a set of European Employment and Industrial Relations Glossaries covering all 15 Member States. These glossaries, which are published in an international English version (and some also in their national language), provide a comprehensive guide to industrial relations institutions and terminology that has already proved invaluable to practitioners and academics alike.

Writing in 1991, Prof. Tiziano Treu stated in his preface to the series: 'The development of social dialogue, and the ever-increasing need for debate and discussion between the Member States, employers and unions, spurred by the prospect of full European economic integration in 1992, have given a fresh impetus to the need for clarity and mutual understanding in this vital subject.' He added that the thousands of potential users across Europe of the glossaries included national and international administrators, academics and researchers, trade unionists and managers, and specialist journalists, amongst others.

As the feedback proves, the series has become a success: 12 of the 15 glossaries are now available, and updating of the earliest ones is under way. They have become an indispensable tool for a large group of users, which has borne out the truth of Prof. Treu's words. In fact, since then, the 'need for clarity and mutual understanding' has dramatically increased. The reasons for this are complex but include the following aspects: the consolidation of the European monetary union programme, which will place even greater emphasis on the requirement for 'flexible' labour markets; the intention of the European Commission to create a social dimension that already includes the rapid development of European works councils and the internationalization of information disclosure and consultation within multinational companies; the sharpening awareness of industrial relations as a productive factor in competitiveness at both national and European levels; and continuing debates about the nature and desirability of convergence of national industrial relations institutions.

Within this context, the Foundation decided to update and revise the introductory essays to each of the glossaries and publish them in two volumes, the first one of which is here before you. It contains contributions on eight of the current Member States of the European Union: Belgium, Denmark, Germany, Greece, Italy, the Netherlands, Portugal and Spain. They were each originally published as the introduction to the respective country volume in the international English language version. However, as outlined in greater detail below, each has now been thoroughly revised and updated.

Contents

The contributions to this book all focus on three principal aspects of comparative industrial relations. The first is an analysis of the strikingly similar **pressures** which have assailed the industrial relations arrangements in each country covered over recent years. The second is the degree to which these institutional arrangements have nevertheless retained their diverse national **identities** under such pressures. And the third is the **development of the institutions** themselves within the context of these pressures. Of course, increasingly convergent pressures do not by any means necessarily lead to convergent institutional outcomes.

The **pressures** referred to here are familiar and well documented, if sometimes controversial. They include structural economic change, such as the trend from manufacturing to services, rising levels of female participation in labour markets and the challenges associated with ageing populations. They include the effects of economic recession and the problem of unemployment. And they include the introduction of new technologies and the apparent shift in manufacturing techniques away from old 'Fordist' paradigms of mass production towards those of 'flexible specialization' (Piore and Sabel, 1984) and 'diversified quality production' (Streeck, 1992). These pressures have themselves mounted in the context of progressive trade liberalization on a global scale and the creation of the single European market and preparations for economic and monetary union. Meanwhile, unemployment, the decline in trade union densities across much of Europe and the crisis of the welfare state have enabled governments of all political persuasions to adopt neo-liberal or deregulatory labour market policies. This has in turn helped to tilt the balance of power within industry and services towards the employers, who have taken the chance to adopt more individualistic employment policies, including a range of human resource management techniques. At the same time, the collapse of the Soviet bloc has led to a greater degree of pragmatism amongst formerly pro-communist trade unions.

This, at any rate, is the composite European picture often depicted by commentators, though there remains a great deal of disagreement over the long-term significance of these trends. For example, some would argue that there is a process of re-regulation of labour markets under way across Europe rather than deregulation. A recent case is that of Italy, where the Employment Agreement signed in 1996, which has since been passed into law, covers the use of temporary agencies, which had hitherto been prohibited, and amends the legal regime governing areas like fixed-term contracts and part-time work in an attempt to both promote and regulate them. In addition, at EU level, it can be argued that recent Directives on parental leave and part-time work are designed to protect workers' interests when employers consider forms of 'flexible' working, not to eradicate them from the equation altogether.

The effects of these pressures on national institutions must be studied country by country. They are empirical matters that require close attention to developments and responses within specific institutional settings, but this requires first of all an accurate and up-to-date understanding of the **structural identities** of the institutions themselves. The structure of employers' associations and unions and their relationships, levels of collective bargaining, the role of the state and the legal framework of industrial relations and methods of resolving disputes, amongst many other institutional arrangements, are the result of lengthy historical processes in each individual country, which makes it possible to speak of the Danish, German, Italian or any other 'system'. Whilst some of these systems may be grouped together according to certain salient characteristics – such as the Roman, German or Nordic model – major differences within groupings remain substantial. For example, in the current volume, though Germany and the Netherlands are often regarded as closely comparable, it is clear that they diverge widely in the structure of their unions, the role of government in pay bargaining and the scope of co-determination at work. In the same way, Italy and Spain, which are often dubbed 'statist' in their approach to economic and labour policies, nevertheless vary greatly in the impact of collective bargaining on their respective systems. Reading the contributions on the eight countries contained in this volume gives a great impression of diversity and individuality in institutional settings.

Yet the interesting question centres on **institutional development**, that is, how these individual national settings adapt to or deal with the range of economic and social pressures noted above. How are concepts like 'flexibility' and 'decentralization' to be understood in countries as varied as Denmark and Greece? How successful are Belgium and Germany – with very different union structures – in creating employment? To what extent can the state in Italy or the Netherlands intervene to rectify perceived rigidities in the labour market? Does the political underpinning of the union movement in Portugal and Spain affect the ability of those countries to reform collective bargaining? Again, these are empirical questions which require close analysis of the institutional and legal frameworks within which governments, employers and unions formulate strategy and policy.

Some examples illustrate the interplay of pressures with institutional settings. Take 'decentralization'. The decentralization of decision-taking to lower levels in the organization is regarded as a way to improve the quality and effectiveness of decisions, since they then more closely reflect the views and interests of those affected. Decentralization, as a facet of flexibility, has affected all the countries covered in this volume to a greater or lesser degree though its contours vary. In Denmark, for example, it means a move away from multi-industry bargaining to sectoral-level bargaining. In the Netherlands, too, central agreements are now rare, and bargaining has moved down to sector or company level. In Germany, by contrast, where sectoral bargaining has always been the norm, decentralization has meant increased responsibilities for the works council at establishment level. Though it is technically against the law, works councils have been increasingly drawn into agreeing pay and conditions below those set at sector level in an attempt to keep the company or plant profitable and in business.

Opposite moves – towards centralized 'social pacts' – are noteworthy in the four southern countries, Greece, Italy, Portugal and Spain, in the 1990s. In Italy and

Spain, these may be seen as ad hoc measures designed to solve specific problems rather than as ongoing institutionalized processes. In Italy, for example, the state promoted a series of central tripartite pacts to help establish the conditions to meet the Maastricht criteria for entry into economic and monetary union (EMU), which in 1995 included reform of the pensions system. Meanwhile, in Portugal, a series of tripartite agreements under the auspices of the Economic and Social Council have covered areas like pay policy, employment, social security and taxation matters, and in Greece national general agreements have focused on a similar range of topics including reform of national insurance and pensions.

The notion of 'deregulation' can also be examined in national settings, with attention focusing on specific areas of perceived rigidity. For example, in Germany, Italy and the Netherlands, the state has lost its monopoly over the job placement service in recent years, whilst in Spain reforms have dealt with a wide range of issues, not least the cost of dismissals, which had been a serious grievance amongst employers for a long time. In Italy, attention focused on reforming and then abolishing the pay indexation system, the butt of employers' criticisms for many years.

Trade union responses to issues like flexibility and deregulation also reflect the influence of national institutional settings. A well-known, but rather elderly, theory categorizes these responses into four groups (Lange et al., 1982). The maximalist response, based on Marxist analysis, refuses to play any role in the management of capitalism, and so adopts an adversarial stance towards any attempts at incorporation. The French CGT and the Portuguese CGTP have traditionally provided examples: the CGTP has traditionally refused any involvement in tripartism at central level. The interventionist response, reflected in the approaches of, for example, the Italian and Spanish unions, assumes that partial intervention, as and when required, could help to alleviate the worst aspects of economic crisis. The defensive response is to refuse cooperation when confronted with job insecurity and pay cuts in an attempt to prevent undesired change: the breakdown of central agreements in Belgium in recent years provide an instance. Finally, a neo-corporatist strategy describes the policies of those unions that have cooperated with the state and employers over pay and employment policies. Amongst the countries represented in this volume, Denmark may be traditionally regarded as falling into this category.

Why do these categories now appear so out of date? This is because union power has weakened during the 1980s and 1990s, and the room for government policy to manoeuvre in the context of the Maastricht criteria and EMU has become increasingly restricted. Unions – of all political persuasions – have correspondingly come to acknowledge that their own opportunities to veto policies with which they disagree have shrunk. They have therefore tended to adopt more proactive, interventionist stances in an attempt to regain influence by sharing it. This to a large extent explains the background to the emergence of social pacts in southern Europe.

The maximalist and neo-corporatist categories, based as they are on an analysis of the years 1945-1980, are now particularly outdated. In Portugal, the policies of UGT and CGTP have gradually converged, as have those of all unions formerly associated with ex-communist parties, whilst in Denmark, and other Nordic countries, multi-industry regulation has broken down, as we saw above.

Layout

As noted above, the contributions published in this volume were each originally published as the introduction to the respective country volume in the English language version of the European Employment and Industrial Relations Glossaries.

However, each contribution has been thoroughly revised and updated – usually by the original author – to the time of writing. In addition, we have attempted to standardize some of the subheadings in the text in order to make it easier for the reader to cross-reference between country sections. However, this has not always been possible. Authors were not writing to a template and, in any case, complex institutional arrangements and procedures cannot always be made to fit neatly under standard headings. For example, there is no heading for 'disputes' in the German contribution; disputes resolution is covered under other subheadings such as 'collective bargaining'. By contrast, an extra section in the German contribution allows greater examination of employee representation on the supervisory board of companies, a subject that barely applies in other countries.

As far as possible, however, the following headings have been used for each country, though sometimes they have been combined, altered or adapted in line with the judgement of each author.

Historical Background

This section covers the major historical determinants of each country's industrial relations structure. These include the process and timing of industrialization and the struggle for union recognition and influence, which moulds the prevailing patterns of consensus and conflict, and often symbolizes the principal characteristics of the system in question. The role of the state is critical in this process, both as employer, legislator and, where appropriate, conciliator. Major historical events also play a key part in determining key features of the industrial relations structure. The post-Second World War settlements in countries like Italy and Germany are obvious examples, but the experience of dictatorship and the transition to democracy in Greece, Portugal and Spain are critical to an understanding of those countries. The oil crises of the 1970s are also crucial episodes in explaining the changing industrial relations climate, marking the switch in emphasis from demand-led economic management to the supply-side policies that characterize the 1980s and 1990s. The conclusion overall is that it is no longer adequate – if it ever was – to treat industrial relations systems as abstracted subsystems. They are inextricably interlinked as a productive factor with the macroeconomic institutions and competitive processes of the country concerned.

Economic and Social Context

The economic and social context includes analysis of the main features of the national labour markets. A central aspect focuses on the structure of the labour force: the proportions employed in manufacturing and services; in the private and public sectors, and in self-employment; in full-time and part-time work; amongst various age bands, and so on. The structure of unemployment is also examined: the proportion of workers who are young, or long-term unemployed or unskilled, amongst other characteristics. Other features of the labour market that vary considerably from country to country include the impact of the informal economy on employment relations, the numbers of disabled people and patterns of emigration, amongst others. Macroeconomic data are generally sketched in as appropriate to provide the backdrop to an analysis of the pressures on the labour market, with particular reference to national approaches to job creation measures. The impact of meeting the Maastricht criteria is a notable determinant in the evolution of labour market policy over recent years, though the ways in which policy is mediated depends very much on the institutional settings in question. Other features of the social and economic context include levels of social security expenditure and the structure of labour costs, insofar as they impinge on labour market policy.

Institutional and Legal Framework

In most of the countries covered in this volume, major pieces of legislation both define and reflect the framework of industrial relations. This framework embraces the rights and obligations of employers and workers, the employment relationship itself (in both its collective and individual aspects), major terms and conditions (such as minimum pay, hours and holidays) and other aspects of labour market regulation (such as job placement, health and safety, equal opportunities and so on). The law often, but not always (for example, Denmark), also structures patterns of collective bargaining, which may impose constraints on its development. In Germany, for example, decentralization is taking place to the level of the works council, even though collective bargaining is technically outside its competence.

Contributions also examine the role of legislation in governing the organization of employers' associations and trade unions and their mutual rights and obligations, as well as the role of case law and the courts in industrial relations (particularly significant in the case of, for example, Germany and the Netherlands). Other institutional aspects covered include the structure of public sector employment, employment services, unemployment insurance and the labour inspectorate and enforcement agencies.

Actors in Industrial Relations

Broadly, there are three sets of actors involved in the processes of industrial relations: employers, unions and the state. This section focuses on the structure of employers' associations and unions at various levels of interaction (multi-industry, sectoral, company and workplace). It looks at the density of union membership and the structure of the union movement, with reference to the degree of unity or fragmentation to be found on ideological, religious or regional grounds. It also reviews the determinants of the changing structure of unions over recent years and analyses notions of 'representativeness' and how this affects union effectiveness. The emergence of unofficial unions, as in Italy, comes under scrutiny, where appropriate.

The changing role of the state, in all its dimensions, is critical in understanding the dynamics of industrial relations in Europe. In some countries it plays a limited role (as in Denmark), whilst in others it has played a key role at crucial moments of a country's history (Portugal and Spain are clear examples). In some it appears to be playing an increasing part (arguably in Italy), whilst in others it is increasingly withdrawing from involvement (such as in the Netherlands).

Collective Bargaining

The backbone of an industrial relations system in any industrialized country is the framework of collective bargaining. These frameworks vary dramatically across the eight countries contained in this volume. Each section under this heading examines the levels at which collective bargaining is conducted, the often complex relationships between levels, the normal length of agreements and the role of 'extensions' (that is, how collective agreements can be extended to cover employers and workers who were not themselves signatories). The decentralization of collective bargaining has already been alluded to above, and it is striking how greatly patterns vary. In Germany, Italy and Spain, for example, there is an important territorial or geographical aspect to the process of collective bargaining, whilst in Greece occupational bargaining predominates. In other countries, the sector or company remain the key bargaining units (such as Denmark or the Netherlands).

Bargaining patterns in the public and, where appropriate, semi-public sectors are examined, as well as other relevant aspects, such as the role of peace obligations and current controversies (such as the debate over the abolition of extensions in the Netherlands).

Participation and Employee Representation at the Workplace

Widely varying forms of employee participation are a further characteristic of European industrial relations systems. Each contribution analyses prevailing forms of employee participation by level, subject and method. They range in scope from the German system, where long-standing arrangements – including worker directors – give employees rights to information disclosure, consultation and co-determination at all levels in many companies (depending on size thresholds), to the Italian system, where forms of participation have been largely absent and employee representation at the workplace takes place through union channels. Systems vary too as to whether they are based on legal regulation (as in most countries) or on collective agreement (as in Denmark) and on location. In Italy, for example, participation has tended to take place in the public rather than the private sector.

With respect to the works council, each contribution examines its relationship with the unions, its competence and its changing role over recent years. This might include its part in regulating new human resource management techniques or total quality management, which has proved controversial in countries like the Netherlands.

Disputes

There has, across Europe as a whole, been a general decline in strike activity since the late 1970s. Contributions generally examine strike trends and the changing pattern of conflict within each country, with particular reference to relevant determining factors. In some countries, such as Italy and Spain, the level of industrial conflict remains comparatively high. In Spain strikes are generally brief and intermittent and designed to put pressure on the public authorities to take action. In other countries, such as Denmark, Germany and the Netherlands, where peace obligations are a normal part of collective agreements, levels of industrial conflict have fallen to historically very low levels, despite the occasional blip.

Contributions also cover dispute resolution and the role of specialist agencies and labour tribunals in the processes of conciliation, mediation and arbitration. These have evolved greatly in recent years, particularly in Greece, where compulsory arbitration has given way to voluntary settlement procedures. The introduction of strike codes in the public sector has also been a notable recent development in the containment of conflict in Italy and Portugal. The issue of lockouts is also addressed, where appropriate.

Prospects and Conclusions

The final section of each country contribution concludes with a discussion of major trends and developments and takes a forward look at future prospects. It examines issues like forms of flexibility, decentralization, the evolving pattern of employment relationships, the changing nature of employers' associations and unions, and other aspects of industrial relations specific to the country in question. The impact of membership of the European Union is a matter of concern to some of the authors.

Key Employment Indicators

During the course of writing their contributions, authors refer liberally to statistics on macroeconomic, labour market and other indicators, usually drawn from their own national sources. However, readers will often want to make comparisons between countries based on common international indicators. Only in this way can trends and tendencies be genuinely contrasted.

For this reason, we have appended a set of tables to the main body of the text at the end of this volume. They cover all 15 Member States of the European Union and draw on two important sources of data: *Employment in Europe 1997*, published by the European Commission, and the *World Labour Report 1997-98*, published by the International Labour Organization in Geneva. The tables cover the following areas:

- key employment indicators (all employees; men; women);
- trade union membership;
- trade union density;
- changes in trade union density;
- number of strikes and lockouts;
- workers involved in strikes and lockouts;
- workdays not worked as a result of strikes and lockouts; and
- collective bargaining structures and their evolution.

Acknowledgements

We should like to thank all the contributors to this volume for the time and trouble they took in updating and revising their entries, and in particular for their patience and good humour in agreeing to a second round of revisions when serious delays held up the prompt submission of the final manuscript.

Hubert Krieger, the research manager for the Foundation, provided the dynamism for the project, and Rita Inston of Cave Translations Ltd. was exceptional not only as translator and reviser but also as valued adviser.

M.G., M.W. – June 1998

Further Reading

Lange, P. *et al.*, *Unions, Change and Crisis: French and Italian Unions and the Political Economy, 1945-1980,* London, Allen & Unwin, 1982.

Piore, M. and Sabel, C., *The Second Industrial Divide: Possibilities for Prosperity,* New York, Harper & Row, 1984.

Streeck, W., *Social Institutions and Economic Performance,* London, Sage Publications, 1992.

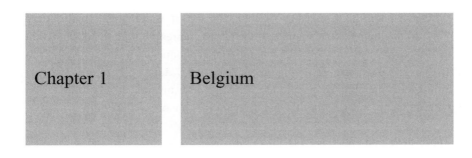

Chapter 1 Belgium

Roger Blanpain and Nancy Luyten

Economic and Social Context

The context in which industrial relations in Belgium are evolving is increasingly international. The factors are well known: globalization of the economy, the introduction of new technologies, especially in the handling of data flows, and demographic development. The result is that decisions are taken over the heads of the national actors – the government as well as the social partners (employers' associations and trade unions). On top of that, there are the Maastricht criteria for EU Member States to qualify for economic and monetary union (EMU): inflation of less than 3 per cent and a national deficit of less than 60 per cent of GDP. This means that Belgium has to follow very rigid budgetary polices, which have led to controls on free collective bargaining and heavy cuts in social policies.

The new emerging information economy is having a dramatic impact on the nature of the employment relationship, which is becoming less hierarchical and more lateral, with the emphasis on teamwork and communication skills.

Belgium is also plagued by very high unemployment and ongoing restructurings, which in 1997 led to massive lay-offs and growing public resentment: Renault (3,100), Nova (420), Forges de Clabecq (1,800). Several job creation programmes have proved unsuccessful and unemployment remains on the increase.

Whereas the official statistics of the Ministry of Employment report only 779,120 unemployed and claim that the figures represent an increase of 30,000 in 1997 over 1996, they exclude a number of economically inactive people who are nevertheless also receiving unemployment benefits. Therefore, the real number of unemployed people can actually be estimated at 1,069,176, even without taking into account the massive lay-offs announced recently.

These developments have led to a dramatic shift in power relations between employers and unions, with the latter striving just to cling on in order to save jobs. Flexibility regarding individual employment contracts, working hours and pay is becoming more and more widespread. These features are of the greatest importance. Although the system remains formally in place, the influence of the industrial relations system on actual pay and employment conditions is losing momentum.

The Belgian economic system may be adequately described as a market economy with active government intervention in its cyclical and structural evolution. The economy is very open to the rest of the world, and two-thirds of all exports go to EU countries. While the 'system', and especially the profit motive, is challenged less nowadays than in the past, its existence has at the same time been repeatedly and explicitly recognized and legitimized. In most of the national multi-industry agreements concluded since the Second World War, the trade unions have recognized the necessity of the employer's legal authority (1944), of not changing the status of the enterprise or challenging the authority of the management (1954), and of respecting the employer's managerial responsibilities and decision-making power (1970). In 1971 and again in 1972 the trade unions recognized, as they had in a 1947 agreement, the necessity of the employer's legal authority, and considered it a point of honour for workers to perform their work dutifully. The latter agreements are still valid.

Belgium is a pluralistic society in which individuals and groups are allowed the freedom to promote their own interests, and in which social conflict is consequently inevitable and indeed an essential element in the decision-making process. This is patently the case in the Belgian industrial relations system, where employers and employees, enjoying a large degree of autonomy, settle their disputes of interest through industrial warfare. Conflict and strife are looked upon as essential to the autonomous decision-making process that characterizes the Belgian industrial relations system: free and effective collective bargaining is in fact impossible if workers do not, for example, have the freedom to withdraw their labour collectively as a means of trying to force the employer to accept their point of view. Or, to put it another way, in Belgium industrial relations are essentially a power relationship in which the decision-making power of the employer is challenged by the collective power that the workers are able to display.

Lately, however, the power relationship has again shifted in favour of the employer, mainly owing to massive unemployment. This has recently been leading to huge demonstrations directed at the creation of more jobs.

It should also be borne in mind that the profile of the 'average' employee has changed dramatically: the average worker is now better educated and has higher expectations, firstly for a (more) interesting job and life, and secondly for a sustained real income. The industrial worker, once the traditional base of trade union strength, is fading into the background; the new worker emerging, with more strongly pronounced part-time, female, white-collar and professional elements in the profile, is less ideologically motivated, more individualistic, and is looking towards a personal career rather than solidarity.

Industrial relations are also shaped by a number of economic factors. Despite its extremely favourable geographical situation, Belgium remains a small economic element in the Western capitalist world; even within the EU Belgium is a small nation, with its 10.1 million inhabitants out of the total Community population of some 373 million.

In addition, Belgium is a host to a great many foreign investors. Over 70 per cent of enterprises with more than 1,000 employees are owned by multinational corporations which take certain important decisions at headquarters located outside Belgium (eg Renault), decisions that are not subject to any local political or social control. It is clear that policies of this kind directly diminish the market power of the unions.

A report published in April 1997 by the Organization for Economic Cooperation and Development (OECD) praises the results gained by Belgium in reducing its budget deficit, but calls for renewed efforts to make the labour market more flexible.

Following an impressive effort at turning the economy round, Belgium has managed to reduce the deficit of its public administration from 7 per cent in

1992 to 3 per cent in 1996, and has made progress in bringing down its ratio of debt to gross domestic product from 130 per cent in 1996 to 127 per cent in 1997 and 124.5 per cent in 1998 (though still far from the 60 per cent mark envisaged under the convergence criteria laid down by the Maastricht Treaty).

In fact, overall, according to the OECD, 'prospects are good, except as regards the labour market'. 'Non-employment remains of great concern', the report stresses. However, 'rises in wage levels and in the individual remuneration of employees in the private sector seem to have been one of the lowest in the OECD area in 1996, and it could be that the unit costs of labour may have fallen, contributing to a quasi-stabilization of employment faced with a slow growth in the GDP'.

The Government has taken various labour market measures: reduction of certain non-wage costs, increased flexibility in the workplace, etc. But this merely serves to increase what is already considerable state intervention in the labour market, whereas the OECD considers that intervention by public authorities should be reduced in addition to 'considerably reducing the impressive number of programmes in favour of employment and assuring greater flexibility on the labour market.' The OECD considers Belgian legislation on job protection to be still too restrictive.

Finally, the report criticizes the lack of competition in some sectors: telecommunications, air transport, distribution, electricity (there are few electricity companies in the OECD area whose power in the market is as extensive as that of Electrabel).

Meanwhile, Belgium remains a country of small businesses. Indeed, in 1995, 97.26 per cent of the total number (226,214) of private employers employed fewer than 50 people. Nevertheless, 28.85 per cent of workers are employed in enterprises with more than 200 employees (0.56 per cent of the total number of private enterprises), 20.73 per cent of workers in enterprises employing between 50 and 199 employees (2.18 per cent of the total number of enterprises) and only 50.42 per cent of workers in enterprises with fewer than 50 employees (97.26 per cent of all enterprises). In 1995, only 103 companies employed more than 1,000 workers (9.21 per cent of the private sector labour force, or 201,169 workers). This has important consequences, and in fact implies a dual labour system in Belgium. Taking the size of the enterprise into account is a long-established practice in employment legislation and industrial relations. A works council has to be set up only in those enterprises which employ, on average, at least 100 employees; a workplace prevention and protection committee (known as a 'health and safety committee' prior to the entry into force of the Welfare Act of 4 August 1996) only where there are 50 employees; and a 'union delegation', depending on the collective agreements in force, only when, for example, 25 or 50 workers are employed. As a result, in the majority of enterprises there are no works councils, workplace prevention and protection committees or 'union delegations', and so, for a significant number of employees, there is no workers' representation at this level. Quite evidently, the unions have less influence in smaller enterprises as compared with larger companies. However, as will be seen later, it has to be remembered that collective agreements covering pay and terms and conditions, whether at national multi-industry level or at industry level, can be extended and thus made binding on all employers operating in the private sector as a whole or in the branch of industry concerned, so that all employees will benefit from the provisions of the collective agreement.

Actors in Industrial Relations

Trade Unions
There are no official figures on trade union membership in Belgium. According to the OECD figures, 53 per cent of employees are organized, which gives Belgium a high level of unionization for a free enterprise economy and the highest of any country with union pluralism. Recently membership has been declining. According to the European Commission-funded survey *Eurobarometer*, the overall unionization rate in Belgium (based on information collected in the spring of 1991) would officially amount to only some 36.7 per cent. The degree of organization is much higher in the industrial sectors (up to 80 per cent) than in service industries, such as banking and insurance (23 per cent). In the major industrial sectors, such as building, metals, chemicals, cement, petroleum and mining, more than 90 per cent of blue-collar workers are organized. White-collar workers tend to organize less (approximately 23 per cent), while managerial personnel are rarely organized, although they are legally entitled to join unions under the 1921 Freedom of Association Act and to bargain collectively under the 1968 Collective Agreements and Joint Committees Act. The most important trade union organizations are the Confederation of Christian Trade Unions (ACV-CSC) and the socialist-inclined Belgian General Federation of Labour (ABVV-FGTB), followed by the less important Federation of Liberal Trade Unions of Belgium (ACLV-CGSLB).

With regard to membership, the Christian trade unions claim to have 1,581,516 affiliated members (1995), the socialist trade unions 1,176,701 (1995) and the liberal trade unions 216,423 (1996).

The respective strength of the three union federations is also reflected in the results that the unions obtain in the 'social elections' for works councils and workplace prevention and protection committees (health and safety committees), which are held every four years. All employees are entitled to vote in these elections, whether or not they are members of a union. In the 1995 elections, there was an expected total of 3,065 works councils and 5,304 workplace prevention and protection committees in the profit-making sector, of which 2,197 works councils and 3,819 workplace committees were finally elected. Actually, 12 per cent of profit-making companies did not proceed with the election procedure for a works council despite the legal obligation to do so (and 21 per cent did not proceed with the election procedure for a workplace committee) because of a lack of candidates or because only one union possessing representative status put forward a list of candidates. National results in the profit-making sector were as follows: Confederation of Christian Trade Unions 51.68 per cent of seats (works councils) and 54.08 per cent (workplace committees); Belgian General Federation of Labour 39.41 per cent (works councils) and 40.08 per cent (workplace committees); and Federation of Liberal Trade Unions of Belgium 1.57 per cent (works councils) and 5.84 per cent (workplace committees).

An innovation in 1987 was that for the first time elections were held for *kaderleden/cadres* (professional and managerial staff) on the works councils. Here, independent candidates and a separate union for professional and managerial staff can participate in the elections, in addition to the traditional representative unions. In the 1995 elections, the division of seats was as follows: independent candidates 21 per cent of seats; separate professional and managerial staff union 19 per cent of seats; Confederation of Christian Trade Unions 35 per cent of seats; Belgian General Federation of Labour 17 per cent of seats; and Federation of Liberal Trade Unions 7 per cent of seats.

Belgian trade unions are not organized on a craft or occupational basis, but by industry. However, both the socialist and Christian federations have a separate division for white-collar workers, irrespective of the particular industry to which they actually belong. The Confederation of Christian Trade Unions and the Belgian General Federation of Labour have essentially the same structure:

both are federations of national trade unions organized, for the most part, by sector of industry (important exceptions being the separate white-collar divisions and the public sector unions). The Federation of Liberal Trade Unions of Belgium has a unified structure.

Employers
The principal Belgian employers' association is the Federation of Belgian Enterprises (VBO-FEB). The Federation was formed in 1973 by the merger of the Federation of Belgian Industries and the Federation of Non-Industrial Enterprises (banks, insurance services and so on). It now comprises 35 industry-level associations covering some 35,000 affiliated firms, of which some 25,000 are small and medium-sized enterprises. These national associations cover most sectors of economic life, with the exception of agriculture, small shops, handicrafts and the nationalized industries. There is also the National Christian Federation of Small Firms and Traders (NCMV), and a number of agricultural organizations. The Belgian employers' associations have a very important role to play: not only do they give legal, fiscal, economic and other advice to their members, but they also engage in collective bargaining. While the Federation is active centrally at national multi-industry level, the industry associations take care of the sectoral level.

Whereas the VBO-FEB consists only of national associations, the NCMV comprises about 81,000 individual employers, of whom some 6,500 are in the liberal professions. Regional employers' organizations such as the Vlaams Economisch Verbond (Flemish Employers' Association), the Union Wallone des Entreprises (Walloon Employers' Association) and the Brussels Federation are becoming increasingly important.

Legal Status of Unions and Employers' Associations
To understand the system of labour relations in Belgium, it is essential to grasp what is meant by the term 'most representative trade union organization'. Only three organizations (the Confederation of Christian Trade Unions, the Belgian General Federation of Labour and the Federation of Liberal Trade Unions of Belgium) are recognized as 'most representative' by the Government and the employers' associations.

The concept of 'most representative organizations' is defined in various laws relating to the National Labour Council (1952), collective agreements and Joint Committees (1968), works councils (1948) and workplace prevention and protection committees (1996). The following are examples of the criteria that an organization must satisfy in order to qualify for 'most representative' status:

a. in the case of trade unions, they must be:

  • multi-industry employees' organizations which are established at national level, are represented on the Central Economic Council and National Labour Council and have at least 50,000 members; or
  • industrial unions affiliated to or forming part of a national multi-industry organization;

b. in the case of employers' associations, they must be:

  • multi-industry employers' organizations which are established at national level and are represented on the Central Economic Council and National Labour Council;
  • organizations affiliated to or forming part of a national multi-industry organization;
  • occupational organizations which, in any given branch of industrial activity, are declared representative by Royal Decree on the advice of the National Labour Council; or
  • national multi-industry and occupational organizations, approved under the Law of 6 March 1964 providing for the institutional structure of small firms and traders, which are representative of the heads of enterprises in handicrafts, small- and medium-scale trades and small-scale industry and self-employed persons carrying on a liberal profession or some other type of professional work.

With regard to these criteria, the ILO Committee of Experts on the Application of Conventions and Recommendations recently called on the Belgian Government to adapt its legislation, in the near future, to ensure by law that objective, predetermined and detailed criteria are adopted in establishing rules for the access of trade unions and employers' organizations to the National Labour Council, since the Act of 20 May 1952 establishing the National Labour Council still contains no specific criteria on representative status but leaves wide powers of discretion to the Government.

The organizations that are recognized as most representative enjoy a monopoly in law and practice in representing workers' interests at national, industry and enterprise level. They are the only organizations represented on the official Joint Committees, composed of employers' and employees' representatives, within which a great deal of collective bargaining is done. The responsible bodies are:

at national multi-occupation or multi-industry level, the National Labour Council; at industry level, the Joint Committee; and at enterprise level, the works council and the workplace prevention and protection committee. The organizations recognized as most representative, which for all practical purposes are the Christian, the liberal and the socialist unions, have to be accepted and negotiated with as the duly authorized bargaining representatives of the workers.

In 1985, however, the Works Councils Act of 1948 was amended in order to pave the way for recognition by the Executive (the Minister for Employment and Labour) of a new category of representative union: a representative union for *kaderleden/cadres,* ie, professional and managerial staff. This is defined as a multi-industry union which is established at national level and organizes at least 10,000 professional and managerial staff members.

Historical and Institutional Background

With more than 50 per cent of employees organized, Belgium has one of the highest levels of unionization of any European free enterprise economy, and the highest of any country with union pluralism. This pluralism is due to the ideological differences that still mark Belgian industrial relations. The various trade unions hold conflicting views on issues such as the role of the State in public life, the place of private enterprise, privatization, and the programmes and goals of the education system; and they seek to win over public opinion to their way of thinking on these and other matters. Ideological conflicts are so deeply rooted that the trade unions themselves also form part of larger movements, as do political parties and cultural organizations that share and defend the same beliefs. More and more often, however, a pragmatic approach prevails and ideological differences tend to fade in the face of the challenges presented by globalization and the introduction of new technologies, which are largely beyond the control of the social actors at national (ie, Belgian) level and often make them look powerless with less and less influence on the course of economic and technological developments.

The close links between the major trade unions and the chief political parties, and the fact that a large number of present or former union leaders are Members of Parliament or even hold government office, are also characteristic of Belgian industrial relations, and partly account for the constant political influences acting on the system. The political power of the trade unions explains the extensive protective labour legislation, the absence of legislation relating to trade unions, and the existence of an almost unrestricted freedom to strike. Industrial relations in Belgium are largely dominated by the two major trade union organizations, which are almost omnipresent. At national multi-occupation or multi-industry level they participate in the shaping of national economic and social policies through formal consultation, generally at the request of the public authorities; at industry level they are represented on the Joint Committees within which collective agreements are concluded with binding effect for that industry as a whole; and at enterprise level they have a presence via the 'union delegations', works councils and workplace prevention and protection committees.

Another feature of Belgium's industrial relations system since the Second World War has been the organized participation of the unions in public life and their cooperation with the employers' associations, especially the Federation of Belgian Enterprises, at both national and industry level. This working relationship is the result of a long evolution in which the events of the Second World War played a special and important role. During the last months of the war, prominent union leaders and representatives of the employers' associations clandestinely negotiated a 'Draft Social Solidarity Pact', establishing the main principles on which a modern industrial relations system should be built. The Pact, which was very explicit, was a blueprint covering the main points of social reform to be developed in the post-war period. It dealt with wages, working hours, social security (pensions, sickness, invalidity and unemployment benefits, and family allowances), annual holidays, the formation of 'union delegations', Joint Committees and a National Joint Council, and the settlement of industrial disputes.

The working relationship thus established led, in 1960, to 'social programming': in other words, the joint programming by employers and trade union organizations of a series of agreements, at both national and industry level, under which the social advances envisaged could be worked out against the background of a realistic assessment of the economic possibilities.

Since 1960, collective bargaining in Belgium has been carried out in accordance with this principle of social programming. The term was first used in that year, and although its meaning has never been clearly defined, it has been generally applied to collective agreements concluded since then. Social programming reflects the need for a special relationship between the social partners based on dialogue and mutual understanding, rather than on conflict. The main idea is that, by working in concert and taking account of objective criteria, the workers' share in the growth of the national wealth will be 'programmed' over a certain fixed period. Collective agreements that result from this mutual understanding are called 'social programming agreements'. There is no doubt that social programming has favoured the centralization of collective bargaining; national multi-industry agreements have had an important effect on the overall climate of industrial relations, while most industrial sectors are covered by a particular national agreement. This centralization has led to agreements that are of longer duration, fixed term, and more comprehensive and technical in their content. In addition, the nature and tone of bargaining have undoubtedly been influenced, especially in as far as union security and the preservation of industrial peace are concerned. Social programming at national level does not, however, automatically exclude bargaining within the enterprise, and bargaining continues to take place at different levels. The first social programming agreement was concluded at national multi-industry level on 11 May 1960. The trade unions and employers' associations laid down three fundamental principles.

- A concerted policy of economic expansion must enable workers to share in a steadily improving standard of living.
- This must be achieved through collective agreements, concluded at national multi-industry level, which programme the share workers are to have in the growth of the national wealth over a fixed period. Additional benefits can be programmed in national agreements for particular industrial sectors and enterprise-level agreements. Programming takes into account state social security benefits financed by employers' contributions.
- Social programming is possible only if industrial peace is observed during the lifetime of a collective agreement.

Thus, one of the fundamental principles of social programming is that it demands the observance of industrial peace while an agreement is in force. Consequently, most agreements contain a no-strike clause under which the unions guarantee industrial peace during the lifetime of the agreement. This peace obligation is generally accompanied by a clause providing special benefits for union members only, and linking the payment of benefits to faithful compliance with the collective agreement and the maintenance of industrial peace during its lifetime. The unions have successfully argued that a situation in which those who do not pay union dues can nevertheless benefit from trade union achievements (secured with the aid of members' dues and contributions) is no longer acceptable. It is only fair, therefore, that the employer should reimburse union dues in the form of a special benefit paid only to the union or its members. The first important agreement reserving benefits for union members only was signed in the cement industry in 1954, as part of an attempt by unions and employers to establish a long-term labour costs budget. It was not until the 1960s, however, that the practice was introduced on a wide scale. Only 45,000 workers were covered by these special provisions in 1961, but the number is now more than one million even though most employers vigorously opposed the unions' demands at first. Special benefits for union members are now customary in most major industrial sectors, such as textiles, clothing, coal mining, cement, petroleum, chemicals, tobacco, laundering and dry-cleaning, gas and electricity, steel and metalworking, and food. The benefits take various forms, such as productivity bonuses and supplementary unemployment and pension benefits, as well as flat-rate payments. There is also a great deal of variety in the ways in which the money involved is administered and distributed to the members. The Belgian Supreme Court has ruled (1981) that the system of reserving benefits for union members only is not necessarily an infringement of freedom of association if such benefits remain proportional to the services (maintenance of industrial peace) provided for the employer(s) by the union(s) or union members concerned.

Since the 1970s, however, social programming has been under strong attack. Workers have struck against it, and the expression itself is used less and less frequently. According to some commentators, social programming leads to a widening gap between workers and their unions by eroding trade union activity at enterprise level, with the consequence that the technicalities of an action taken at the top are not always understood by the rank and file.

Impact of the Economic Crisis

The economic turbulence triggered in 1974 by the oil crisis has had a dramatic impact on Belgian industrial relations in general and collective bargaining in particular, notably through unemployment reaching record levels.

As a consequence of the crisis, from 1975 until 1986 no traditional national multi-industry agreements were concluded. Initially, the Government tried to bring the trade unions and employers' associations together in order to conclude such an agreement. One such attempt in 1980 on the occasion of a National Labour Conference met, like the others, with failure. The Government then had

Parliament adopt a Social Recovery Act on 10 February 1981 providing for pay restraint. This Act specified that its projected measures would not apply if employees and employers, at national level, could conclude (under more moderate terms) a comparable agreement. Such an agreement was concluded on 13 February 1981 and made generally binding by a Royal Decree of 14 February 1981. This pay restraint agreement ran from 1 January 1981 until 31 December 1982.

The period 1981-1986 was characterized by a far-reaching incomes policy, with the explicit goal of making Belgian enterprises more competitive on the international market: a pay freeze (with the exception of the national minimum wage) and changes to the cost-of-living clause to be calculated over a period of four months.

Although the Government severely curbed the freedom to negotiate, it also encouraged collective bargaining in an attempt to absorb unemployment, by obliging employers and unions to negotiate on the reduction of working hours and the hiring of additional employees. It imposed the following '5-3-3' formula on the social partners: a 5 per cent reduction in working hours and the hiring of 3 per cent additional employees on the basis of the numbers employed as of 31 December 1982. If no agreement could be reached, 3 per cent of the wage bill had to be paid into a Central Employment Fund. Enterprises which were in difficulties or operating under serious economic circumstances were exempted.

Mention should also be made of Royal Decree No. 179 of 30 December 1982 allowing for agreements that could deviate from protective mandatory labour standards in establishing, by way of experiment, flexible arrangements on working time. The purpose was to create additional jobs. These agreements, to be concluded between an employer and the 'union delegation' or, in the absence of the latter, other representatives of the employees appointed by them within the enterprise, had to be submitted for approval to the Minister for Employment and Labour, who co-signed the agreement. They became known as the Hansenne Experiments, named after the Minister of the time.

A law of 11 April 1983 introduced for the first time a guideline on the level of competitiveness in Belgian industry compared with the industries of the major trading countries. This guideline was confirmed in Article 26 of the Social Recovery Act of 1985, which laid down the guideline for 1985 and 1986 as follows: the competitiveness of Belgian industry should be at least maintained at the 1982-1984 level. The development of competitiveness was to be measured on the basis of two criteria:

- labour costs as compared with the weighted average of those of Belgium's seven most important trading partners; and
- the degree of improved flexibility in the use of the factors of production in Belgium.

This latter criterion marked the definite introduction into Belgian industrial relations of deregulation and flexibility, the start of which had already been contained in the Hansenne Experiments on working time. Flexibility features in various amendments that the Social Recovery Act of 1985 made to the 1978 Contracts of Employment Act (ie, relating to replacement contracts; the possibility of paying compensation in lieu of notice in monthly instalments when the enterprise concerned is in economic difficulties; extension of the duration of the probationary period for white-collar workers; and adjustment of the pay ceilings governing the period of notice), and to the legislation on works councils and workplace health and safety committees (now called 'prevention and protection committees'), *stage* (traineeship) working time (yearly workload), pay protection, work rules, closure of enterprises, etc.

Under a Royal Decree of 14 December 1984, most of the pay ceilings governing the calculation of the period of notice for white-collar workers, the validity of non-competition covenants, the probation clause, etc, were raised considerably: from BEF 250,000 to 650,000; from BEF 300,000 to 780,000; and from BEF 500,000 to 1,300,000.

The beginning of the second half of the 1980s was likewise characterized by incomes policies, efforts to improve the employment situation, and 'flexibility'.

The Government continued to intervene in collective bargaining. The Emergency Powers Act of 27 March 1986 allowed the Executive, in the absence of a national multi-industry collective agreement (concerning competitiveness, employment, flexibility, incomes and purchasing power) for 1987-1989, to lay down a guideline for the competitiveness of Belgian enterprises and to enforce its observance.

The Executive was also given the power to determine under what conditions free negotiations could take place on profit-sharing for employees.

On 12 April 1986 a national multi-industry agreement was concluded for the period 1987-1988. It was a framework agreement, containing guidelines for further negotiation at Joint Committee level. The Joint Committees were recommended to allocate 0.5 per cent of wages to improving the unemployment situation in general, and of young people in particular. Other points concerned in-service courses, post-school vocational training (for young people aged 18-21) and *stage* training opportunities (of the 3 per cent quota, 1 per cent to be for the hardest hit groups of young unemployed people, preferably on a half-time basis). The 1983-1984 and 1985-1986 employment agreements under the 5-3-3 scheme (see above) to absorb unemployment were continued; the reduction of working hours was left to negotiations at enterprise level.

With a central agreement of 18 November 1988, the tradition of national multi-industry bargaining was resumed. The agreement covers 1989 and 1990 and deals mainly with employment and vocational training.

The 1990s: Difficult Years

Whereas the employers had found the 1980s rather easy, as high unemployment shifted the balance of power in their favour, the early 1990s proved more difficult for them.

First, there was a pronounced shortage of skilled labour. Secondly, there was a growing contradiction between the continuing need for flexibility on the one hand and a sense of job security for employees on the other, and between the need to get labour costs down for competitive reasons and the fact that costs are bound to rise, owing to the lack of skilled labour. Thirdly, international economic competition, intensified by the advent of the single European market provisions in 1992, meant that the restructuring of enterprises would have to continue, as companies need to become efficient and adaptable in the field of international economic warfare. Adding to the difficulty is the fact that those workers who are dismissed as part of the rationalization process often do not possess the required qualifications to fill the job vacancies available. Fourthly, professional groups such as pilots, air traffic controllers, nurses and the like are going to make increasing use of their market strength and engage in industrial action, not necessarily within the framework of traditional trade union action.

All in all, industrial relations were back on the agenda even more than before, combined with a greater emphasis on human resource management. The latter is certainly the case since the new 'knowledge workers' are more loyal to an (exciting) job than to the company, and need to be given an incentive not only to be creative in their jobs but also to stay with the company.

Flexibility was increased. One example is Collective Agreement No. 46 concluded within the National Labour Council on 23 March 1990, which deals with shift work and night work. Another example is an agreement concluded within the same arena on 23 April 1986 to make the Hansenne Experiments part of normal practice, whereby the Introduction of New Working Arrangements Act was adopted on 17 March 1987. This Act allows economic reasons as justified grounds for enterprises (with the exception of retail distribution) to operate for 12 hours per day, and for Sunday working, night work for men and work on public holidays, provided a collective agreement can be concluded on the matter.

Flexibility is topical in Belgium as elsewhere. The reasoning that too much protection is counter-productive, kills jobs and harms the long-term interests of workers, has some following. The eternal question remains the same: how to find an adequate balance between flexibility and individualization on the one hand and appropriate protection on the other.

After a short economic recovery at the beginning of the 1990s, the crisis struck again. The unions asked for a general 38-hour week, which the employers refused. Nevertheless, on 9 December 1992 a tripartite agreement was concluded for the years 1992-1994. The main points concerned:

1. an increase in the national minimum wage; and

2. the obligation of enterprises to contribute, in 1993 and 1994 respectively, 0.25 per cent and 0.30 per cent of the wage bill for the promotion of employment:

    •   0.10 per cent for financing the counselling of unemployed people;
    •   0.05 per cent (1994 only) for financing childcare; and
    •   0.15 per cent to be agreed upon in sectoral or enterprise agreements.

Enterprises not contributing up to 0.25 per cent in 1993 (0.30 per cent in 1994) of the wage bill to increase employment would be obliged to pay 0.15 per cent to a national employment fund.

The 1992 agreement also contained proposals for government action concerning: apprenticeship, positive action for female workers, early retirement, career break arrangements, holiday allowances, overtime, the informal labour market, shift work, night work, part-time work, etc. Some of these proposals were enacted by way of an Act of 10 June 1993.

When taking office in March 1992, the Government pledged that it would give priority to working with the social partners on an overall agreement to improve Belgium's international competitiveness and the employment situation, while at the same time containing pay and social security expenditure. In August 1993, it started negotiations for a tripartite meeting on these issues, but no agreement could be reached. In particular, the unions opposed government proposals to adjust earlier collectively agreed pay settlements, and the socialist unions walked out.

The Government then unilaterally introduced its 'overall plan'. This was countered by national strikes during which some factions illegally blockaded industrial premises, provoking much anger among employers and leading to a debate on ways of exercising the right to strike and the role of the courts in dealing with industrial disputes, especially by way of an employer's unilateral request for an injunction against illegal picketing, blockading of industrial premises and the like.

Finally, the Government succeeded in passing an amended overall plan. The main elements related to:

- a pay freeze for the period 1995-1996;
- a youth employment plan;
- changing the terms of notice for white-collar workers;
- consecutive fixed-term employment contracts;
- more flexible employment contracts for younger employees (up to 30 years of age);
- community employment agencies for longer-term unemployed people;
- redistribution of available work through collective agreements on the organization of working hours; and
- measures to combat undeclared employment in the informal labour market.

First, the pay freeze. In accordance with the Act of 6 January 1989, a Royal Decree of 24 December 1993, confirmed by the Act adopting the overall plan, adjusted the automatic cost-of-living clause as regards pay indexation, heading towards a so-called 'health cost-of-living clause', in which increases in the price of tobacco, alcohol and fuel could no longer be included. More importantly, a pay freeze was imposed prohibiting, for a period running from 1 January 1995 until 31 December 1996, new pay increases or benefits, of whatever form or nature, awarded either through an individual contract or collective agreement or unilaterally by the employer.

However, in the case of enterprise plans providing for the redistribution of work, partial compensation for loss of income (working fewer hours to allow the hiring of more people) would not be considered as a new benefit.

In 1994-1995, 230 enterprises signed collective agreements on work-sharing, thereby creating 2,800 new jobs. Each new job was rewarded by a social security rebate of BEF 100,000.

The youth employment plan involved a drastic cut in social security contributions – paid on top of wages – for a period of three years for younger (up to 26 years of age) unemployed people who had been out of work for more than six months.

The measure undoubtedly had some measure of success, since (in 1994) 44,652 young people obtained a job within the framework of this scheme. However, there were many reverse effects. Job-seekers older than 26 had no chance of finding a job, while many (more expensive) older employees were pushed out in order to be replaced by cheaper young employees. It seems that there was a net employment gain of only some 25 per cent.

The plan came to an end on 31 December 1994. However, a new plan was introduced by the Act of 21 December 1994 providing for a reduction of all or part of social security contributions in the case of hiring certain specific categories of long-term unemployed people.

The overall plan also provided for ways of giving a helping hand to those unqualified unemployed individuals who have particular difficulties in (re)joining the labour market. These included community employment agencies where private citizens or non-profit organizations can call upon the services of long-term unemployed people to do casual work such as gardening, repairs, etc. These unemployed people are paid by cheques written by the recipients of their services, covering not only payment of the unemployed individuals concerned but also taxes and social security contributions. Such unemployed individuals may do up to 45 hours of such work a month and receive this payment as additional income on top of their unemployment benefit. Those who have been unemployed for more than three years are obliged to take up these offers of work. The community employment agencies are on the whole quite successful. However, some local authorities refuse to organize them on the grounds that it amounts to forced labour and does not provide real jobs. It is, nevertheless, self-evident that these schemes are a move in the right direction; all possible avenues have to be explored in order to integrate unemployed people as usefully as possible into gainful occupation.

The fight against undeclared employment in the informal labour market, which is widely spread throughout Belgian society, is another important point. The reason is obvious: in the construction industry, for example, it is possible (illegally) to save two-thirds of expenses by engaging such labour, since official labour has become so expensive that it is pricing itself out of the market. An official construction worker can, for example, easily cost BEF 1,300 an hour. This means that national and, especially, sectoral employers' social security contributions amount to not less than 114-116 per cent of the wage bill. The Act of 23 March 1994 relating to labour law against the informal labour market provides for stiff increases in penal sanctions and fines in cases of social fraud. In the construction industries, a social identity card has been introduced and every worker has to carry it when at work. The informal labour market nevertheless continues to flourish.

Employment Programmes since 1995

On 7 December 1994, the social partners concluded a new social agreement, after difficult and protracted negotiations, with backing from the Government. Once again, employment is the centre of attention: the parties agree to concentrate collective bargaining on the preservation or promotion of employment. The same goes for bargaining at enterprise level.

These employment agreements will be facilitated by the lowering of social security contributions and the introduction of early retirement schemes at the age of 55.

The Government agreed to back and implement the national social agreement 'given the fact that there was a guarantee not to take measures, which would increase labour costs or affect the organization of work. The search for a climate of industrial peace was considered by all parties involved to be an essential element for the success of the national agreement.'

In June 1995, the newly elected Government, composed of Christian Democrats and Socialists, agreed on its programme for the next four years. Again employment was said to be the first priority: strengthening employment and reducing unemployment through more new, redistributed work in the creative economy of tomorrow.

The 'multi-annual plan for employment' was introduced by an Act of 22 December 1995 designed to promote employment through the following measures:

1. reduction of labour costs: reducing employers' social security contributions for the low-paid;

2. redistribution of available work:
    *   job plans in enterprises;
    *   career break arrangements;
    *   promotion of part-time work; and
    *   partial early retirement;

3. targeting of special risk groups:
    -   first work-experience contracts;
    -   better use of the 0.05 per cent social security contribution for risk groups;
    -   jobs to assist absorption into employment; and
    -   targeting of low-income groups;

4. new labour markets: in the non-profit sector by lowering employers' social security contributions; and

5. the social audit: this is an annex to the annual account with the purpose of gathering additional information about the impact of employment measures on the numbers of employees in enterprises.

Government, Employment and Competitiveness

A special act (1996) on the promotion of employment and the safeguarding of the competitiveness of Belgian enterprises is part of a global plan, whereby the

Government received special powers from Parliament regarding employment, the modernization of the social security system and the entry of Belgium into economic and monetary union according to the Maastricht Treaty of 1991, namely by controlling inflation and the public debt.

The framework act is characterized by drastic government intervention in free collective bargaining with respect to both pay and working hours with the priority to control pay trends.

The point of departure is the degree of competitiveness of Belgian industry. The trend in pay has to be controlled and this will be done in relation to three reference States, namely Germany, France and the Netherlands, which are Belgium's most important trading partners. The strategy is as follows:

National multi-industry level

Twice a year (before 31 January and 31 July) the Central Economic Council and the National Labour Council report on trends regarding employment and wage costs in Belgium and the three reference countries.

- Every year (before 30 September) the Central Council presents a technical report on the maximum available margin for labour cost expansion, including the possibilities for real pay increases.
- Every two years (before 31 October) the social partners conclude a national multi-industry agreement, including measures to promote employment and the maximum available margin for wage cost development. This agreement has to take forecasts in the countries of reference into account, but will guarantee as a minimum a predictable indexation to the cost of living and scale increases.
- Because no such agreement between the social partners could be reached before 31 October 1996, the Government provided for mediation.
- Because this did not succeed, the Government fixed the maximum pay increase which will be allowed at 6.1 per cent.

Failing a collective agreement, the Government can also take employment-related measures concerning:

- redistribution of available work, such as reduced working hours, part-time work, career break arrangements and measures for young people; and
- a more flexible organization of the labour market.

The following are not taken into account for the calculation of possible increases:

- profit-sharing; and
- increase in the wage bill due to an expansion of employment in the enterprise.

Sectoral, enterprise and individual level

At sectoral level, before 31 March, and at enterprise level, before 31 May of the first year of the term of the national multi-industry agreement, collective agreements may be concluded relating to employment and to wage cost development. The latter must observe the maximum available margin with a minimum cost-of-living indexation and a scale increase. In doing so, the cost-of-living mechanism and the economic potential of the sector have to be taken into account.

The maximum available margin for wage cost development must be observed by the agreements concluded at national multi-industry, sectoral and enterprise level, and by individual contracts. Employers who fail to do so will be penalized.

Before 30 November every year, a Supreme Council for Employment is to make recommendations regarding the collective agreements at national multi-industry or sectoral level if the measures they propose regarding employment are insufficient. The Government can take the necessary measures on the basis of these recommendations.

The collective agreements at national multi-industry or sectoral level must contain a mandatory clause providing for an adjustment mechanism if wage cost developments in Belgium or in the sector concerned prove de facto to be higher than those in the countries of reference. If the social partners do not act, the Government will. A strict timetable is also provided for here.

If the growth in employment is weaker than in the three reference countries, the social partners or the Government are allowed to take additional measures.

The framework act of 1996 also envisages measures relating to:

- full early retirement;
- partial early retirement;
- employment plans in enterprises (financial incentives);
- annualization of working hours;
- part-time work;
- temporary work; and
- reduction of working hours.

Sectoral employment agreements could be concluded up until 15 May 1997. Negotiations took place in 116 of the 164 joint committees and subcommittees. This led to 85 agreements covering 1,444,050 employees, 70 per cent of the private sector total. The figures reveal that the social partners paid special attention to employment, after wages and conditions. Twenty-eight agreements, covering 700,000 employees, dealt with part-time work.

Finally, the Act of 13 February 1998 concerning the promotion of employment contains various measures including:

- the prohibition of stipulating age limits when hiring an employee;
- promoting the use of consecutive fixed-term contracts;
- changes in the regulation of apprenticeships;
- using unemployment benefit as part of the wage to be paid by the employer; and
- measures on collective dismissals, as a reaction to the Renault case, where some 3,100 employees were dismissed without proper information and consultation.

Collective Bargaining

Although collective bargaining may be described as one of the ways in which workers can participate in managerial decision-making (by regulating pay and terms and conditions of employment through agreement between their representatives and the employers), national differences in approach, procedures and scope are so extensive that a general definition is almost meaningless. The characteristics of the Belgian policy-making, social and economic scene have undoubtedly had a great influence on collective bargaining in Belgium and have determined its main features. Two factors that are obviously important are the degree of unionization and the close links between the trade unions and the major political parties. Using these links, the unions have succeeded in pushing through Parliament detailed legislation concerning individual relations between employer and employee. As regards the sources of employment law, there is in fact so much employment legislation that there is less room for collective bargaining. Collective bargaining must, of course, observe the mandatory legal provisions, but this does not mean that certain aspects of industrial relations (in their broadest sense) are excluded, either in theory or in practice, from the collective bargaining process. In many cases the law lays down a minimum standard of protection upon which collective agreements may then build. Moreover, there are no legal restrictions on managerial prerogatives, which could exclude certain items from the bargaining process. At enterprise level particularly, the scope of bargaining is expanding in line with the increasing strength of the unions, and topics such as changes in work organization (especially when dismissals are involved), subcontracting, the closure of enterprises, transfers of undertakings, etc, are the subject of negotiations with the unions, 'union delegations' and works councils.

The Belgian social partners, and especially the trade unions, believe in free collective bargaining without any government intervention, particularly with regard to pay.

Free collective bargaining has been one of the major characteristics of Belgian industrial relations over the past 35 years, with certain major exceptions.

In June 1977, the Government, after a 'summit meeting' with the social partners, decided that collective agreements providing for pay increases in excess of the foreseeable increase in the gross national product (approximately 3.5 per cent) would not be extended by Royal Decree, and that these agreements would not be taken into consideration in deciding pay increases. As indicated earlier, however, the economic crisis has obliged the Government to intervene drastically in the wage formation process: in 1981, a major national multi-industry agreement providing for pay restraint was concluded under very heavy pressure from the Government, and in 1982 it made use of special powers to intervene in the cost-of-living clauses. Subsequently, government intervention continued until the end of 1986. However, it encouraged the social partners to bargain on the reduction of working hours and the hiring of additional labour. Since 1 January 1987 freedom of collective bargaining has been restored.

A Parliamentary Act of 6 January 1989, however, provides for opportunities for the Government to intervene indirectly in collective bargaining on pay in order to preserve the country's economic competitiveness. It can intervene to restore the competitiveness of the Belgian economy when, after granting the social partners a limited period of time to take the necessary measures themselves, competitiveness is still threatened.

A new pay freeze was imposed firstly for the period 1995-1996, and has been extended for an indefinite period since 1 January 1997 in order to safeguard Belgium's competitive position. Clearly, the Government is calling the shots in co-determining the bargaining agenda: no additional labour costs.

The political influence of the trade union movement has also made its mark on the legal measures that are of the greatest importance for collective bargaining. The 1968 Collective Agreements and Joint Committees Act restricts the right to conclude legally binding collective agreements to the most representative unions, and stipulates that a union cannot be sued for a claim for damages even if it calls a strike in the face of a peace obligation. The Act also provides for the possibility of extending collective agreements and making an agreement as such into a binding minimum for an entire sector of economic activity or for the whole of private sector industry, thus giving collective bargaining a law-making function.

The fact that collective agreements fix only minimum conditions provides for the possibility of concluding agreements at different levels, and for the development of a system of cumulative bargaining or different rounds of bargaining: at national multi-industry level, at industry level, possibly at regional level, and finally at enterprise level. The practice of concluding national multi-industry agreements began before the Second World War, and was continued and even expanded after the war. These agreements were not, of course, all of equal importance, but some have influenced the overall picture of industrial relations in the post-war period up to the present. One example is the aforementioned Social Solidarity Pact, through which employers' and employees' representatives expressed their willingness to cooperate loyally and constructively. The Pact laid down a number of fundamental principles and, among other similar matters, resolved on the revival of the Joint Committees and the idea of the 'union delegation'. Another important national multi-industry agreement, concluded in 1947 and since replaced by Collective Agreement No. 5 of 24 May 1971, concerned the establishment and functioning of the 'union delegation'. We need only mention the social programming agreement of 11 May 1960 described earlier, and the numerous agreements concluded within the National Labour Council, to indicate the very real importance of these agreements.

The regular national multi-industry agreements that had mostly been concluded at two-year intervals since 1960 came to a stop in 1975. A variety of contributory reasons explained this turn of events. One was that, as a consequence of the economic crisis, the difference between stronger and weaker sectors of the economy became so pronounced that the idea of an overall agreement which could also be meaningful for the stronger sectors became less realistic, since trade unionists in those sectors did not want to give up their comparative advantages. To add to this, over the years the overall agreements had come to deal with a growing number of issues, leaving less room for bargaining at lower levels more appropriate to the particular needs and aspirations of each sector or enterprise. A second reason seems to have been the lack of consensus between employers and unions, mainly owing to radicalization of the differing views held by the two sides, their respective thinking on the role of free enterprise, managerial prerogatives, taxes, social security, the cost of living, industrial democracy and the like being poles apart. Another factor appears to have been the diminishing control of the central employers' and trade union organizations over their member federations as a consequence of a more critical attitude on the part of their members, demanding that agreements should be ratified by them beforehand. The language issue, with its increasing social and economic overtones, was another separating factor.

This breakdown did not, however, prevent master agreements, covering more technical and less dramatic issues, from continuing to be concluded within the National Labour Council. Many of the national agreements include peace obligations stipulating, for example, that no additional claims whatever may be put forward, either at national, regional or enterprise level (textiles sector, blue-collar workers, absolute clause), or no additional claims concerning matters already covered at national level (metalworking sector, blue-collar workers).

This description indicates that bargaining is usually done separately for blue-collar and white-collar workers. Only in a few cases is there real coordination between the two categories. Most workers are covered by collective agreements, especially in the case of national or regional agreements, since the Joint Committees cover all enterprises in that industry and all their employees, and agreements can be made generally applicable by Royal Decree.

Agreements rarely contain provisions relating specifically to senior managerial staff.

Recently, since 1988, the tradition of central agreements has been resumed. The latest covers the years 1995-1996, as stated above (though there was no agreement in 1997 or 1998). Overall they seem difficult to reach nowadays, since negotiators have less of a mandate from their constituents.

The importance of the reduction of working hours and the creation of new jobs has already been stressed in connection with the role of government intervention in collective bargaining.

In the main, collective bargaining is still separate for blue-collar and white-collar workers in Belgium. This is largely due to the clear-cut and far-reaching differences between the two groups. Indeed, almost all the important structures in the industrial relations system reflect these differences: there are separate 'union delegations' for blue-collar and white-collar workers, separate Joint Committees, separate chambers of the labour courts and, most important of all, separate trade unions. White-collar workers are not, as already noted, organized by industry; instead, each central trade union body has its own multi-industry white-collar division. Senior supervisory personnel are not involved in collective bargaining. This is not due to the absence of bargaining machinery, since the Joint Committees for white-collar workers represent all white-collar employees. But scrutiny of the collective agreements concluded within the Joint Committees shows clearly that the pay and employment conditions of senior supervisory personnel above the level of first-line supervisor are generally omitted. The main reason for this is that senior supervisory personnel do not join representative trade unions.

Participation

In addition to collective bargaining, workers' participation in Belgium operates by way of the works council and the workplace prevention and protection committee. The works council, however, which is made up of representatives of the employer and a specified number of elected employees, is mainly a channel for information and consultation. It has little or no decision-making power, and certainly none in economic matters, where such powers consequently remain entirely in the hands of the employer.

In Belgium there are few supporters of the German model whereby employees, or their trade union representatives, have seats on the supervisory board of a large enterprise. Although there are proposals along these lines, they appear to meet with little success.

Disputes

Industrial conflict in Belgium is characterized by the almost complete freedom of the social partners to engage in industrial warfare, and also by the lack of legal rules laying down a particular course of action. This does not mean that there are no rules, but that the rules are decided between the social partners themselves as the most visible expression of their autonomy. And again, these rules are not legally enforceable in court. Lately the number of strikes has declined considerably, among other reasons because employees are afraid to strike with a view to gaining new advantages, given the unemployment situation and the actual measures on pay restraint, or to harm the enterprise. It should also be noted that both the Christian and socialist unions have substantial strike funds at their disposal.

Since strikes have less to do with gaining new advantages for employees and more to do with reorganization, restructuring of enterprises, collective dismissals, delocalization, closing-down and the like, it is clear that most of them are of a defensive nature.

The first half of the 1990s was, as far as industrial disputes were concerned, overshadowed by two main features. The first was a general strike in November 1993, the first one since 1936, whereby the socialist and the Christian unions, in their fight against the Government's overall plan, virtually paralysed the country, and almost all public services and all larger private companies were shut down nationwide. Trade union leaders indicated they wanted to discuss employment, cost of living and tax fraud with the Government.

The roads to the national airports and to industrial areas were blocked, bringing many small and medium-sized enterprises (SMEs) to a standstill and angering most employers. Some strikers engaged in random vandalism, damaging plants and offices.

1994 and the first half of 1995 were rather quiet, with strike activity low throughout 1995. Most of these strikes were part of the renegotiation of two-year sectoral and enterprise-level agreements. Many of the strikes were either in older steel, automobile or textile sectors or in the public sector.

Lately, in 1996 and in the first quarter of 1997, (defensive) strike activities increased dramatically because of collective dismissals and closures. Again these strikes mainly concerned the older steel sector (Forges de Clabecq) and the automobile sector (Renault).

The second feature is the use of legal injunctions against certain forms of industrial strife other than withholding labour or peaceful picketing. Whereas the courts previously had little or no part to play in the settlement of collective disputes of interest, they have recently started to play an important role. Before, the settlement of industrial disputes lay within the sphere of relations between the social partners and intervention by the Government, which has an excellent team of conciliators at its disposal. Since these conciliators also chair the Joint Committees, where most of the negotiating activity at industry-wide level is carried out, they are familiar both with the industry in question and with the actors concerned. While the normal conciliation procedure goes on at the level of the Joint Committee, more and more employers have applied to the President of the civil court in order to obtain an injunction against the blocking of entry to enterprises by employees or suppliers, customers or other third parties, forms of paralysing the production process, etc. These legal procedures are introduced on the basis of an individual application, meaning that the other party to the conflict is not to take part in the proceedings before the President. The reason this is done by way of individual application relates to the fact that the individuals blocking entry to an enterprise are not necessarily employees of the enterprise concerned, and would in any case be easily replaced if they had to be identified beforehand and then named before the President. These injunctions are often granted and impose a fine on any individuals who take part in these actions or continue to do so.

The unions dislike this trend and see it as an attack on the right to strike. The employers say that their legal actions have nothing to do with the right to strike, which they respect, but with the freedom of work and of industry, access to the enterprise and the right of property. They defend their right to go to court, like any other individual whose rights are not respected. Employers claim that trade unions should be liable for damages and, to that end, should be legally incorporated, which they are not.

Academia is also divided. Some defend the opinion that trade unions are entitled to blockade enterprises and the like, and that the courts should not intervene in disputes between employers and trade unions, as these issues have to be based upon market strength and resolved by way of negotiation within the framework of the autonomy between the social partners, with the Government intervening as mediators/conciliators only. Others assert that although the right to strike, including the right to peaceful picketing, undoubtedly has to be respected, the right to strike has definite limits, eg, it does not include the right to block entry to enterprises, and that the civil court judges also have a role to play in deciding the rules of the game.

The Government has pledged to try to amend existing legislation regarding unilateral application to the President of the court, the imposition of fines, access to enterprises and industrial areas in cases of industrial conflict, and the safeguarding of essential services.

Since the Act of 1921 which abolished the provisions of the Penal Code outlawing strikes, complete freedom to strike has existed in Belgium. A strike would amount to an offence only if it infringed upon the freedom of association or if ordinary offences, such as violence, were committed during its course. Moreover, the Act of 19 August 1948, dealing with essential supplies and services, stipulates a procedure by which the public interest and equipment are protected in the event of a strike.

The Supreme Court (1981) decided that the 1948 Act implies the right of the employee not to fulfil his obligations under the individual contract, namely the duty to work, in the event of a strike. Participating in a strike does not in itself constitute an unlawful act. The Court also decided that employees can participate in strikes that are not recognized by their trade unions.

In 1991 Belgium also ratified the European Social Charter, which contains in its Article 6 (4) the right to strike and to lock out, which means that since then the right to strike has been a fundamental social right. *De jure* and de facto the right to strike is part of a triad which also includes the right to associate and the right to bargain freely on the basis of industrial action. The right to bargain, without the right to strike, is reduced to collective begging.

Employers are as free to resort to locking out as employees are to striking; the lockout is the legal counterpart of the strike. In practice, however, lockouts occur only exceptionally. A lockout can be described as the refusal of an employer to provide work for his or her employees, used as a means of coercion. It may sometimes be possible to distinguish between defensive and offensive lockouts, but, in Belgium at least, this distinction has only academic implications and no legal consequences.

Conclusions

Belgium could be described as a country where a pragmatic consensus was achieved on the basis of a true balance of powers. This has changed dramatically over the last five years owing to the globalization of the economy and the Maastricht criteria for economic and monetary union (EMU), which leave governments and social partners less and less room to agree. To date, the political process of regionalization has had no great influence on industrial relations, although such a prospect cannot be ruled out in the future.

Further Reading

Blanpain, R., *Codex Arbeidsrecht (Codes of Labour Law)*, 26th edition, Bruges, Die Keure, 1996.

Blanpain, R. (ed.), *Arbeidsrecht (Labour Law)* (loose-leaf), Bruges, Die Keure.

Blanpain, R., *Schets van het Belgisch Arbeidsrecht,* 14th edition; *Principes de droit du travail belge,* 6th edition *(Outline of Belgian Labour Law)*, Bruges, Die Keure, 1996.

Blanpain, R., *Labour Law in Belgium*, Brussels, The Hague and Bruylant, Kluwer Law International, 1996.

Dekeersmaeker, I.F. and van Steenberge, J., *Bibliografie van het Belgisch sociaal recht (Bibliography of Belgian social law)* (loose-leaf), Deventer, Kluwer.

Engels, C., *Het ondergeschikt verband naar Belgisch arbeidsrecht (The Concept of Subordination in Belgian Labour Law),* Bruges, Die Keure, 1996.

Jamoulle, M., *Le contrat de travail (The contract of employment)*, 2nd edition, Liège, Faculté de droit, d'économie et de sciences sociales de Liège, 1987.

Lenaerts, H., *Inleiding tot het sociaal recht (Introduction to social law),* 4th edition, Ghent, Story Scientia, 1988.

Les Codes Larcier, Tome II, *Droit Social (Social Law)*, Brussels, Larcier.

Mergits, B., van Eeckhoutte, W., Vanachter, O. and Votquenne, D. (eds.), *Aanwerven, Tewerkstellen, Ontslaan (Hiring, Employment, Termination of Employment)* (loose leaf), Antwerp, Kluwer Rechtswetenschappen.

Steyaert, J., *Arbeidsovereenkomst handarbeiders en bedienden (The contract of employment for blue-collar workers and white-collar workers)*, Ghent, Story Scientia, 1988.

Chapter 2 — Denmark

Ole Hasselbalch

Historical Background

Since the middle of 1849, Denmark has been a constitutional democracy characterized by a non-adversarial political scene. There are numerous different political parties: in recent years between eight and ten parties have regularly been represented in the Folketing itself (Parliament), with no single party in a position to secure an absolute majority. As a result, Danish politics have also been characterized by the art of compromise.

In modern times, the different groups within Danish society have to a large extent solved their problems themselves, through a joint, organized approach. In this sense the labour movement has been a driving force behind social and industrial relations developments.

Denmark is by nature (and historical tradition) an agricultural country and remained predominantly so right up to the middle of the nineteenth century, with the majority of the working population employed in food production. Following a process of industrialization lasting until after the Second World War, however, only a modest proportion of the population now work in agriculture and horticulture. Yet neither this shift in employment nor a significant increase in the number of white-collar workers compared with that of manual workers (and, in particular, a dramatic expansion of the public sector) has led to any fundamental changes in the system of industrial relations as it was created at the end of the nineteenth century.

Public law provisions relating to seafarers and to agricultural and domestic workers (*medhjælpere*) existed from earlier times. In the 1850s rules on the latter category were collected together in a special Master and Servant Act, nowadays continued in the form of the Agricultural and Domestic Workers' Act (1994). In the 1880s, provisions regulating the employment of apprentices were likewise collected together in a special Apprentices Act, which has now become the Vocational Training Act (1997).

In the case of skilled and unskilled manual workers, the advent of freedom to earn a living in a chosen occupation brought with it a liberalization of their relations with the employer during the second half of the nineteenth century, giving rise to a widespread movement among workers to organize with a view to the collective negotiation of their terms and conditions of employment. This trend stabilized in 1899 when, at the end of a period of bitter conflict in the labour market, confederations representing the two sides of industry reached an agreement known as the September Compromise, which laid the foundations for future collective relations. This led, in turn, to the establishment by law in 1910 of both a central labour court charged with the task of adjudicating cases involving the breach of collective agreements (the Permanent Court of Arbitration) and an Official Conciliation Service given responsibility for helping the social partners to negotiate the renewal of collective agreements. In addition, the two confederations adopted what are referred to as the Standard Rules for Handling Industrial Disputes, intended to serve as a basis for inclusion in the collective agreements covering individual sectors. The industrial relations model thereby created has been in existence ever since, and the same collective bargaining system has spread to both white-collar and public sector employment.

Among white-collar workers, unionization was originally low. Development of the law was therefore in the hands of the courts, based on the parties' own (individual) contracts of employment and any general principles that could be applied by inference, for example, from the Master and Servant Act. In 1938 these rules were collected together into the White-Collar Workers' Act, and are now consolidated in amended form in Act 642 of 28 June 1996.

From the end of the 1930s the legislators took an increased interest in the labour market and there were new laws including the Annual Holidays Act and, subsequently, the Sickness Benefits Act and a Supplementary Earnings-Related Pension Act. The trend accelerated from the 1970s, with a string of scattered laws.

This was accompanied by a growing body of legislation on health and safety at work and social security aspects. Starting with the first Machinery Safety Act of 1889, rules on the protection of workers' health and safety were gradually extended to cover all sectors and all types of risk, and are now collected together in a general statute, the Work Environment Act (1995), since amended on several occasions. Supplementary to this, a system of industrial accident insurance was introduced in 1898 for certain groups and has since been made generally applicable and mandatory.

Economic and Social Context

On the employers' side, the private sector in Denmark is dominated by numerous small and medium-sized enterprises, one reason being that a large proportion of firms originated in the craft trades sector. During the 1990s, however, the need to ensure competitiveness in international markets has prompted a number of company mergers along with many instances of company collaboration in other forms.

The labour force (defined as the total number actually in work plus unemployed people who are available for work) currently amounts to over 50 per cent of the country's population, the remainder consisting mainly of the young and the elderly. Women in particular have increased their presence in the labour market to the point where they nowadays represent some 50 per cent of the labour force, although much of this increase is in the form of part-time work.

In 1994 normal working hours were reduced to 1,687 hours per annum (calculated on the basis of weekly working hours excluding mandatory public holidays and annual holiday entitlements).

Hourly earnings are relatively high in Denmark. In addition to pay in the strict sense, the employer contributes a sum in the form of holiday pay, social security contributions, etc, amounting in all to around 21 per cent of pay for white-collar workers and 26 per cent for manual workers. There has, however, been a sustained effort to restrict pay increases and to reduce pay inequalities between the high and low paid. In general, over the period starting from the mid-1970s, real earnings (the purchasing power of pay taking into account the effects of inflation) have been eroded for all groups, but with public employees suffering the largest drop.

Ever since the first oil crisis in 1973, Denmark has suffered from unemployment to a varying extent. During 1995, for instance, according to official figures some 780,000 individuals were registered as unemployed for differing periods, although when calculated as an average over the whole year the number was less than 300,000 (fewer than 100,000 of whom were classed as long-term unemployed). This level of unemployment must, of course, be viewed not only in the light of the economic recession but also in relation to the growth in the total labour force and a steady increase in productivity: at the end of the 1980s, every person in employment was producing, on average, twice as much as in the late 1950s.

Government measures designed to combat high unemployment and mitigate its consequences have taken various forms. Legislative initiatives have included enterprise start-up allowances and other job creation programmes. Favourable state-funded early retirement schemes for the older section of the working population have been introduced in order to open up employment opportunities for younger workers. Training provision has been offered in order to improve the employability of those without work by equipping them with new skills. And, of course, these measures have included preserving the earning capacity of unemployed people by paying them unemployment benefit during periods of unemployment.

Unemployment insurance as such is administered by private Unemployment Insurance Funds, which are attached to the trade unions and are, in principle, private benevolent societies. Subject to the fulfilment of certain criteria regarding the administration of unemployment benefits, these funds have traditionally received substantial public subsidies. As a result, they nowadays operate, broadly speaking, within a common framework set out in a special Unemployment Insurance Act (1997).

Alongside this general system of unemployment insurance, special schemes have been introduced to create jobs for groups of long-term unemployed and young people, such as incentive payments to employers who hire these groups and grants towards job creation.

Institutional and Legal Framework

The formal legal order and respect for tradition have always been important features of Danish society. This is one of the reasons explaining the fact that labour legislation has never undergone systematic rationalization. Also, in contrast to the situation in many EU Member States, the law plays a relatively minor role in the Danish system compared with the leading role accorded to central agreements reached through the process of collective bargaining.

Labour Market and Employment Legislation

A series of separate laws single out particular categories of employees according to the kind of work they do and outline their rights and obligations. These are: white-collar workers employed in shop and office work and managerial posts, who are covered by the White-Collar Workers' Act; public employees who possess 'crown servant' status and are bound by a special duty of allegiance to the State (or local government authority) as their employer, covered by the Crown Servants' Act (1991), as amended on several occasions, and similar provisions; certain agricultural and domestic workers, for whom there is a special Agricultural and Domestic Workers Act; vocational trainees, who are covered by a Vocational Training Act regulating their special employment relationship; and seafarers, who are covered by the Seafarers' Act (1995).

In addition, there are other laws regulating particular aspects of the employment relationship that are applicable to all employees. These relate, for example, to annual holidays, sickness benefit, freedom of association, equal pay, equal treatment for men and women, and transfers of undertakings.

Certain rules relevant to the employee's legal position are also scattered throughout the general legislation on quite different matters (such as the laws on bankruptcy, compensation, etc). And some social security legislation is, of course, relevant to the labour market, such as the laws on the Supplementary Earnings-Related Pension Scheme, industrial injury insurance, etc.

In general, it is left up to the individual employee to protest against any infringement of the employment laws and, where appropriate, to initiate legal proceedings.

There are also a few laws on the collective bargaining system, ie, those introduced for the purpose of its formalization (see above). Lastly, there is the legislation on the work environment, which, in addition to regulating health and safety at work, contains a number of general rules on working hours and the employment of young workers.

Collective Agreements

The Danish system of collective bargaining is essentially based on what is agreed between the parties themselves and the general rules of contract law. For example, there is no special legislation regulating how collective agreements are entered into, or terminated, etc. As a result, under Danish law a collective agreement need not be in any particular form and may even be tacit.

A collective agreement is thus regarded as a private undertaking from the employer concerned to the trade union to provide (at least) the pay and conditions stipulated in the agreement (for both unionized and non-unionized employees). An employer who is bound by a collective agreement can therefore quite validly contract something different with an individual employee, but if so is committing a breach of the agreement with respect to the union. Conversely, a collective agreement constitutes an undertaking from the trade union and its members to the other party that no industrial action will be taken by those covered by the agreement while it remains in force (this is referred to as the 'peace obligation'). On the employer's side, since the right of assertion in relation to this undertaking lies with the direct party to the agreement, this means that if the agreement has been entered into via membership of an employers' association the right lies with the association, not the individual employer. Consequently, if such is the case it is the association that must challenge any contraventions of the peace obligation.

The effect of a collective agreement is also determined in accordance with the general rules of contract law, ie, the principles on interpretation and development by inference.

These principles mean that express (usually written) clauses in an agreement may be adjusted and supplemented (sometimes even deviated from) in the light of what has taken place between the parties during the period since the agreement was entered into. As a result, something which has been an established practice (custom) between the parties regarding the application of the agreement may be deemed to represent a binding part of the agreement on a par with its written clauses.

In addition, the successors to the September Compromise, ie, the overarching collective agreements referred to as *hovedaftaler* (basic agreements), establish a number of principles governing relations between the parties which must also be observed in ordinary collective agreements between the employers and unions covered by the basic agreement in question. The principles laid down in such a basic agreement serve as a general guideline for the interpretation of ordinary agreements on pay and other conditions and for their development by inference. Consequently, a collective agreement that does not expressly provide otherwise is, for example, deemed by virtue of the basic agreement to contain the presumption of the employer's managerial authority (*ledelsesretten*), ie, the right to make detailed decisions on directing and allocating work and other matters relating to the workplace.

The decision as to whether a collective agreement exists at all lies with a central Labour Court, which was established under the Labour Court Act (1997) to replace the Permanent Court of Arbitration. However, disagreements regarding the implications of existing collective agreements (ie, their interpretation and development by inference) are, ultimately, settled by industrial arbitration tribunals set up in the various sectors in accordance with the Standard Rules (see above) or corresponding rules on dispute resolution contained in the agreement in question. If one party is in breach of the obligations deemed to be inherent in an agreement, a complaint may be brought before the Labour Court, which has the powers to impose a special penalty on the guilty party. This applies whether the breach is in the form of underpayment on the part of the employer or contravention of the peace obligation, ie, the obligation not to strike which the agreement imposes on employees.

The penalty is a financial one, which is assessed by taking into account all the circumstances of the case, and may therefore be greater or smaller than any actual loss caused by the breach in question. It is paid to the injured party to the agreement. Where this party is an organization, it is up to the organization itself to decide whether the money should be passed on to those of its members who have suffered loss. A trade union will not normally pass on money it has been awarded in a case concerning underpayment if the employees who have been underpaid are non-union members. The latter may, however, bring a claim against their employer before the ordinary courts for the amount by which they have been underpaid in relation to the collective agreement. But such a claim will be successful only if there has been a breach of their individual contract of employment (which, since terms and conditions different from those in the collective agreement may be contracted expressly or implicitly between employer and employee, is not necessarily the case simply because the collectively agreed provisions on pay have been contravened). Union members do not have this option of asserting their own claim of underpayment before the ordinary courts on the basis of their individual contract if their union takes the case to the Labour Court on the grounds of underpayment in relation to the rates stipulated in the collective agreement. However, where a union is paid a sum by way of a penalty imposed by the Labour Court, the money is usually passed on to the individual member(s) concerned. In fact, the organizations representing both sides are entitled to act on behalf of their members in all matters relating to a collective agreement, including arriving at a compromise on the amount payable for contravening an agreement.

The parties to an agreement may have established special arbitration bodies for the settlement of disputes concerning specific issues. For instance, cases involving the contravention of collectively agreed rules stipulating that individual dismissal must be justified by reasonable cause are usually dealt with by special dismissal tribunals.

Individual Employment Relationship

The relationship between employer and individual employee is in principle regulated by what has been contractually agreed between the two parties. Where nothing else has been expressly agreed between them, however, the terms and conditions of employment laid down in the relevant collective agreement are deemed to have been adopted.

In addition to this, the employment legislation mentioned earlier is applicable (and as a general rule may not be set aside by the parties either in the individual contract of employment or by collective agreement).

The statutes on particular types of employment relationship (the White-Collar Workers Act, the Agricultural and Domestic Workers Act, etc) normally regulate aspects such as termination of employment, entitlement to severance pay, and the most common instances of absence from work (illness, pregnancy and maternity leave). There are also rules on breach of contract and compensation for termination of the employment contract without notice. In the case of manual workers, for whom no generally applicable legislation exists, these matters are regulated by collective agreement.

In the absence of other statutory or collectively agreed rules, the effects of the employment relationship follow from the general rules on the interpretation and development of the contract of employment and the principles of contract law regarding the consequences of breach of contract. The employment legislation and collectively agreed rules on terms and conditions of employment are extensively shaped by these principles.

Right to Organize and Bargain

The right to form or join an organization, and to participate collectively through that organization in safeguarding and improving employment-related interests, is regarded as a fundamental principle in Danish law. This fact, coupled with the high union density in Denmark (see below), means that in reality it is possible for the trade unions to close down an enterprise which refuses to enter into a collective agreement. As a result, employers usually join the employers' association for the sector concerned and thereby become covered by the relevant agreement, or they adopt the agreement covering the sector through a separate agreement with the particular trade union.

There is no general legislation in Denmark governing trade unions and employers' associations. The functioning of such organizations and internal relations within them are based on what has been agreed between the members themselves in the organization's constitution (sometimes called the 'rule-book' in the case of a union). However, from considerations deriving from general legal principles (including the fact that these organizations exert a decisive influence on the individual's freedom to earn a living in a chosen occupation) the courts do lay down certain mandatory rules on their activities. For example, a trade union or employers' association is deemed to be obliged to admit all applicants seeking to join it who fall within its area of coverage, to be prohibited from expelling a member without substantial reason, and to be generally obliged to ensure that their members receive proper consideration while participating in the life of the organization. Conversely, members are deemed to be obliged to exhibit solidarity, including adherence to the rules adopted by the organization (such as those regarding the initiation of industrial action).

Actors in Industrial Relations

Degree of Organization

The Danish labour market is, as indicated, dominated by the employers' and employees' organizations. In the case of manual workers, it is estimated that just under 90 per cent are union members. Among white-collar workers, although effective unionization began late, their union density (depending on sector) is nowadays estimated at almost 80 per cent.

Although only 25 per cent of all private sector employees are employed by enterprises belonging to the DA (the main private sector employers' organization: see below), numerous non-organized employers have, as mentioned above, undertaken to accept the general industry-level agreements as binding by way of special adoption agreements. Overall, as indicated by the findings of a recent survey conducted by Socialforskningsinstituttet (Social Affairs Research Institute), some 75 per cent of all employees are covered by collective agreements.

Structure of the Organizations

The Danish industrial relations system is characterized by strong collective organizations with national coverage which conclude the collective agreements for the various industries or sectors of activity, and which are mostly grouped under central 'umbrella' organizations. Another feature is its single-union system (ie, with single unions organizing specific occupational or professional categories horizontally across sectors); there are only a few instances of autonomous unions covering the same categories. In addition, the organizations characteristically operate with a high level of internal discipline in regard to all their activities, including collective bargaining.

The traditional **trade union movement** has its roots in local unions (*fagforeninger*) representing each occupation in the various geographical areas. These local unions went on to form national unions covering the entire country (*fagforbund*), to which in most cases the capacity to negotiate collective agreements for the employees concerned has nowadays been transferred. In turn, the national unions then united to form one central 'umbrella' organization, which groups together the unions for numerous occupational categories and concludes basic agreements with the employers' central organizations. These provide a framework for ordinary collective agreements and stipulate fundamental rules for workplaces which are intended to apply throughout the central organization's domain. Also, within an individual enterprise, employees who are members of a particular local union may form an organization referred to as a *klub*, and a number of such enterprise-level union organizations sometimes then form a combined union organization called a *fællesklub* to safeguard their shared interests within the enterprise in question.

Along the same lines, the **employers** are generally grouped in national collective organizations which unite local or sectoral associations and are, in turn, affiliated to a central organization (of which there are several). In recent years, the number of separate employers' associations has become much smaller as a result of a process of amalgamation. Nowadays, for example, the whole of manufacturing industry is covered by one major organization (Dansk Industri, ie, the Confederation of Danish Industries).

In those areas of employment that have only more recently begun to make use of collective bargaining (especially among white-collar workers and public employees), the structure of the organizations may differ from the traditional model. In particular, the unions concerned have been national unions from the outset, and by no means all of them are affiliated to a central organization possessing the capacity to conclude basic agreements. In such cases, an agreement on the issues that are normally regulated by a separate basic agreement is concluded by the individual union itself, typically in a collective agreement which is still called a basic agreement, alongside its ordinary collective agreement on pay and conditions.

At enterprise level, communication on collectively agreed issues is usually channelled through a workplace union members' representative (*tillidsrepræsentant*), elected in accordance with rules set out in the relevant collective agreement, and the local union (or local branch of the national union). The day-to-day administration of agreements entered into by a national union is therefore undertaken by this local organization, not the national union itself. It is only when disputes concerning the application of an agreement have proved unresolvable at this level that the next step becomes involvement of the national union (and the employers' organization).

On the **employers' side**, in the private sector the Danish Employers' Confederation (Dansk Arbejdsgiverforening, widely referred to by the initials DA) is the main organization uniting a number of employers' associations in the commercial sector, small-scale craft trades, manufacturing industry and the service sector. Major employers' organizations outside the DA include the Confederation of Agricultural Employers' Associations (Sammenslutningen af Landbrugets Arbejdsgiverforeninger, referred to as SALA) and the Finance Sector Employers' Association (Finanssektorens Arbejdsgiverforening, referred to as FA), and the cooperatives are likewise not affiliated to the DA. In the public sector, the employers' side is represented mainly by the Ministry of Finance, the National Association of Local Authorities (Kommunernes Landsforening), the Association of County Authorities (Amtsrådsforening), the Copenhagen Municipality and the Frederiksberg Municipality.

On the **employees' side**, the most important central organization is the Danish Confederation of Trade Unions (Landsorganisationen i Danmark, widely referred to by the initials LO). The LO has close ties with the Social Democratic Party and groups together a number of large and smaller national unions (both manual and white-collar) with a combined total of some 1.5 million members, skilled as well as unskilled. These member unions include, in particular, the National Union of General Workers (Specialarbejderforbundet, referred to as SiD), the Union of Commercial and Clerical Employees (Handels- og Kontorfunktionærernes Forbund, referred to as HK) and the Union of Danish Metalworkers (Metal). There are often demarcation agreements between unions, defining the boundaries of their respective areas of interest. But any demarcation disputes between LO-affiliated unions over which areas of employment the various unions should cover in collective bargaining are settled through a special demarcation tribunal.

Many employees' organizations have members in both the public and the private sectors. One particular central organization that mainly (but not exclusively) covers public employees is the Confederation of White-Collar Workers and Crown Servants (Funktionærernes og Tjenestemændenes Fællesråd, referred to as FTF). It unites various white-collar and crown-servant unions such as the Danish Teachers' Union (Danmarks Lærerforening), the Union of Finance Sector Employees (Finansforbundet), the Danish Nurses' Organization (Dansk Sygeplejeråd), etc, but does not possess any capacity to bargain.

Under the Crown Servants Act, at central government level pay and conditions for crown servants (tjenestemænd), whose employment is governed by special legislation, must first be negotiated with four specially authorized crown-servant unions that have been granted the capacity to bargain. These central organizations are the CO I (representing low-paid crown servants), CO II (representing middle-income crown servants), the National Association of Teachers (Lærernes Centralorganisation, referred to as LC) and the Danish Confederation of Graduate Employee Associations (Akademikernes Centralorganisation, referred to as AC), which collaborate through the Danish Central Federation of Crown Servants and Public Employees (Centralorganisationernes Fællesudvalg, referred to as CFU), a joint negotiating body which also covers ordinary public employees. At local government level, the pay and conditions of crown servants are not necessarily negotiated through the central organizations but with the individual organizations, which have formed the Association of Local Government Employee Organizations (Kommunale Tjenestemænd og Overenskomstansatte, referred to as KTO) to perform this function.

In addition, there is the Organization of Managerial and Executive Staff (Ledernes Hovedorganisation), which is united with two smaller organizations, the Association of Engineers (Maskinmestrenes Forening) and the Association of Supervisors (Formandsforeningen), in the Danish Confederation of Managerial and Technical Staff Associations (Fællesrepræsentationen for Arbejdsleder- og Tekniske Funktionærforeninger, referred to as FR). Mention should also be made of the AC (see above), which unites a number of graduate employee associations.

Significance of Labour Market Organizations

The combined effect of the high union density on the employees' side, the single-union structure of the trade union movement, and the well-established and effective system of collective bargaining, has meant that in Denmark collective agreements have traditionally carried more weight than legislation in the industrial relations system, and that the labour market organizations play an important role in society. In fact, the collective organizations have been accorded a function that amounts to their being (co-)administrators of the labour market, with frequent involvement in the preparation of new labour legislation and representatives in the statutory advisory bodies on policy-making.

Despite a general wish to leave the labour market organizations to regulate their own affairs as far as possible, there has inevitably been a need to harmonize their bargaining activities with the country's general economic and social policies and, in general, to ensure a good understanding between the State and the organizations in regard to labour market policy. Since the DA and LO have traditionally been the two major confederations that have set the trend for the whole of the labour market, successive governments have therefore maintained close contact with them during the regular, synchronized negotiations on the renewal of collective agreements. Governments have also participated in these negotiations in an advisory capacity, putting forward proposals based on incomes policy accompanied, on occasion, by intimations that taxes will be raised unless these proposals are accepted. 'Tripartite' negotiations of this kind have sometimes even resulted in agreements to the effect that a specified pay ceiling will be observed in return for an undertaking by the Government to pursue a certain economic policy.

Apart from this, the legislators have occasionally intervened directly in the collective bargaining process, prompted either by the need to prevent industrial action in areas providing essential services (in which case government intervention may have been deliberately provoked by one of the parties) or by general socio-economic considerations. Such legislative intervention has sometimes taken the form that a mediation proposal put forward by the official conciliator (ie, a proposal for a compromise between the negotiating parties) that the latter have rejected is subsequently enforced by law. Or that collective agreements have been prolonged in their existing form but with certain amendments acceptable to the legislators. Alternatively, such intervention has sometimes been to decree that the outcome of negotiations must be determined by a specially appointed arbitration body (compulsory arbitration). Lastly, there have been instances where provisions that have been agreed for all those falling within the ambit of the DA and LO have been written into law and so made applicable to other areas of employment threatened by conflict. Legislative intervention has, in fact, frequently been based on a direct or implicit understanding between the social partners.

In addition to the contact that takes place when collective agreements fall due for renewal, since the end of the 1980s there have been various instances of ongoing tripartite negotiations between the government and the labour market's central organizations on major issues of labour market policy, including general economic policy. These negotiations have in many cases been conducted on the basis of government surveys and studies.

Collective Bargaining

As indicated above, collective agreements on terms and conditions of employment (pay, working hours, etc) are mainly concluded between the various national occupational unions and the corresponding national employers' organizations for the industry or sector of activity in question. At one time, when agreements between unions and employers' associations affiliated to the DA and LO were due to be renewed, these two central organizations selected certain claims that were common to many industries or sectors of activity and regarded as particularly important (such as the general cost-of-living adjustment of pay, reduction of working hours, annual holidays, etc) for direct negotiation and settlement between the DA and LO themselves at central level (referred to as 'general' claims). Nowadays, however, the usual procedure is 'decentralized' bargaining, with the organizations for each individual industry or sector negotiating all issues directly between themselves.

The bargaining process takes place within a fixed framework. For example, the parties have the assistance of an Official Conciliation Service established by law (see below). In addition, the basic agreements contain rules on the termination of industry-level agreements and the initiation of industrial action in this context (notice period, authorization by competent bodies, etc).

Since basic agreements are intended to provide a more permanent basis for relations between the parties, the nature of their content means that they typically remain valid despite the notice of termination or actual termination of ordinary collective agreements. In cases where the organizations within an industry or sector are affiliated to a central organization, it is the latter which normally acts as the party that negotiates the relevant basic agreement. In the private sector, where the unions come under the umbrella of the LO and most employers' organizations are members of the DA, it is these two central organizations that have traditionally concluded the basic agreement, and the DA/LO Basic Agreement serves as the model for other basic agreements.

An employer who is covered by an industry-level agreement (and basic agreement) often supplements their provisions with what is referred to as a local agreement, ie, an agreement with the union in the geographical area in which the company is located. Such local agreements regulate the many aspects that need to be tailored to the individual company, such as the scheduling of working hours, incentive payment schemes, etc. Indeed, many industry-level agreements presuppose that such supplementary local agreements may or should take place. For example, there has been a marked trend in recent years for general industry-level agreements specifically to provide that their pay provisions should be negotiated further at local level (over and above minimum levels stipulated by the organizations in question). Local agreements also rank as de facto collective agreements, which incur the imposition of a penalty in accordance with the general rules on the breach of an agreement. Obviously, however, a local agreement may not contravene the industry-level agreement covering the sector of activity concerned.

In the public sector, collective bargaining is conducted at central government level by the Ministry of Finance and at local government level by the individual local government associations (the Association of County Authorities, the National Association of Local Authorities, etc: see above). In the case of local government, however, this is done under the supervision of a joint body called the Local Authorities Pay Board (Kommunernes Lønningsnævn), which is responsible for approving both bargaining proposals and the outcome of negotiations. The system of collective bargaining in the public sector basically reflects that in the private sector. Because the local administrative authorities have traditionally not been allowed to manage their own financial affairs, binding provisions on pay and other conditions have usually been fixed at central level with only non-financial matters regulated by local agreements. In recent years, however, there has been a growing trend for pay determination to be left to decentralized bargaining based on pooled local funding.

Participation

A wide range of matters which would otherwise fall within the scope of the employer's managerial authority are regulated in advance through the ordinary system of collective agreements. Beyond this, some measure of influence over management decisions taken by virtue of the rest of the employer's freedom of management is secured for employees by way of legislation and also special collective agreements dealing exclusively with employee involvement and cooperation within the workplace.

For example, the DA and LO have concluded, at basic agreement level, a special agreement on employee involvement and cooperation within the individual workplace called the Cooperation Agreement (1986). This provides for the establishment of a workplace-level cooperation committee (*samarbejdsudvalg*) composed of equal numbers of management and workforce representatives, who are responsible for participating in the formulation of company policy (ie, guidelines which the employer undertakes to follow) in matters affecting employees. They have the right to information on management's views on the consequences of planned changes on the economic and employment prospects of the company. This arrangement has served as a model for similar cooperation agreements between unions and employers outside the ambit of the DA and LO.

Most collective agreements also provide for a system of union members' representation. This entitles unionized employees to elect a workplace union members' representative to act as their spokesman in matters arising in the day-to-day management of their work. These workplace union members' representatives normally enjoy special protection against dismissal under the terms of the relevant collective agreement. Under the Work Environment Act, this system of union members' representation has been extended to include the election of safety representatives for the particular purpose of protecting employees' interests in matters relating to health and safety at work.

In addition, company law in Denmark contains provisions which ensure that employees in public and private limited companies, funds, etc, are entitled to elect representatives to sit on the board of directors. The principal laws are the Public Limited Companies Act (1996) and the Private Limited Companies Act (1996). These representatives participate on equal terms with other board members in general management functions and decisions (except for decisions on matters such as the negotiation of pay and other conditions, and the initiation of industrial action).

Lastly, special provisions in collective agreements may impose obligations on employers in regard to the information, consultation and participation of employees in certain specific situations (eg, in connection with collective dismissals).

Dispute Resolution

In Denmark, the fundamental idea is that disagreements relating to the establishment or renewal of collective agreements should, as explained above, be resolved by negotiation between the parties concerned, possibly under the pressure of threatened industrial action. The Official Conciliation Service is available to assist in the negotiations, and the official conciliator can intervene actively by postponing (in certain circumstances) the initiation of notified industrial action or by putting forward mediation proposals aimed at securing an amicable settlement between the parties in accordance with certain rules. Basically, however, it is up to the parties in dispute themselves to reach agreement, and only in a few cases has the State actually intervened and imposed a settlement by means of legislation.

Once a collective agreement has been concluded, however, the situation is quite different. All collective agreements in Denmark are based on the presumption that, while the agreement is in force, no disputes between the parties may give rise to industrial action: the 'peace obligation' prevails.

The principle of the peace obligation is stated expressly in the DA/LO Basic Agreement of October 1992 and in many corresponding agreements. It also follows, however, from the Standard Rules for Handling Industrial Disputes agreed between the DA and LO. Under the Labour Court Act (§ 22), these Standard Rules apply in all cases where the parties to an agreement have not explicitly agreed on some other 'adequate' procedure for dealing with disputes.

And situations where a dispute of rights is settled not by a judicial ruling but through industrial action (or settled by a body which is dominated by one or other of the parties or follows procedural rules not carrying the guarantee of due legal process) would certainly not be regarded as adequate.

The Standard Rules prescribe that the settlement of disputes arising while a collective agreement is in force must first be negotiated between the local parties concerned and then, if this proves unsuccessful, between their respective organizations. If this still proves unsuccessful, and if the dispute concerns the interpretation or application of the agreement, the final decision on the matter is made by an industrial arbitration tribunal. Such a tribunal is established by the parties to each particular collective agreement, in accordance with rules set out in the agreement itself. However, if the case concerns a breach of the agreement, it must be referred to the central Labour Court, whose powers and procedural rules are laid down in the Labour Court Act.

Prospects

In recent years the trend in collective bargaining has been towards increasing decentralization, with the collective organizations in individual industries or sectors of activity gaining a dominant position at the expense of the DA and LO, the traditional central organizations, which nowadays are but a shadow of their former selves. In the wake of this trend the location of pay determination has shifted to the individual workplace. This development has been accompanied by greater emphasis on the individual employment relationship, to some extent also because of the increased importance of legislation on the contract of employment as a result, for example, of the need to implement EU Directives. In addition, the system of industrial organization has come under pressure from the declining interest in trade unionism among the young.

These developments, and the turbulent times experienced by Danish enterprises in adjusting to the more open international market, combine today to place a large question mark over how the collective bargaining system will develop in the years ahead and what consequences this will have for the country's traditionally stable industrial relations model.

Conclusions

The Danish labour market has traditionally been characterized by stability based on a system of regulation of the conclusion, application and negotiation of collective agreements that has been established by the social partners themselves through collective bargaining. The reason for this is the high level of collective organization (particularly the high union density among employees) coupled with internal discipline within the organizations and a centralized bargaining process. The major organizations have had the final say in this and the Official Conciliation Service has often played an important mediatory role in the creation of new agreements. Collective agreements concluded in this context essentially cover the whole of the labour market and are supported by an effective system of regulation for their application, extending to cases where a party to an agreement fails to fulfil the obligations it imposes on them. At the same time, collective agreements act as a finely meshed net which regulates virtually all aspects of working life. As a consequence, the legislators have traditionally felt it necessary to intervene in the industrial relations system to only a limited extent.

The organizations (especially the DA and LO, the two traditional central organizations in the private sector) occupy a semi-official position and exert a strong influence on government labour-market policy, including the formulation of new legislation and application of the law, and on social policy, fiscal policy, etc. Through this influence, practical experience from everyday working life has, in effect, been integrated into the law-making process as well as the administrative apparatus, making the collective bargaining system an important influential factor in Danish society (and indeed a pillar of the Danish welfare system).

Another characteristic of the collaborative nature of the industrial relations system is the fact that the social partners traditionally refrain from attempting to impose on each other any conditions that seriously undermine the other's interests, either by way of law or collective agreement. Their collaboration has always been based on consensus.

The resulting stability is reflected in the low level of industrial conflict. Although the escalating crisis in the early 1970s did spark an increase in the number of unlawful strikes, since then the number has dropped again. Viewed over a period of years, the majority of the working days lost through stoppages have been due to the relatively rare occasions when a dispute has spread to the whole of the DA/LO domain in connection with the renewal of collective agreements. Over the last 40 years or so this has occurred only in 1961, 1973 and 1985.

Further Reading

Bruun, J.R., *Usaglig afskedigelse (Unfair Dismissal)*, Copenhagen, Gads Forlag, 1996.

Carlsen, H.G., *Dansk Funktionærret (Danish Law on White-Collar Workers)*, 5th edition, Copenhagen, Gads Forlag, 1994.

Due, J., Madsen, J.S., Jensen, C.S. and Petersen, L.K., *The Survival of the Danish Model. A Historical Sociological Analysis of the Danish System of Collective Bargaining,* Copenhagen, Juristforbundets Forlag, 1994.

Galenson, W., *The Danish System of Labor Relations. A Study in Industrial Peace,* Cambridge (Mass.), Harvard University Press, 1952.

Hasselbalch, O., *Arbejdsret med tilknyttede dele af skatteretten og socialretten (Labour Law, with Related Parts of Fiscal Law and Social Security Law),* 6th edition, Copenhagen, Juristforbundets Forlag, 1997.

Hasselbalch, O., *Arbejdsrettens Almindelige Del (The General Part of Labour Law),* Copenhagen, Juristforbundets Forlag, 1984.

Hasselbalch, O., *Ansættelsesretten (Employment Law)*, 2nd edition, Copenhagen, Juristforbundets Forlag, 1996.

Hasselbalch, O., *Kollektivarbejdsretten (Collective Labour Law)*, Copenhagen, Juristforbundets Forlag, 1987.

Jacobsen, P., *Kollektiv Arbejdsret (Collective Labour Law)*, 5th edition, Copenhagen, Juristforbundets Forlag, 1994.

Nielsen, R., *Employers' Prerogatives – in a European and Nordic Perspective,* Copenhagen, Handelshøjskolens Forlag, 1996.

Schaumburg-Müller, P., *Forligsmandsloven med kommentarer (A Commentary on the Official Conciliators Act)*, Copenhagen, Nyt Juridisk Forlag, 1995.

Statistisk Arbog (annual statistics with English translations), Copenhagen, Danmarks Statistik.

Waage, N., *Arbejdsretsloven (The Labour Court Act)*, 2nd edition, Copenhagen, Juristforbundets Forlag, 1997.

Working Papers from Centre for Labour Market and Social Research, University of Aarhus and the Aarhus School of Business.

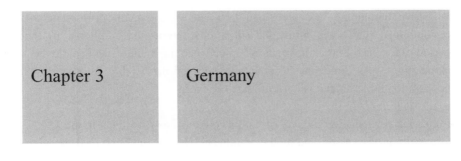

Chapter 3   Germany

Manfred Weiss

Historical Background

The origins of today's labour law and industrial relations date back to the time before the foundation of the German Reich in 1871. The first protective regulation in Prussia in 1839 refers to the prohibition of child labour. The trade unions emerged in the second half of the nineteenth century. The labour movement was at that time fragmented into socialist, liberal and Christian trade unions. At the turn of the century, the socialist trade unions had some 680,000 members, whereas the liberal trade unions amounted to only about 92,000 members, and the Christian trade unions to only about 77,000 members. This ideological fragmentation lasted until 1933, when the trade unions were disbanded by the Nazis. One of the main goals of the labour movement after the Second World War was to overcome these ideological differences and to establish an amalgamated trade union structure.

The origins of the employers' associations date back to the last decade of the nineteenth century. Originally these associations were founded to fight the socialist trade unions, which were still pursuing a revolutionary strategy attempting to overthrow capitalism. Only after the socialist labour movement changed its strategy to a reformist one, and only after the very same labour movement acted in a patriotic way during the First World War, did it become recognized by the employers' associations as a legitimate representative of the labour force. This led in 1918 to the so-called Central Commission of Cooperation between the federations of both sides of industry. Since that time collective bargaining has developed into one of the main instruments of regulation of employees' terms and conditions, interrupted, of course, by the period of the Nazi State. The relationship between trade unions and employers' associations over time has become a pattern of partnership in a spirit of cooperation rather than a pattern of mere conflict.

Employee participation by way of works councils has its origins in the 1870s. Originally it was established by the employers with the intention of weakening the socialist labour movement. Whereas the first very fragmentary statutory regulation on the matter was therefore strongly opposed mainly by the socialist trade unions, the first comprehensive Act on Works Councils of 1920 was backed by the very same group. This had to do first with the change of strategy within the socialist labour movement, and secondly with events during and after the First World War. Abolished by the Nazis, this system of employee participation was reintroduced after the Second World War. The original animosity between trade unions and works councils has in the meantime been replaced by close cooperation.

Employee representation on the supervisory boards of large companies has been realized only since the Second World War. The concepts, however, were already developed in the Weimar period as an essential element of industrial democracy.

The system of labour courts as a specific branch of the judicial system was established in 1926. This was prompted by recognition of the fact that labour law constitutes an independent field with specific structures, rather than a mere subdivision of civil law. Nowadays this special branch of jurisdiction is a three-tier system with local labour courts of first instance, *Land* labour courts as the appeal instance and the Federal Labour Court as the judicial review instance. (The *Land* is the regional state within the German federal system.) At all three levels the courts include, in addition to professional judges specializing in labour law, unpaid lay judges who represent the employers and the unions.

From 1949 to 1990 Germany was separated into two States: the Federal Republic of Germany (FRG) and the German Democratic Republic (GDR). Labour law in the GDR was totally different from that in the FRG. It was mainly focused on three functional goals: fulfilment of the plan, full employment, and workers' education in the spirit of 'socialist morality'. In the course of reunification, all the legal and institutional patterns of labour law of the former GDR were abolished. They were simply replaced by the institutions and legal structures of the former FRG. Trade unions and employers' associations likewise extended their scope of activity into the territory of the former GDR.

Economic and Social Context

The labour market is subject to ongoing change. Therefore it is pointless to rely on exact figures which quickly lose their significance. What is important, rather, is to focus on trends. Since the labour markets in the territories of the former FRG and the former GDR are still very different, it seems appropriate to sketch them separately.

In the territory of the former FRG, the period from the 1950s until the mid-1970s was characterized by full employment. Although the number of jobs rose steadily in the 1980s, unemployment did not decrease to the same extent. It has fluctuated around a level of about 7 per cent. Owing to waves of immigration (mainly *Aussiedler*, ie, ethnic immigrants from Eastern Europe) unemployment did not fall in spite of the fact that from 1950 to 1992 the number of jobs grew from 20.4 million to 29.5 million. In the meantime even this influx is increasing, leading to a further rise in unemployment. At present the number of jobs ranges around 28 million. The rate of unemployment has risen to more than 10 per cent. A further increase is to be expected. It has to be stressed that the official figures do not correspond with the total number of those who are without jobs: individuals who are in retraining programmes, women who do not register as unemployed, people who take early retirement, etc. In short, the real figure is much higher than the number of those who are officially registered as unemployed.

Equally as frightening as the absolute number of unemployed is the fact that the rate of long-term unemployment is increasing dramatically. In 1996, more than a third of those who were unemployed had been in this situation for more than a year. Particular groups are over-represented among unemployed people: unskilled workers, young workers after their vocational training, women, foreigners and people with health problems.

In the territory of the former GDR, the size of the original labour force of about 9.8 million was drastically reduced in the course of the restructuring of the planned economy into a market economy. The present number of jobs amounts to about 6.3 million. The unemployment rate has reached a level of more than 15 per cent. Here also, it must be stressed that the real figure is higher than the official one. And a further increase is to be expected.

As far as the structure of unemployment in the territory of the former GDR is concerned, the groups who are over-represented are basically the same as in the West. The proportion represented by women is, however, significantly higher. In the GDR 85 per cent of women in the respective age groups were integrated in the labour force. Since then the percentage has dropped to about the same as in the territory of the former FRG: about 60 per cent.

In the former FRG, in 1950 about 15 per cent of the working population were self-employed. This number fell drastically and now ranges below 10 per cent. In the same year the percentage of participating family members was about 15 per cent, but has now fallen to a negligible level. More than 90 per cent of the working population are employees. Corresponding figures for the territory of the former GDR are not available.

For a very long time in Germany the great majority of the working population were employed in manufacturing. Now the most significant trend is the shift from manufacturing to services. In the territory of the former FRG the volume of jobs in services already exceeds 60 per cent, and in the territory of the former GDR it is already close to 75 per cent. This trend is continuing. About 20 per cent of the labour force in Germany are still employed in the public sector. This percentage will, however, decline owing to the privatization of public services (railways, telecommunications, postal services, etc). It must, however, be stressed that there is no significant difference between manufacturing and services or between the public and private sectors as regards the level of employment conditions and the regulatory framework. Trade unions are equally strong in all these sectors. And the regulatory framework (minimum conditions, employee participation, etc) is basically the same, even if there are differences in detail.

Germany does not have a statutory minimum wage. Collective agreements are therefore the main instruments for defining basic pay. In the case of other minimum conditions, there are statutory minima which may be improved to the benefit of employees by collective agreements. There is still a significant gap between all the employment conditions fixed in collective agreements in the territory of the former FRG and the former GDR respectively.

The basic feature of the employment structure is still full-time employment for an indefinite period. Atypical forms of employment, such as fixed-term contracts or part-time work, are nevertheless gradually increasing. However, this global trend is much slower and weaker in Germany than in most other industrialized countries.

The main feature of the German economy is its strong export position. At the same time, however, many goods are imported, including a large quantity of raw materials, because Germany lacks many essential resources. While in 1950 in the former FRG imports still exceeded exports, by 1960 the relationship was already reversed. This has remained the case after unification. Even if it is relatively low, the German economy still shows a growth rate, but this has no positive effect on the job situation.

Institutional and Legal Framework

In Germany, almost all problem areas of working life are covered by statute law or executive orders based on statute law, providing a minimum level of protection. This minimum level of protection applies to all employees, whether they are trade union members or not. Consequently, collective agreements are able to build on a statutorily guaranteed foundation and so have the function purely of improving still further the protection that exists in any case. As already indicated, this does not apply to pay: there is no statutory minimum wage in Germany.

The principal feature of formalized industrial relations in Germany is the highly elaborated system of institutionalized employee participation. In the private sector, employee interests are protected by works councils, company works councils and group works councils. In the public sector, the system of staff representation provides a corresponding representation of interests at all levels of the hierarchical structure of state administration. An important point to note in both cases is that these representative bodies safeguard the interests of all employees: here again, trade union membership makes no difference. Although separate statutes regulate employee participation in the private sector and the public sector respectively, establishing formally different structures, the position of employees is essentially the same in both sectors. Another channel for influencing management's decision-making is employee representation on the supervisory boards of large companies. This instrument, however, applies only to the private sector.

Most of the protective legislation makes no distinction between the public and private sectors. Collective bargaining policy in the two sectors is closely aligned. In some instances unions in the private sector (notably IG Metall, the Metalworkers' Union) act as trendsetters for particular areas of regulation, and in other instances it is unions in the public sector (notably ÖTV, the Public Service and Transport Union) which perform this role. The very fact that the function of pacemaker is interchangeable points to the relatively high degree of homogeneity of collectively agreed conditions in the two sectors.

There is, however, one particular group in the labour force to whom none of this applies: career public servants (*Beamte*). Career public servants are not employed under a normal contractual employment relationship, but a public-law service relationship. They are not covered by the rules of labour law, but by career public service law which falls under public law. Their terms and conditions of employment are regulated solely by statute. Although career public servants have the right to form associations, these associations are not permitted to conclude collective agreements. According to prevailing legal opinion, career public servants are not only excluded from the freedom to engage in collective bargaining but also, in contrast to employees in general, do not possess the right to strike. In recent times, growing doubt is being voiced regarding the legally binding nature of this presumption of a prohibition on strike action. Such doubt is founded mainly on the fact that the special position of career public servants is becoming less and less justified by the function they perform. Nowadays, they are employed not only in posts in the traditional public administration but also, for example, in the education sector (schools, universities) as well as in the postal service, the railways and other service sectors. In these areas of activity, it appears increasingly difficult to understand why it is necessary to accord the individuals concerned the special status of career public servants. However, being equated in law with other employees would not just bring these career public servants advantages (such as the right to strike and collective bargaining autonomy). They would also acquire a whole series of disadvantages, since from many individual aspects they are in a far better position than other employees. Whatever the various considerations, the debate concerning career public service is a many-layered one and as yet unresolved. Quite possibly, only moves to achieve standardization in the context of the European Union will eventually lead to fresh thinking on the legal status of this category.

The labour courts system mentioned above not only performs an essential role in the interpretation of existing law, but also in the making of law. The Labour Courts Act, which has been amended many times since its original enactment in

1953, expressly empowers the Federal Labour Court to undertake the function of further development of the law. Since the legislature is obviously not in a position itself to make the normative adjustments necessitated by social change, and since it is obviously hesitant itself about regulating such contested areas of collective law as the right to strike, the Federal Labour Court has no alternative but to step into the breach and perform the role of 'substitute lawmaker' which is thrust upon it. Alongside statute, judge-made law or case law has consequently become an important element of labour law.

In view of the fact that fundamental rights as contained in the Constitution play a major role in labour matters, the function of the Federal Constitutional Court has become increasingly important. This Court examines whether legislative measures, administrative measures or judicial decisions are compatible with the Constitution. To an increasing extent, the Federal Constitutional Court has to draw the demarcation lines in the area of labour law.

The Employment Service (Bundesantalt für Arbeit) is the most important institution in the context of labour administration. It is a combination of a state agency and a tripartite organization. It is organized on three levels: at the top the Federal Employment Office, in the middle the *Land* Employment Offices, and at the lowest level the local Employment Offices. The Employment Service not only administers the system of unemployment insurance, but also performs major functions involving active intervention in the labour market. Until recently it had the monopoly of job placement; it also organizes and finances training and retraining programmes and can provide temporary employment for unemployed persons, stimulate employment by providing subsidies to enterprises, etc. Last but not least, it has a research institute which continuously studies the problems of the labour market and develops strategies for its future management.

The Labour Inspectorate is established in each of the *Länder* on three hierarchical levels. Its offices have the task of inspecting and enforcing the implementation of a whole range of protective rules, mainly those relating to safety hazards, working hours, maternity protection and youth employment protection. In addition to their inspection function, they are also expected to take the initiative and advise employers on the effective observance of protective regulations.

Collective Bargaining

Freedom of association (in this context, the specific right to form collective industrial organizations) and hence collective bargaining autonomy are guaranteed by Article 9(3) of the Constitution. The salient aspects of collective bargaining law are regulated in the Collective Agreements Act which dates from 1949, but has been amended many times since.

In theory, and according to the letter of the law, collective agreements may be concluded not only between trade unions and employers' associations but also between the unions and individual employers. Although such company agreements do exist, they are the exception. The normal pattern is the so-called association-level agreement, concluded between individual unions on the one side and individual employers' associations on the other. These association-level agreements cover either the entire territory of the former FRG or the former GDR for a given sector of activity or a particular region within a given sector of industry. The reason why collective bargaining policy is so geographically extensive lies in the structure of the organizations on both sides.

In Germany the unions are industry-based, in accordance with what is known as the principle of industrial organization. This means that in principle there is only one union for each sector of activity. Bearing in mind that, of the now 13 unions (formerly 16) affiliated under the umbrella organization of the German Federation of Trade Unions (DGB), four fall within the public sector, leaving only nine for the entire private sector, it becomes very apparent how wide-ranging their radius of operation must be in order to provide the necessary coverage. For instance, the Metalworkers' Union encompasses such diverse sectors as the automobile industry, the electrical and electronics industry, the engineering industry, the shipbuilding industry and the steel industry, to name but a few. Where there is doubt as to which union is responsible for which area of activity, the DGB itself issues a decision in order to avoid any overlap or competition. Owing to privatization the number of trade unions in the public sector will decrease further. The number of trade unions as a whole is decreasing and will continue to do so as a result of union mergers. These mergers are carried out in order to strengthen weak trade unions. The latest event of this kind was the merger between the Metalworkers' Union and the Textile Workers' Union. Furthermore, six unions are now considering a merger to form just one mega-union for the service sector as a whole: the union of science and education employees; the union for commerce, banking and insurance; the union for public service and transport; the union of post and telecommunications workers; the union of white-collar employees; and the union of workers in the media. Debate centres on whether it should be a merger in the strict sense or whether it should involve merely more intensive forms of cooperation. However, the chances of a real merger are good. At the turn of the century this would not only change significantly the organisational structure of the German unions but would also – and in particular – change the balance of power within the union movement itself. Only a few powerful players would remain.

All the unions are organized on a national basis. There are regional and local subdivisions, but the power centre is the central union body, with its Executive Committee. It is there that strategies are developed and major decisions are taken. Given this structural background, it is immediately evident that the unions pursue a predominantly macroeconomic perspective rather than a microeconomic one. Their concern must inevitably lie not with the situation of employees within a particular establishment or company but with the overall situation of employees in the sector of activity, industry or service concerned. To avoid jeopardizing solidarity within the organization, union leaders also have a manifest interest in achieving relatively uniform standards for the employment conditions of all their members.

Throughout the period when elsewhere trade union movements were weakened, the German trade unions succeeded in remaining strong. The fact that at least in principle there is only one union for a given sector of activity, and that there is no competition between trade union movements of different ideological orientation, has proved to be a rather resistant organizational structure. The rate of unionization in the member unions of the DGB remained practically unaltered over the period between 1970 and 1990. In 1970 about 6.7 of the 22.1 million employees were unionized in DGB unions, and in 1990 the figures were 7.9 out of 25.5 million. This means that the percentage remained almost the same: 30.5 per cent in 1970 compared with 31 per cent in 1990. This does not, incidentally, represent the total rate of unionization in Germany. There are some minor unions of marginal relevance not linked with the DGB (white-collar workers' union; Christian unions; unions for executive staff, etc), comprising in all another 5 per cent of the labour force. Owing to the fact that after unification employees in the territory of the former GDR joined the trade unions to an astonishing extent, the rate of membership in the DGB unions climbed to about 38 per cent. Subsequently, owing to the reduction of the labour force in East Germany and the fact that many people had unrealistic expectations when joining the union, the rate went back to normal. It is still relatively stable, even though in the last few years the figures show a slight decrease.

On the employers' side the organizational structure is essentially the same. The employers' associations which are united in the Confederation of German Employers' Associations (BDA) are also industry-based in accordance with the principle of industrial organization, and likewise pursue a macroeconomic rather than a microeconomic perspective. For these associations, the interest in establishing relatively uniform employment conditions for all members rests on considerations relating to competition.

A geographically extensive bargaining policy is able to accommodate the particular circumstances within individual companies only to a very limited extent. In many cases, collectively agreed provisions, which are therefore inevitably generalized and vague, still need to be translated into a more specific form relevant to individual establishments and companies. However, it is possible for the collective bargaining parties to delegate regulatory powers to the works council and the individual employer and at the same time to define the limits within which these actors may operate at establishment level. Increasing use has been made of this possibility in recent years. During the 1980s, such collective agreements combining geographically extensive bargaining policy with decentralized regulation were concluded, in particular, on the arrangement of working time. As will be shown later, the relationship between sectoral bargaining and establishment-level bargaining is still problematic.

Under collective bargaining law in Germany, there is neither an obligation to negotiate nor a compulsory arbitration procedure in the event of a breakdown of negotiations. The question of whether and in what manner dispute resolution bodies should be established, and which powers should be conferred on them, rests entirely in the hands of the collective bargaining parties themselves. On this basis, joint dispute resolution agreements exist for all collective bargaining regions, in which the joint dispute resolution procedure is regulated in specific detail. Under the vast majority of these agreements, the parties are free to choose whether to refer a dispute to the dispute resolution body and, in particular, whether to agree to abide by its settlement proposal. In these circumstances, industrial action is the sole remaining instrument for achieving the conclusion of a collective agreement. This key role of industrial action in the functioning of collective bargaining means that the law on industrial action, in giving dimension to the respective strength of the two sides, is of outstanding importance. In its capacity as a 'substitute lawmaker', the Federal Labour Court not only developed the structures of this area of law more or less autonomously during the 1950s, but since then has made a number of significant adjustments. In doing so, the Court has sought on each occasion to base its reasoning on the practical experience of previous labour disputes and to develop rules that take the needs of both sides into account. Recently, however, this pragmatic and compromise-minded strategy as adopted by the Court has met opposition from the employers and the unions. This lack of acceptance is most clearly indicated by the fact that almost all major rulings on industrial action during the 1980s led to appeals to the Federal Constitutional Court, whether by the employers or by the unions.

The relative peace obligation is understood in Germany to be an inherent element of collective agreements. It means that, for the duration of the agreement, neither of the parties is permitted to engage in any form of industrial action with the intention of altering the existing content of the agreement.

Regulations laid down in a collective agreement on the formalities of entering into or terminating an individual employment relationship, and on the conditions determining its content, have a normative effect. They are directly and compulsorily applicable to those members of the contracting union who are employed by an employer who is, in turn, a member of the contracting employers' association. Although these standards established by collective agreement may be improved to the employee's benefit under an individual contract of employment, they may not be worsened. In cases of contravention, employees have the opportunity of taking the matter before the Labour Court. The Collective Agreements Act makes provision for an official procedure whereby, subject to certain conditions, the applicability of a collective agreement can be extended to include non-union members as well. In practice, however, this official extension of collective agreements plays only a marginal role. But it is important for all practical purposes to note that, even though only union members formally enjoy the benefit of the normative effect of collectively agreed terms, employers usually extend them voluntarily to non-union members. Thereby, for more than 90 per cent of the labour force in Germany, employment conditions are in practice defined by collective agreements.

Regulations laid down in a collective agreement which refer to matters beyond the scope of the individual employment relationship and are of collective relevance (*Betriebsnormen*, ie, normative provisions relating to the establishment), or which refer to the powers of employee representation at establishment level (*betriebsverfassungsrechtliche Normen*, ie, normative provisions relating to the law on the works constitution), likewise apply directly and compulsorily. In this case, however, there is no distinction between union members and non-union members; provided that the employer belongs to the contracting employers' association, such collectively normative provisions cover employees regardless of whether they are union members or not. A number of collective agreements from the 1980s broadened the participation rights of the works council on matters concerning working hours and training, and in this way created structures in which non-union members are included whether they like it or not.

Participation

System of Works Councils

Owing to the historical background mentioned above, works councils in the private sector and staff councils in the public sector are, to this day, institutionally separate from the trade unions. The unions have, nevertheless, succeeded in the meantime in exerting considerable influence on the recruitment of members of these representative bodies. Some 85 per cent of works council and staff council members are union members. To that extent there is no difference between the works councils in the territories of the former FRG and GDR. In addition to achieving this tie-in with the actual composition of the councils, the unions have since been granted specific powers by statute. An important example is, in particular, the union's supportive function with respect to works council and staff council activities. Of utmost importance is the fact that trade unions offer training programmes to which works council members are entitled in accordance with the relevant statute.

Since such differences as exist between the respective systems of employee representation in the public sector (the Staff Representation Act of 1974) and in the private sector (the Works Constitution Act of 1972) are of no significance for the purposes of the context under discussion here, it will suffice to outline the principal features of the works constitution (Betriebsverfassung).

A works council should be formed in every establishment where there are at least five employees entitled to vote (ie, aged 18 or over) of whom at least three have been employed there for six months or longer. In many small establishments, however, this statutory regulation is not followed. The question of whether or not a works council is formed depends on the employees of the particular establishment. If they refrain from forming such a body, they forgo the opportunities for participation that are provided for by statute. There are all kinds of reasons why employees in small establishments forgo these rights of their own accord, ranging from simple lack of information to varying degrees of gentle pressure from the employer.

In companies with several establishments that each have a works council, a company works council must be formed. However, the individual works councils are not subordinate to the company works council; the latter is responsible only for matters which cannot be dealt with at individual establishment level. In the holding company of a group of companies a group works council also may be formed, which is then responsible for matters that can only be dealt with at group level. Although provided for by statute, this opportunity is very rarely used in practice.

In 1990 the term of office for the works council was increased from three to four years. No limits are imposed on re-election, which is common practice. For works councils above a specified minimum size (governed by the number of employees in the establishment), the council may demand that a certain number of its members be given full-time release from work so that they are able to devote themselves exclusively to works council activities. All other works council members are also entitled to carry out their works council duties during working time and to be released from their work to the extent necessary for this purpose. Comprehensive guarantees regarding pay, employment and protection against dismissal enable council members to pursue a non-opportunistic and consistent policy in the representation of employee interests. The fact that members are entitled to attend training courses during working time and, furthermore, to be provided with the forms of information and reference material necessary for their activities fosters professionalism in works council policy. An important point to note in this connection is that all costs necessarily incurred for works council activities must be borne by the employer concerned.

The specific participation rights granted to the works council are defined in detail by statute. These rights cover personnel, social and economic matters, and are most extensive in the area of social matters and least extensive in that of economic matters. They range from mere information and consultation rights to rights of control and veto and, beyond this, to what is the most important legal position of all: the true right of co-determination. In matters where the works council possesses such a right of co-determination, the employer may not take any action without its consent. What is more, the council itself can take the initiative and require that certain action be taken. In cases where no agreement can be reached, both sides are free to refer the issue to what is called an establishment-level arbitration committee (*Einigungsstelle*), whose decision takes effect as a substitute for agreement between the employer and the works council.

This establishment-level arbitration committee, which is almost always set up purely on an ad hoc basis, consists of equal numbers of assessors appointed by the employer and the works council respectively, and is presided over by an impartial chairperson. The choice of this impartial chairperson may either be agreed between the works council and the employer or, failing such agreement, be left to the decision of the Labour Court under a special procedure. The committee's discretionary powers are delimited solely by consideration of the interests of the employees concerned on the one hand and those of the establishment on the other. Its decision requires only a simple majority of the votes recorded. Both the employer and the works council have the formal option of referring the committee's decision to the Labour Court for examination. However, the fact that the committee's discretionary powers are so wide makes it extremely unlikely that its decision would be overturned. In practice, therefore, in the vast majority of cases the committee's decision prevails.

The importance of the establishment-level arbitration committee cannot be emphasized strongly enough. Since there is no way of knowing in advance who will chair it and hence who will have the casting vote, it is impossible to predict the outcome of its deliberations. Furthermore, from the employer's point of view, the committee not only entails a loss of time but also incurs substantial expenditure on costs. It is therefore hardly surprising that the committee's function is mainly a preventive one: in many cases the mere possibility of its being called in leads to early compromises that would otherwise not come about.

The matters in which the works council possesses a right of co-determination are specified exhaustively by statute. They are of varying significance and in total are not all that numerous. However, the mere existence of such a right in particular matters has considerable implications as regards the works council's position in general. Since the employer has to take care to avoid unnecessary conflicts with the council, in order to be able to count on its cooperation in matters that are subject to co-determination, this greatly strengthens the council's position even in areas where, under the statutory provisions, its position is in fact comparatively weak. The works council may conclude works agreements with the employer which have a normative effect in the same way as collective agreements and concern the same matters that are also open to regulation by collective agreement. The question of conflict between collective agreements and works agreements is one of the most difficult problems of labour law.

The legislators have sought to prevent any element of competition between the works councils and the unions, since this could weaken the system as a whole in the representation of employee interests. In matters where the works council has no right of co-determination and is therefore able to achieve the conclusion of a works agreement only on a voluntary basis, it must not be able to act as a competitor of the unions, which in any case possess, as collective bargaining parties, the means of exerting pressure in the form of strike action. It is therefore laid down by statute that the conclusion of a works agreement on material terms and conditions of employment, which in the sector of activity and geographical region concerned are regulated (or usually regulated) by collective agreement, is prohibited even if the collective agreement does not apply to the employment relationships within the specific establishment concerned. The mere fact that the union has made the regulation of a particular matter its own business is enough to constitute an absolute ban on its regulation by the works council. In establishments where employment relationships are not covered by the collective agreement (ie, where the employer and employees are not members of the contracting organizations), it means that there can be no form of collective regulation at all. Even in the period of full employment, however, this very rigid provision was already being steadfastly ignored. Despite the statutory rule, works councils and employers persisted, for example, in fixing by works agreement outline pay scales which in many cases were higher than the rates set by collective agreement. Such contravention of the law was always tolerated by the unions, for the simple reason that any protest on their part would annoy their own members, who benefited from these unlawful agreements.

In the last few years, however, the situation has changed dramatically. Works councils and individual employers have gone much further in ignoring the provision concerned. Works councils confronted with the employers' demand to reduce costs in order to save jobs have concluded works agreements to an increasing extent, ignoring the minimum standards fixed in collective agreements. As a trade-off for the guarantee that there would be no redundancies for a certain period, they have agreed to employment conditions below the level laid down by collective agreements. Of course, such agreements are against the law. But there is no plaintiff: the employees affected agree because of the chance of thereby keeping their jobs, and the employer and the works council obviously support the solution they have agreed upon. Trade unions in most cases do not dare to challenge these works agreements in court: they would run the risk of losing members as a result. In the territory of the former GDR this situation has been even more dramatic than in the territory of the former FRG. There the parties to collective agreements tried to make up the gap in the level of employment conditions between West and East relatively quickly. This led to an explosion of labour costs which turned out to be too high, especially for medium-sized and small companies. Therefore it was not surprising that quite often such collective agreements were undercut by works agreements. The parties to collective agreements reacted by adapting the latter to reality, prolonging the process of harmonization and including provisions to allow individual companies to fix employment conditions below the level of minimum standards for a certain period in cases of specifically defined hardship. This has at least led to a decrease in the number of works agreements violating the minimum protection provided by collective agreements.

These events have led to a very intensive debate on the future of sectoral collective bargaining. The crisis of sectoral bargaining has become the key issue of the 1990s. For the employers' associations it is a question of survival: without sectoral bargaining they would be deprived of their main function. For the trade unions the question is equally important. Owing to their centralized organizational structure it would be very difficult for them to renounce sectoral bargaining entirely and shift from a macro- to a micro-perspective. Therefore, it is not surprising that both employers' associations and unions are making every possible effort to rescue the system of sectoral bargaining. Both reject the legislature's intervention in this particular area. In the meantime both sides have repeatedly declared their willingness to modify the policy of collective bargaining by merely concluding framework agreements. This would allow them to accept to a much greater extent the inclusion of the legally permitted clauses known as 'opening-up clauses' (*Öffnungsklauseln*), which authorize the works council and the individual employer to make the provisions of collective agreements more specific and even to deviate from them under certain conditions, within certain limits and subject to criteria contained in the collective agreement concerned. This policy of flexibilization could ultimately lead to a new relationship between sectoral bargaining and establishment-level bargaining, establishing a meaningful division of labour in a pragmatic way. The first steps in this direction can be observed mainly in the chemical industry, which is acting as a sort of forerunner in this respect. The success of the policy will be a test of the adaptability of the so-called German model of industrial relations. The signs are very promising.

The relationship between the collective agreement and the works agreement is regulated quite differently in matters where the works council possesses, from the start, a right of co-determination and hence a strong position. In this case, only a collective agreement that covers the employment relationships in the particular establishment concerned (ie, where the employer and employees are members of the contracting organizations) can affect the right of co-determination and hence the possibility of concluding a works agreement. Even then, the right of co-determination is supplanted only where the collective agreement regulates the matter in question in such detail and so exhaustively that there is no margin left for more locally appropriate decisions in implementing it. Where some scope remains for such decisions, the works council retains its right of co-determination and hence the possibility of concluding a works agreement. The reason why the relationship between the collective agreement and the works agreement is differently defined in these matters which are subject to co-determination is perfectly simple. Where the works council's position is a strong one, it must not be reduced without any replacement, since this would create a decision-making vacuum leaving room for a revival of the employer's unilateral decision-making power, ie, precisely what the right of co-determination was intended to remove.

Employee Representation on the Supervisory Board

Under the traditional system of company law there was no provision for employee representation on company-level decision-making bodies. In meeting the unions' demand for a voice in company policy, the approach adopted was not a complete reshaping of the company constitution. Instead, the traditional structure was retained and employee representation was simply fitted into the existing company bodies. This has given rise to a whole range of problems and inconsistencies, by no means all of which have been satisfactorily resolved. For example, the duty of secrecy traditionally imposed on shareholders' representatives applies in exactly the same way to employee representatives, although in their case the interest in communicating information necessarily takes a quite different form. Secondly, the sole formal obligation on employee representatives, as on shareholders' representatives, is to be guided by the interests of the company, which means that the objectives seen as falling within this category have to be redefined. Thirdly, employee representatives receive the same payment as shareholders' representatives, and this has prompted special arrangements to prevent too wide a gulf from opening up between them and the rank and file whom they represent. This catalogue of problems could be continued at will. All that matters in the present context is to point to the consequences of the fact that the company constitution was not fundamentally restructured but simply maintained as it was, with employee representation added on.

In a system where it is confined to the supervisory board, employee representation does not mean participation in management. Responsibility for the business management of the company lies solely with the management board. The powers of the supervisory board are restricted to supervising the activities of the management board, plus the task of appointing and removing its members. This latter function must not be overestimated, however, given the limited choice of personnel available. As far as the real scope for supervision is concerned, in at least most instances the management board, with its full-time members and constant access to staff experts, is so well-equipped to prepare and present decisions that it is difficult for the supervisory board, whose members are engaged full-time in other functions and which normally meets only at intervals of several months, to impose alternative positions or introduce modifications.

Only in the system operating in the coal, iron and steel industry does employee representation extend into the management board. Here, the member of the management board who is responsible for personnel and social matters, the so-called 'employee director', cannot be appointed against the votes of the employee representatives. This extension of employee representation into the management board is not, however, without its problems; it confronts the management board member concerned with a conflict of loyalties which quite often resolves itself in the direction of streamlined integration with the board's group identity.

Employee influence is at its strongest in the system of employee representation in the coal, iron and steel industry, where there is statutory provision (initially under the 1951 Coal, Iron and Steel Industry Co-Determination Act) for true parity on the supervisory board and an 'impartial' chairperson whose function it is to tip the balance in the event of deadlock. In other industries, the system as established by the 1952 Works Constitution Act for companies of a specified legal form with at least 500 employees limits the proportion of employee representatives on the supervisory board to only one third. These two systems represent extremes in another respect as well: whereas the presence of external union representatives is a strongly developed element of the system in the coal, iron and steel industry, it plays almost no role in the 1952 system.

The Co-Determination Act of 1976 should be seen as a kind of compromise between the other two systems. It gives the shareholders' side a slight advantage and relegates the influence of the unions farther into the background than in the coal, iron and steel industry. The Act covers all companies of a specified legal form with at least 2,000 employees, and thus almost all large companies in the private sector. Whereas the practical importance of this system is, if anything, growing, that of the coal, iron and steel industry system is dwindling, for the simple reason that the industries that it covers are becoming less and less important. Although the legislators have attempted on a number of occasions to check its only too dramatic decline, this does not alter the fact that the system will be of only marginal importance in the long term.

Whereas the employers failed in their application to the Federal Constitutional Court to have the 1976 Co-Determination Act declared unconstitutional, on the other hand the unions have likewise remained unsuccessful in their efforts to raise the 1976 system to the level of co-determination in line with the coal, iron and steel industry system. So it looks as if there will be no change in the situation, at least within the foreseeable future.

The practical importance of employee representation on the supervisory board can be understood only if it is seen in relation to the representation of employee interests by the works council. In almost all cases, those employee representatives on the supervisory board who belong to the workforce of the particular company concerned are also members of the works council, usually leading ones. This provides a channel whereby information obtained within the supervisory board can be utilized for the works council's activities, and vice versa. For the reasons outlined above, the management board obviously has an interest in maintaining good cooperation with the works council; in many cases, therefore, an informal structure has evolved in which the management board holds preliminary discussions with the internal employee representatives to clear up difficult matters. In this way, the supervisory board is never really confronted with particularly controversial issues. Any such plans are revised before they reach this stage, in order to avoid conflict with the works council members. Here too, the effect is therefore mainly a preventive one.

Conclusions

German industrial relations are characterized by a high degree of juridification – that is, legal rules cover almost every area, together with a multiplicity of institutions. Therefore, industrial relations can be described only by putting special emphasis on legal issues. This will continue to be the case in the future.

To an astonishing extent the institutions developed in the former FRG have now been implemented in actual practice in the territory of the former GDR. However, the fact that the headquarters of all the trade unions and employers' associations are still situated in the territory of the former FRG undoubtedly creates problems on a psychological level. In this connection it is important to note that in the near future the Federal Labour Court will move from the territory of the former FRG (Kassel) to the territory of the former GDR (Erfurt). The population in East Germany was used to a comprehensive Labour Code which contained all the rules of labour law in a very accessible form. Therefore, it is not surprising that there are problems in getting to grips with the very scattered structure of the FRG labour law, which is not only fragmented into numerous statutes on specific matters but is also to a great extent case law. In spite of an ongoing discussion on developing at least a comprehensive code on employment contract law, there are no signs of any quick realization of such a project. Hence the present situation will continue for at least the immediate future.

In the 1990s, the post-war pattern of industrial relations in Germany is being exposed for the first time to a severe test. It has to cope with the implications of German unification and with a steady increase in unemployment. This has led to a search for new strategies. For example, the concept of reducing working hours in order to distribute the available jobs among more people has lost much of its attraction. Flexibilization of working time has become the focus instead. All the actors are engaged in shaping the face of the welfare state without questioning its basic value. Excessive labour costs accumulated in the boom periods up to the mid-1970s are to be reduced. Especially for the trade unions, this is a difficult task: they have to be very careful not to lose members by supporting this goal. But in the meantime they have already demonstrated the first steps in how to cope with this goal.

Legislative interventions in the area of labour law (relating to protection against unfair dismissal, the relaxation of restrictions on fixed-term contracts and the hiring-out of temporary workers, the facilitation of early retirement, the lowering of sick pay, etc) have not led to an essential change in the traditional protective structure. These amendments remain largely symbolic. They demonstrate, however, the lack of a comprehensive concept of how to fight unemployment. The same is true of legislative activities in the area of unemployment insurance: there, cost reduction has become the decisive guideline for legislation.

In 1995, on the initiative of the Metalworkers' Union an attempt was made to form a tripartite 'Alliance for Employment'. After promising first steps the arrangement proved to be a failure. This was mainly due to internal problems within the trade unions and especially within the employers' associations. For the employers' associations, the integration of representation of the interests of big business on the one hand and those of small and medium-sized enterprises on the other has become a very serious challenge. In the meantime, however, there are signs that these organizations are succeeding in coping with the problem. Both trade unions and employers' associations are in an ongoing process of becoming better adapted to the needs of their respective membership. Even if the 'Alliance for Employment' was a failure, informal tripartite arrangements continue to survive. And, after a period of some disorientation, the spirit of cooperation between the unions and employers' associations has turned out to remain a characteristic feature of the German industrial relations scene.

As already mentioned, the main problem in German industrial relations nowadays consists in the question of how to develop a new relationship between sectoral bargaining and establishment-level bargaining. There are, however, strong indications that this problem will find a satisfactory solution in the near future. In this connection it is important to stress that a purely individualized approach, leaving everything to individual contracts and thereby largely renouncing collective representation and protective regulation, is not at all a realistic alternative in Germany. The system of employee participation is uncontested, even if there are debates about modifications in detail. It will continue to play an important role alongside sectoral bargaining and protective legislation. To that extent at least, it may be predicted that the so-called German model will survive.

Further Reading

Halbach, G., Paland, N., Schwedes, R. and Wlotzke, O., *Labour Law in Germany: An Overview,* 5th edition, Bonn, Federal Ministry of Labour and Social Affairs, 1994.

Hoffman, R., Jacobi, O., Keller, B. and Weiss, M., *German Industrial Relations under the Impact of Structural Change, Unification and European Integration*, Düsseldorf, Hans-Böckler-Foundation, 1995.

Hoffman, R., Jacobi, O., Keller, B., and Weiss, M. (eds.), *The German Model of Industrial Relations between Adaptation and Erosion,* Düsseldorf, Hans-Böckler-Foundation, 1998.

Jacobi, O., Keller, B. and Müller-Jentsch, W., 'Codetermining the Future' in A. Ferner and R. Hyman (eds.), *Industrial Relations in the New Europe,* Oxford, Blackwell, 1992, pp. 218-269.

Weiss, M., 'The Transition of Labour Law and Industrial Relations: The Case of German Unification – A Preliminary Perspective', *Comparative Labour Law Journal*, Vol. 13, No. 1, 1991, pp. 1-17.

Weiss, M., 'Workers' Participation: Influence on Management Decision-Making by Labour in the Private Sector', *Bulletin of Comparative Labour Relations*, Vol. 23, 1992, pp. 107-122.

Weiss, M., 'Industrial Relations in Medium and Small-Sized Companies in the FRG', *Bulletin of Comparative Labour Relations*, Vol. 26, 1993, pp. 107-117.

Weiss, M., 'Employment Security in Germany' in Blanpain, R. and Hanami, T. (eds.), *Employment Security in Belgium, Bulgaria, France, Germany, Great Britain, Italy, Japan and the European Communities,* Leuven, Peeters, 1994, pp. 141-158.

Weiss, M., 'Strikes and Lockouts in Germany', *Bulletin of Comparative Labour Relations*, Vol. 29, 1994, pp. 67-81.

Weiss, M., 'The Future of the Individual Employment Contract in Germany' in Betten, L. (ed.), *The Employment Contract in Transforming Labour Relations*, Deventer/Boston, Kluwer, 1995, pp. 29-42.

Weiss, M., *Labour Law and Industrial Relations in Germany*, 2nd edition, Deventer/Boston, Kluwer, 1995.

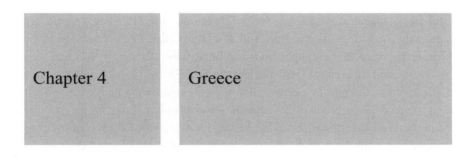

Chapter 4 Greece

Yota Kravaritou

Historical, Economic and Social Background

Industrial development in Greece has been, compared with most other EU Member States, belated and limited. Up to the 1950s, the economy was markedly agricultural: the primary sector accounted for the highest proportion of workers. Also, the Greek development model was directed externally, with no production machinery manufactured at home and industrialization directly dependent on the importation of technology from abroad. Furthermore, investment in Greece has traditionally been in sectors other than manufacturing, with a pronounced emphasis on commerce, banking, the historically established shipping sector and, more recently, tourism.

Mobility of the labour force has been very high: first, geographical mobility, both in the form of emigration during the 1960s, mainly to northern European countries (especially Germany), and in the form of a strong movement towards urban centres; and then, occupational mobility, which is still in process: an exodus from the agricultural sector into the tertiary and industrial sectors, and later a shift from the industrial sector into the tertiary sector. The most distinctive feature of the Greek labour force is the particularly high proportion represented by the self-employed (around 40 per cent), while no more than 45 per cent are employees.

Since 1970, under the impact of the economic crisis, the Greek economy has entered an era of de-industrialization, with a halt in the pace of industrialization and an expansion of the service sector. There has, however, been a significant rise in the proportion of employees and, to a large extent, an improvement in the manner in which their employment is regulated, which for many years had been unilateral and autocratic. Until the enactment of Law 1876 of 1990 on free collective bargaining, the primary aim of legislation on collective agreements was to serve the purposes of government incomes policy. But with the growing importance of the proportion of the labour force represented by employees in conjunction with the post-dictatorship struggles, pay and pay settlement have become central elements of the Greek macroeconomy.

Greece always has been, and still is, the realm of small and medium-sized businesses. The economic structure of the labour market is sharply fragmented, owing to the multitude of small and very small enterprises and, in addition, to the recently intensified tendency towards decentralization through the development of subcontracting and, in particular, homeworking. The spread of atypical forms of work, which are increasing rapidly in certain areas, and the growing extent of the informal economy in general (which represents a significant proportion of the Greek national product), add to the traditionally wide-ranging diversity of employment relationships. The same applies to the loose manner in which these forms of work are regulated. And despite the fact that they exist, the rules of labour law are frequently not implemented even in the case of employment relationships that strictly fall within their scope.

One of the other factors shaping the present-day form of the Greek industrial relations system is undoubtedly the entry of women, by now irreversible, into the employee market and into gainful employment in general, which is characterized by all the special features well known throughout Europe: concentration in certain sectors, restriction to a small number of occupations, limited vocational training and qualifications, and lower pay than their male counterparts. Also, it has always been the case in Greece that a very large proportion of women work in family businesses, either as paid helpers or as unpaid family workers. In this connection it should be stressed that, although the enterprise has not become established as a fundamental institution in industrial relations (as has happened in other European countries), the reverse is true of the family: it has always played a decisive role in terms of workers' incomes. The continuation of this role is associated with the preponderance of family enterprises and the close ties between members of the family. Given the absence of an appropriate social infrastructure, the Greek family also fulfils the function of the welfare state. Female work is in general considered auxiliary and is usually unpaid; responsibility for the care of other family members lies exclusively with women and takes precedence over their professional activity. The fabric of Greek society still maintains its equilibrium largely through the multiple economic relationships and exchanges that are carried on between its members, and this is not merely within the context of the vast number of family enterprises.

Unemployment has reached dangerous levels, especially during the past few years with the economic recession, the closure of many marginal and small enterprises, the resultant loss of jobs and the new employment policy, the cutback in hiring in the public sector, the closure of so-called 'problematic' enterprises, privatizations, and a tendency on the part of the multinationals to relocate their production units outside Greece. As in other countries, those hit hardest by unemployment are young people and women. In the second half of 1996, the level of unemployment rose to 10.41 per cent of the total labour force, with the large urban areas particularly badly affected: 12.52 per cent in Athens, 10.64 per cent in Thessaloniki and 14 per cent in other large towns. One third of all young people are unemployed, and for qualified individuals the figure is more than double. Among young women the unemployment rate is as high as 42 per cent, while for young men it is 31 per cent. Given the extent of undeclared employment and atypical forms of work, however, the real proportions may be different. The picture of employment is made more complicated by the fact that it is also bound up with profound changes in workers' way of life and values. Large numbers of young people nowadays prefer to remain in the town in which they have grown up (thereby opting for unemployment) rather than take agricultural jobs that are on offer. Many of these young people may have a part-time or precarious temporary job, which does not make them financially self-sufficient or independent. In such cases either they continue to live at home with their parents even after completing their studies and vocational training, or their parents support them. Despite the fact that their families have spent a great deal of money on the education of this younger generation in the expectation of an improved employment situation, there is as yet no sign of it. Lastly, a further catalyst is the arrival of foreign workers (immigrants), which has begun in the past few years and is now increasing in the aftermath of recent political developments in neighbouring and former Eastern bloc countries.

The profound changes and processes that the industrial relations system is undergoing, particularly since Greece's accession to the European

Communities, do not appear to be levelling out the contrasts (or heterogeneity) of its elements or relaxing its constraints. The tendency is more in the opposite direction, with differentiations becoming still sharper. The fragility of industrial relations not only persists but is increasing. Inequality, as measured by any indicator, exists not between north and south (as in Spain and Italy) but between the urban centres (ie, Athens and, to a somewhat lesser extent, Thessaloniki) and the rest of the country. The inequality between those employed in the public sector and those who work in the private sector is in some ways becoming even more pronounced. Additionally, there is differentiation not only between the various categories of employee within the private sector (above all, since the recent formal recognition of new forms of employment such as temporary work and part-time work), but also between employees within the public sector, who enjoy considerable advantages regarding pay, job security and other privileges. The employees of public enterprises still exert a particular influence (more strongly in some respects) on the shaping of the climate of labour conflicts, although it has been somewhat reduced during recent years.

The system is still characterized (although less markedly) by traditional trade union structures, which do not facilitate union activity within the enterprise, and above all by the strong political factionalism that has always governed trade union activity and, from the outset, trade union structure itself.

Institutional and Legal Framework

Industrial relations in Greece are subject to a comprehensive framework of legal regulation. In contrast to what happens in, for example, the UK, Italy or Denmark, the legislator intervenes in trade union organization and in regulating fundamental rights, like the right to bargain collectively and to strike. Greek labour law, which was created in the early part of this century, was largely enacted at the initiative of the State. Intervention by the social actors themselves in the shaping of rules relating to labour matters is, generally speaking, very limited in Greece. Although the primary source of regulation is legislation, the State also intervenes in industrial relations in many other ways, both formal and informal, although the last two decades have seen some moderation of the more excessive aspects of intervention.

In its present form, the industrial relations system began to take shape mainly after 1974 following the fall of the seven-year military dictatorship. That date marked the onset of a number of far-reaching changes, a tendency towards decentralization, democratization and a greater degree of representation. Certainly, it was the 1975 Constitution that affirmed and gave impulse to a major change of direction, because it establishes principles and defines values that are to the benefit of workers, such as respect for the personal rights of the individual and for human dignity. Alongside the right to work or the right to equal pay for equal work, it also recognizes the right to bargain collectively, the right to trade union freedom and the right to strike. Although a new framework for industrial relations is beginning to take shape following the 1975 Constitution and Greece's accession to the European Communities, it must be said that the process is a slow one; there are no developments as strongly marked as those in Spain or Portugal, for example. The processes of change in the labour sphere are slow-moving, with trends towards modernization engendered by the actual practical reality of industrial relations being deflected or even reversed in some cases. In many instances, it is the legislators themselves who resist and impede trends towards modernization. A typical example is the exercise of the right to unionize within the enterprise and the right to bargain collectively at this level: these first appeared as part of industrial relations practice in 1974, but were not recognized and regulated by law until 1982 and 1990 respectively. Their formal confirmation had not been helped by the virtual non-existence of collective bargaining on any issues other than pay. Nowadays, however, a comprehensive range of legal provisions is in place regulating all contemporary institutions of collective labour relations. The actual implementation of this modern legislation (which puts Greece on a par with the other European countries) is, nevertheless, a different matter. It has long been known that, in Greece, the existence of labour legislation does not necessarily mean that it is implemented, or implemented fully.

Individual employment relationships are also subject to legal regulation, and have evolved mainly by way of an abundant corpus of case law which has contributed significantly to the development of labour law. It should be noted that Greek labour legislation has not been codified, although there have been some unsuccessful attempts to do so. Furthermore, the various laws (as well as court decisions and all relevant texts such as works rules) are characterized by widely differing forms of language, and indeed in many cases the language is incomprehensible to the workers themselves. Depending on their date, some texts are written in *katharevousa*, that is, highly formal legal language incorporating archaic elements, others in the plainer form of this official language, and the most recent in a particularly inelegant form of *demotic* contemporary language.

The capacity to represent employees at the national level, as well as to participate in various bodies and committees and to engage in dialogue with the government, is restricted to unions possessing 'most representative' status. Historically, the criteria of such representativeness have evolved in a rather questionable manner to the extent that they were ultimately decided by party political and policy factors.

The traditionally difficult relations between the government on the one hand and the trade unions and their factions on the other (due among other things to the consequences of the requirement of 'representativeness') have to a certain extent eased in comparison with how matters were in the past, although in the spring of 1997 the old-established conflict between government and factions reappeared. Over the last 15 years in particular, relations between the State and the social actors have been tending to improve, with meetings, discussions and consultation. The views of the employee representatives are given a hearing, even if they are not acted on. In 1994, the Economic and Social Committee was set up for the purpose of promoting social dialogue and its role is one of compulsory consultation. A certain element of dialogue is cautiously entering the structure of Greek industrial relations, in the context of this institution, among the classical protagonists, with some redefinition of the balance of power despite its meagre results. The governments of recent years have adopted various legislative and administrative measures, both at enterprise level, on vocational training and the adaptation of employees to new technologies and to the requirements imposed by the organization of production, and at local or national level on the retraining of unemployed people. The latest of this series of enactments is Law 2434/1996 providing for measures to combat unemployment. Certain new provisions on employees' health and safety have been added to the existing system of regulation: Presidential Decrees Nos. 16 and 17 of 1996, laying down measures for the improvement of health and safety at work and defining minimum standards in the workplace in implementation of EC Directives Nos. 89/391, 91/383 and 89/654. Another recent development has been the ratification of ILO Conventions Nos. 151 and 154, opening up the possibilities for collective bargaining in the public sector as well. Lastly, a number of enactments are being issued in connection with Law 1975/1991 regulating the legal status of foreign workers, providing for a temporary residence and work permit, and establishing criteria for the grant of a residence and work permit proper.

Fundamental changes in the legal framework of industrial relations (completed by Law 1876/1990 on collective bargaining and flexible working hours) have coincided with the emergence of the new and modernized industrial relations system, while at the same time the framework is being influenced and reshaped by factors such as the economic recession, the effects of history and the sweeping political changes taking place all over Europe. As things settle down a clearer picture is emerging which indicates that some of the recent legislative measures appear to be state intervention prompted solely by the wish to accommodate the new demands of the market and the economy, even at the cost of destroying the positive traditional features of the Greek industrial relations system. Its legal modernization is giving the system a quite different content from that of the 1980s.

Actors in Industrial Relations

The employers' organizations and the trade unions are represented at national level on the employers' side by the Federation of Greek Industries (SEV), the General Confederation of Greek Small Businesses and Trades (GSEVEE) and the Federation of Commercial Associations of Greece (EESE), and on the employees' side by the Greek General Confederation of Labour (GSEE). They appear to be in a phase of some degree of *rapprochement* and initiation of relatively constructive discussions. It is well known that for many years the two sides each directed their separate demands and their separate pressures towards the State, which in the Greek context is such a decisive actor in industrial relations. Also, the unions are in a phase of unitary representation, with their one major confederation representing all tendencies. The existence of a dual union structure, ie, the official one, which is recognized at national level by the government of the day and embodied by the GSEE, and the unofficial one, which is made up of union factions attached to political parties, has long been a peculiar feature of Greek trade unionism. This is because the trade union movement in Greece does not consist solely of unions possessing formal status as collective industrial organizations, which from the moment they are formed are organized and regulated in very considerable detail by the legislators (exemplifying one of the forms of state intervention in the sphere of union autonomy). It also comprises union groupings, or organized political factions, which do not possess legal personality and therefore do not have the right either to bargain collectively or to call a strike, but which exert substantial influence and control over union matters.

Trade Unions

The establishment and operation of trade unions in Greece is regulated by Law 1264/1982. Trade union freedom is evolving in a context of relative 'heteronomy', ie, subjection to regulation from outside. In order to exercise the right to strike, unions must, according to the Constitution, 'be legally constituted' and, according to prevailing opinion, must possess legal personality. Only unions that meet these criteria (and in particular are deemed to be representative) possess the capacity to bargain collectively, although all of them, even ordinary employee associations (usually within a small enterprise), are recognized as collective organizations within the meaning of the provisions on the right of association. Representativeness is a fundamental concept in Greek law and also has a central function in industrial relations; it has existed since as far back as 1937, and characterizes the status (identity) of unions which enjoy certain rights and, more generally, privileges. These include, for instance, the facilities and protection provided for by Law 1264/1982 on the exercise of trade union freedom and Law 1876/1990 on collective bargaining.

Most unions in Greece have traditionally been organized on the basis of occupation; industrial or sectoral unions are the exception, and unions at enterprise level are a newer phenomenon which is still being consolidated (see below). National federations constitute the main stem of the unions, forming the vertical structure of trade unionism in the Greek context. Together with the Labour Centres, some of which (such as the Athens Labour Centre and the Thessaloniki Labour Centre) are very powerful, they make up the second-level trade union organizations (a labour centre consists of at least two unions or union branches that have their headquarters in the same locality). The 'primary' unions (the basic level of organization) are individual unions or local branches of unions with wider or national coverage, and are either enterprise-based or occupation-based. These exist in very large numbers, one reason being that there is no limit on how many are formed provided they meet the minimum requirements laid down by law and that they are independent and therefore have no organic connection with the higher-level union organizations. The result is fragmentation but also disorder, with a lack of systematic structure and action. Despite the hierarchical structure of trade union organizations which is actually provided for by law, with confederations (and so essentially the GSEE, ie, the Greek General Confederation of Labour) at the peak, second-level organizations (federations and Labour Centres) in the middle, and primary unions at the base, in practice the interdependence between the three levels is loose, and in some instances may even be non-existent. This is because many of them do not engage in genuine trade union activity but serve other purposes, including even personal interests.

Although the average union density in Greece is around 30 per cent of employees, it should be noted that in the private sector the percentage is very low (and tending to decline further), whereas in public sector enterprises and utilities it is extremely high and growing. The same applies to the civil service, where there is a separate confederation, the Confederation of Public Servants (ADEDY), which groups together all the federations, national unions and local branches and represents all direct employees of the state administration. In fact, public servants recently claimed the right to negotiate on their pay (as happens in other countries), rather than have it imposed by administrative decree. In any event, the phenomenon of de-unionization has not (as yet) been observed in Greece, but rather the opposite: throughout the past decade the number of union members has increased.

Without question, the structure of Greek trade unionism is outdated and does not correspond to the changes that have taken place in production methods or to social developments. The strength of the unions' party dependence makes for further ineffectiveness. Law 1876/1990 was intended, indirectly and without explicit acknowledgement of the fact, to intervene to promote modernization of the structure by encouraging organization at sectoral level and enterprise level. So far, however, it has had no significant effect, even at enterprise level; there are numerous flourishing and profitable small enterprises which meet the legal requirements but have no form of union within them. Nevertheless, the unity which at present characterizes the trade union movement at the top, an element of *rapprochement* created through shared and feasible demands, and a lessening of the ideological weight governing the stances adopted by the major factions, are all factors that demonstrate that the trade union movement is in a phase of rearrangement.

Employers' Organizations

Greek employers are traditionally organized by sector of economic activity: manufacturing industry, commerce, shipping, banking and small businesses and trades. They do not have a unitary organization at national level to represent them as a whole. This role is performed by the well-known SEV (Federation of Greek Industries), which is the most important employers' organization although its membership covers only about 50 per cent of Greek enterprises. The larger enterprises, as well as other independent employers' organizations such as the powerful SVVE (Association of Industries of Northern Greece), support the SEV's policies and attitudes. On the other hand, there is frequently opposition to it from the organizations of the multitude of small and medium-sized enterprises, whose membership is made up of owners of small businesses and other self-employed practitioners; these organizations exist at all levels, ie, primary unions, federations and confederations. The absence of unitary central representation (although in the final analysis this function is performed by the powerful SEV) does create certain problems, one example being in the negotiation and signing of certain collective agreements.

Among their other functions, the employers' organizations (always those with most representative status, exactly as in the case of employees) represent their members' interests in various bipartite and tripartite committees or bodies responsible for deciding matters of social and labour policy, have consultative functions, put forward claims and engage in collective bargaining. It must not be forgotten that in Greece, the State is the employer of a very large number of employees, ie, both public servants directly employed by the administration and the employees of public organizations and enterprises, whose numbers would be reduced by the projected privatization programme. It should also be noted that the State has been tending to introduce the principles that prevail in the private sector into those areas of industrial relations over which it has authority in its capacity as an employer, in order to reduce bureaucracy and improve efficiency. It also features as an actor elsewhere, however, since it has multiple identities and plays a decisive role in the sphere of industrial relations.

Current Phase

The employers' organizations and trade unions now appear to be in a final phase of reorganization and rearrangement: a relatively stable internal context has been achieved, despite the surrounding context of instability and the economic crisis associated with globalization.

The new SEV leadership (of the past few years) speaks in modern terms, has certain long-term plans, appears to be pursuing more meaningful relations with employee representatives, and refrains, up to a point, from resorting separately and unofficially to the government of the day and to the powers at its disposal (legislative or otherwise) in order to resolve shared problems.

The trade unions (and their political factions) likewise find themselves at the end of a transitional period, which has also been marked by the collapse of the socialist countries and the abandonment of the vocabulary traditionally used by them. Like their counterparts elsewhere in Europe, Greek unions too are, of course, seeking contemporary goals as well as language. The various factions, uncompromising a few years ago, appear to be drawing closer together in adopting a common long-term strategy with universally acceptable claims, goals and requests. They are redefining their relations with the other actors, while tending not to give up their party mentality. Yet they still lack adequately trained officials, long-term plans and research facilities. For them the period of transition will take longer, as it will for many trade unions in Europe facing similar problems (although possibly to a lesser extent).

Employee Representation at the Workplace

Nowadays, employees in Greece may be represented within the enterprise either by enterprise-level trade unions, or by ordinary employee associations (usually in small enterprises) or by works councils. In addition, in public sector enterprises covered by Law 1365/1983 (the so-called 'socialized' enterprises), employee representatives also sit on bodies responsible for control and administration.

However, all these possibilities are provided for by legislation which has been in place for less than ten years. Greece has been the last European country (eastern or western) to accept the institution of employee representation within the enterprise. After the end of the civil war, representation was effected through higher-level, occupation-based unions; unions within the enterprise did not exist. In isolated instances strike committees or action committees did appear, but it was with the fall of the dictatorship in 1974 that the **factory union movement** began to develop in large industrial enterprises, mainly in Athens and Thessaloniki but elsewhere as well. This was a spontaneous movement which began with **initiative committees** aiming to resolve labour-related problems by way of meetings with the employer and cooperation. These committees evolved into factory unions after overcoming obstacles and difficulties that were due, in large measure, to the lack of a relevant tradition or industrial culture. In the euphoria of that era, they carried on successful campaigns of action outside the confines of the traditional trade union organizations and, removed from the tutelage of the political parties, united all employees, operated democratically, and put forward new claims previously unseen in the sphere of Greek industrial relations. Although at a later stage these factory unions fell under the influence of the familiar and constant features of Greek trade unionism, and although many of them disappeared or ceased to function effectively, they marked the affirmation of workplace representation as an institution and its establishment as part of Greek industrial relations practice.

Eight years after its appearance following the fall of the dictatorship, the exercise of trade union activity within the enterprise was given formal recognition by Law 1264/1982. In a series of provisions designed to encourage workplace representation, it granted to unions within the enterprise (which may be either trade unions proper or ordinary employee associations subject to certain conditions) the right to be provided with office space, to put up noticeboards, to have meetings with the employer and to distribute announcements. Protection was provided for the founder-members of such unions in order to help reinforce the establishment of the institution, with further support coming from the newly formed Federation of Factory Unions (OVES).

In public sector enterprises and public utilities and services, although employees were represented by very powerful (and numerous) unions, Law 1365/1983 on 'the 'socialization' of enterprises of a public nature or public utility' introduced new forms of employee representation into their administration. These provisions expressed the particular climate of that era, as influenced by the concepts of 'self-management' and 'workers' control', which were much favoured in Greece, as well as in other countries. They provided for employee representatives to occupy one third of the seats on the administrative board (which has significant powers), and also one third of the seats in the Representative Assembly of Social Control (ASKE), which was introduced as the organ of social control of a 'socialized' enterprise.

These rules on employee representation and participation in public enterprises have actually been implemented in fewer than 10 cases, well below the number intended. The projected and widely discussed privatizations have been one of the factors in paralysing these already difficult processes provided for by Law 1365, which in the final analysis, despite what might be termed its grandiose wording, provides essentially for a form of employee representation that contributes to industrial democracy.

In private sector enterprises, the enactment in the spring of 1988 of Law 1767 on **works councils** (simultaneously with ratification of ILO Convention No. 135 on the protection of workers' representatives within the enterprise) introduced the possibility of general representation of the workforce as a body, by way of the new mechanism of unitary representation. The works council is invested with a group of rights regarding participation, meetings, consultation, information, proposals and joint decision-making in very important matters. Since Law 1767/1988 did not provide for group-level works councils, and the implementation of EC Directive No. 94/45 on European Works Councils now requires the election or appointment of employee representatives in both Community-scale enterprises and Community-scale groups of enterprises, an appropriate bill is in preparation.

Thus, a **dual system of representation** now exists in Greece: the union, which is the vehicle for claims, and the works council, which is the vehicle for cooperation and may be established at the initiation of employees in all enterprises with more than 50 employees. Contrary to the expectation of government and unions, and to a lesser extent employers, that the majority of enterprises with a workforce exceeding the stated threshold would acquire this mechanism of unitary employee representation, this has not in fact happened. Most enterprises and their workforces have done nothing about the idea. There are a number of reasons for this. In the private sector, in many cases employees fear that to insist on a works council in the face of employer hostility could lead to victimization or dismissal. However, where works councils have been established, fears that this dual system would result in representation by the works council at the expense of the unions in the enterprise have proved groundless. There has as a rule been admirable cooperation, with trade unionists themselves becoming council members. Only in a few enterprises has a diversionary tactic been attempted against the unions through the establishment of employer-controlled councils.

The limited development and spread of works councils in Greek enterprises may perhaps be due to the fact that for many decades they did not exist at all and that, as viewed at present, there is widespread uncertainty about the consequences of setting them up: the lack of an industrial culture and the autocratic attitudes that formerly characterized labour relations in Greek enterprises have left a lasting impression.

Consequently, representation is effected mainly through trade unions within the enterprise (with the average enterprise having two or three), which as a rule are controlled by the union political factions. There are very few ordinary employee associations in small enterprises functioning as trade unions (see above). And except for those provided for by law, workers' committees or action committees rarely appear. The dual system has not yet really been experienced in practice, and no alternative rank-and-file bodies exist in Greece to oppose it, although isolated criticisms are voiced and the occasional 'independent' action committee is encountered. Despite the importance of the existence of a legal context for employee participation, the current development of participation bodies and procedures in Greek enterprises is not satisfactory.

Collective Bargaining

At present, the Greek bargaining system is at a transitional stage; the new features of its structure are taking shape following Law 1876/1990 on free collective bargaining, which introduces numerous innovations. Collective agreements as provided for by Article 22(2) of the Constitution (which establishes that general terms and conditions of employment shall be laid down by law and supplemented by freely concluded collective agreements) have in fact never played a primary or decisive role in Greece. The structure of collective agreements has traditionally been strictly centralized and hierarchical, and their content exceptionally limited in comparison with the situation in other European countries.

In industrial relations practice, however, the fall of the dictatorship and the spread of the factory union movement saw the development of enterprise-level bargaining as a new bargaining level on the basis of Legislative Decree 186/1969, which was aimed at averting conflict at this level. In large enterprises, negotiations were conducted between the employer and the representatives of the union in the enterprise, without the intermediation of the relevant occupation-based organizations as formally required by law. This resulted in informal bilateral agreements or, in certain circumstances, 'tripartite minutes' drawn up in the context of a tripartite cooperation committee involving the Labour Inspector. In this way the scope of collective bargaining was enriched and a dual bargaining structure was created: the formal system, centralized by law, and alongside it, an informal system based on the enterprise level, which first appeared in 1974 and has been functioning ever since. In essence, this has signified decentralization of the bargaining structure and new possibilities for its development.

The Sisyphean task of modernizing the legislative framework of collective bargaining achieved its goal at a significant moment in Greek politics: the new Law 1876 on free collective bargaining was passed in 1990 under the then three-party Conservative/Socialist/Communist coalition Government. As its very title implies, in expressly mentioning **free** collective bargaining (as does the relevant Article in the Constitution), this new Law is intended to mark the start of the new era and its distancing from the past system of constrained bargaining. According to its Preamble, it has a threefold purpose: full and unreserved recognition of the right to free collective bargaining; decentralization of collective bargaining; and settlement of industrial disputes free from state intervention. It is important here to outline the new regulations, as follows:

Collective bargaining is to be undertaken by the most representative unions, whose role is strengthened. The Law's scope of application is very wide: it also covers workers employed in agriculture and livestock-rearing, homeworkers and individuals who, although not working within an employment relationship involving a situation of 'subordination' to the employer's authority, perform their work in circumstances that incorporate the elements of such a relationship.

The range of issues covered by bargaining is now greatly expanded: topics relating to individual contracts of employment, exercise of the right to unionize within the enterprise, the check-off system for deducting union dues, certain elements of social insurance, and matters pertaining to the pursuit of company policy in so far as it directly affects labour relations, may all be the subject of bargaining. This also extends to the topics made subject to joint decision-making under Article 12 of Law 1767/1988 on works councils, ie, works rules, health and safety regulations, programmes concerning new methods of organization and the use of new technology, and further training and continuing training, and includes the interpretation of both the normative and the obligational provisions of a particular collective agreement. Under Law 2224/1990 the range of issues covered by bargaining also includes specifying emergency staff requirements, such as skeleton staff to guarantee plant safety during a strike.

Furthermore, in order to be valid, any peace obligation, ie, an obligation on trade unions not to take industrial action, can now exist only through express agreement of the parties. The normative provisions of a collective agreement have direct and mandatory application. Individual contracts of employment, as well as legislation, take precedence only in cases where they provide **greater protection** for employees.

There are **five types** of collective agreement: national general, industry or sector of activity (a new level), enterprise or company (also new in the formal sense), national occupational and, lastly, local occupational. Their applicability differs according to the type concerned. National general agreements apply to all employees and all employers, whether organized or not. The other types of agreement, generally speaking, apply as a matter of principle to those employees and employers who are members of the signatory organizations; there is an exception in the case of enterprise or company agreements, whose normative provisions are compulsorily applicable to the entire workforce, whether or not they are members of the unions in the enterprise. There are also the institutions of adoption and extension, whereby an agreement is rendered applicable to other or all employees whom it concerns.

The minimum duration of a collective agreement is one year. Many collective agreements are still concluded only for this minimum duration, owing to the persistent attitude that the main bargaining issue is pay, which needs to be adjusted every year. As yet, there has been little real change in either the scope of bargaining or the duration of agreements. A two-year term has been adopted in the particular case of some national general agreements, such as the National General Collective Agreement signed for 1996-1997 and the recent one signed for 1998-1999, and there is also a tendency for such a two-year term to be extended to the agreements for banking and for a number of other sectors. However, in some instances the content of agreements is more restricted than it was formerly. The 1990 Law's attempt to stimulate activity at the two new bargaining levels of enterprise and industry, in preference to the traditional occupational level, has so far had only a limited impact. Occupational agreements continue to predominate, and company agreements are still concluded as before, ie, only in the large enterprises where this tradition already existed. The Law's indirect aim of restructuring and modernizing the trade union movement through the establishment of the two new bargaining levels has not (yet) been realized.

The Greek legislative framework in force is, of course, fully in harmony with the relevant ILO Conventions and in general follows the same lines as European models. Indeed, one of its provisions on exceptions stipulates that, in the event of conflict between agreements where an occupational agreement exists alongside a company or industry-level agreement, the company or industry-level agreement takes precedence even if its provisions are less favourable than those of the occupational agreement. This provision of the 1990 Law exemplifies today's 'post-modernist' thinking, which is taking over from what has formerly been the traditional purpose of bargaining (or at least of decentralized bargaining), namely, straightforward improvement of workers' terms and conditions of employment. As yet, however, novel approaches to bargaining have not been implemented in Greece; certain of the 1990 Law's basic aims have not yet been put into effect. Company-level bargaining, where it does take place, has not yet developed the possibilities for expanded scope and confines itself to its traditional issues. Even the linking of pay with productivity, although it often exists in practice, is not expressly mentioned in the company agreement. A large number of small and medium-sized enterprises, which fulfil the criteria laid down by the 1990 Law for the conclusion of an individual company agreement, totally ignore the idea. They continue to use other methods, namely, informal arrangements and agreements between employer and employees, still taking the relevant occupational agreement applicable to them as their main basis. Nor has the mechanism of the national agreement yet begun to be used as a means of deciding institutional matters autonomously.

In terms of the number of agreements, the pattern of collective bargaining is distributed as follows. The total number of collective agreements, which stood at 171 in 1992, increased to 254 in 1993 and 287 in 1994. Of these, in accordance with the aims of the 1990 Law, the number of industry-level and company agreements is increasing steadily as compared with that of local occupational agreements, which have decreased as the basic bargaining level after being duplicated at national level. The combined total of collective agreements and arbitration awards, ie, including all bargaining levels, which stood at 208 in 1992, increased to 285 in 1993 and 325 in 1994. Against this background of a rise in collective bargaining activity, which is due mainly to intervention by the mediators of the Mediation and Arbitration Service (OMED) in encouraging and assisting the parties to arrive at the conclusion of a collective agreement without having recourse to arbitration, direct collective bargaining shows only a modest increase. Since the successive entry into force of agreements covering the various industries or sectors results in cumulative provisions that create problems for those concerned, the Mediation and Arbitration Service has codified collective agreements and arbitration awards.

In addition to the 1991 National General Collective Agreement, which included clauses on institutional topics, that for 1993 regulated contributions for unemployment insurance and the creation of the Committee on Equality. The 1994-1995 National General Agreement regulated severance pay for skilled workers and the implementation of works councils, at least as regards their information function, and created an Environment Committee. The 1996-1997 National General Agreement, which like the previous one had a two-year term, covered a wealth of topics. It proposed the reform of the insurance and pensions systems, set up a committee to study the effects of the possible reduction of working hours, instituted an official agent with responsibility for equality, and referred to drugs and alcoholism, childcare, the need for policies on equal opportunities and equal treatment to combat racism and xenophobia, and (a topic of special interest) the implementation of the 1995 European framework agreement on parental leave. In May 1998, the 1998-1999 National General Agreement was also signed for two years. It regulates, besides pay issues, increases in annual holidays and severance pay, the extension of leave for working students, and medical cover for non-insured unemployed young people under the age of 29 by means of a common fund administered by employers' and employees' organizations. It stresses the need for policies to combat racism, prevent discrimination and respect cultural and religious differences.

The welcome impression created by the extreme breadth of this content is somewhat marred by the restricted content of the overwhelming majority of collective agreements, which still deal essentially with pay. Equality between men and women is the only topic that enriches their content. The various types of leave provided for, even that granted to an unmarried father, are always focused on the family. Equal opportunities actually consist in time off work to deal with domestic demands: genuine equal opportunities do not exist because women's professional development is constantly hindered by their commitments in the home.

Apart from this interesting new facet of bargaining, whose outcome remains to be seen, it could be said that the Greek bargaining system is in a period of confusion and transition. The practices of the past weigh heavily upon it and are self-perpetuating, while ahead of it lie the fresh challenges offered by the new framework, for the most part untried.

Disputes

The forms taken by industrial conflict in Greece are evolving and changing. The era of heroic strikes with a strongly politicized content, usually organized by union factions attached to opposition parties and involving broadly sweeping demands and generalized mobilization (throughout the Athens area or the entire country), has given way in recent years to an era in which strikes of this kind occur much less frequently.

The majority of strikes in Greece are of brief duration and many are unofficial, ie, are not sanctioned by the appropriate trade union authority and are deemed unlawful unless subsequently approved by a union. The most widespread form of strike is unquestionably the short workplace stoppage, which has the advantage that it limits the amount of pay lost by employees, is effective and can be initiated quickly: provided that such stoppages last only for a few hours and are not repeated more often than once a week, the decision to stop work can be taken by a primary union's executive council.

During the past decade most strikes have been related to the maintenance of acquired rights, particularly jobs, rather than to pay increases. Also, general strikes with a clearly political content have been tending to disappear and to be replaced by strikes of a mixed nature with a broader socio-economic content, ie, which are simultaneously political and employment-related. Recently, however, this kind of strike has again assumed a more pronounced political character. Apart from the agricultural 'strike' with its spectacular protests during the autumn and winter of 1996 (and also industrial action by both maritime workers and teachers), the most important example has been the strike by lecturers in higher education in the spring of 1997. In addition to its claims regarding pay, this eight-week strike concerned some of the most important issues relating to higher education in Greece and expressed severe criticism of government policy on the matter. Although such strikes were, needless to say, supported by those political factions not included in the present Government, this is just one dimension of the industrial action concerned.

The **lockout** has traditionally been much used by Greek employers and still is today, despite being expressly prohibited by Law 1264/1982. This lack of enforcement is explained by a judicial attitude that is still imbued with the notion of a 'balance of bargaining power' and demonstrates a reluctance to adapt to the philosophy of the more recent legislation. The fact that there are no special labour courts or specialist labour judges in Greece is significant in such cases.

The new method of dispute settlement introduced by Law 1876/1990 is at the opposite end of the spectrum to that of the previous regime based on compulsory arbitration: the whole purpose is now the establishment of a voluntary set of settlement procedures. It thus provides for successive stages of conciliation, mediation and arbitration (arbitration pure and simple, not compulsory arbitration). The **conciliation** procedure is available for any kind of difference occasioned by the employment relationship. The conciliator is a public servant from the Ministry of Labour, whose role is to reconcile the viewpoints of the two sides as quickly as possible and so put an end to the dispute. The new **mediation** procedure is of particular interest to the Greek system of dispute settlement in that it includes an opportunity (unprecedented in Greece) for the actual parties concerned to decide on the conditions and procedures of mediation (and also arbitration) through negotiation. They are also able to record the matters on which agreement has been reached in a minute of conciliation, rather than incorporating them in the collective agreement. However, practical experience to date shows that mediation is not effective enough to resolve complex disputes or disputes arising from serious conflict (strikes). In such cases, referral to arbitration is provided for by law.

Arbitration now represents the final settlement procedure. Its main version is voluntary arbitration, and during negotiations recourse may be had to this at any stage by mutual agreement between the two sides or unilaterally by either of them in cases where the other refuses to take part in mediation, or by the unions when the employers reject the mediator's proposal. Like the mediator, the arbitrator is selected by mutual agreement between the two sides (or, failing this, drawn at random) from a special list maintained by the Mediation and Arbitration Service. The latter is an entirely new institution, governed by private law, which has its headquarters in Athens and is administered by a Council composed of 11 members.

This new spirit of dispute settlement had still not been fully assimilated, when, as a consequence of major strikes in the public utilities and services, Law 2224/1994 amended Law 1264/1982. The new law covers emergency staff and the staff required to maintain essential services for the community, and has recourse to consensus procedures, collective bargaining, the conclusion of agreements and (compulsory) referral to arbitration. These methods basically organize and 'rationalize' the stages of conflict and dispute settlement, restricting the spontaneous and unforeseen element. Law 2294/1994 also established, or rather reformulated, **public dialogue** that means, in essence, consultation under the threat of strike action or during a strike, on a mediator's initiative. It is voluntary for public enterprises and marks a new era in the manifestation of collective disputes, which are declining both quantitatively and qualitatively, and in their regulation by democratic methods – consensus, agreements, bargaining, dialogue – and informal procedures.

Prospects and Conclusions

The Greek industrial relations system is undergoing a period of significant transformation as a result of its accession to the European Communities. The impact is expressed in the form of deregulation, flexibility, a tendency towards the restriction of trade union presence (mainly in the private sector), increased female employment, growth of the informal labour market, a crisis and deterioration of the welfare state, and state intervention to encourage privatizations. The extent of all these changes has not yet become clear or finalized.

The Greek system has emerged from the isolation that formerly characterized it and is beginning to exhibit a wider interest. At the same time, it is seeking to establish its own special features amid the general confusion of remapping and globalization. What is at stake is the enhancement, rather than the loss, of its authentic and positive elements linked to values, expectations and the future of Greek society. At present, the future development of industrial relations in Greece is not at all clear. For the time being the system is making efforts to absorb the new phenomena, without having yet elaborated long-term employment policies and concrete fresh proposals. Discussions between the social actors are still mostly dominated by an adopted and as yet undeveloped European rhetoric. This blurred perspective is perhaps also connected with the fact that it is only during the past few years that indigenous knowledge in the field has been produced and the academic discipline of industrial relations has started to progress in Greece.

Beyond this consolidation of institutions at what is still mainly a level of legislative regulation, there is also some change in the attitudes and thinking of the social partners. Over the past decade in particular, the State has appeared to adopt a fresh stance towards workers and their representatives, lending a 'listening ear' to their demands and approaches.

The more modern generation of Greek employers has reacted positively to European Community exhortations urging social dialogue, but social dialogue is still not in general practice. The opportunity to settle industrial disputes and resolve current problems by this democratic method, respecting conflicting interests in an innovative manner, seems to have been lost. Even the State itself, while indicating formal agreement with the principles of social dialogue and indeed recommending that they should be followed, tends on occasion to behave in the familiar autocratic manner by suddenly passing laws which profoundly concern employees without any prior arrangement, dialogue or attempts to arrive at consent or acceptance. However, by this formula of social dialogue the Government attempted in spring 1997 to introduce, with the unions' consent, new regulations reducing protection against collective dismissals and providing for more flexible working time and new forms of work with no improved social protection: new regulations to facilitate the Maastricht economic convergence criteria, introducing an industrial relations policy quite different from that of the preceding decade.

Such instances trigger, by way of a chain reaction, the old patterns of bitter conflict on the part of the unions. Thus, the fragile and conflict-prone nature of the Greek industrial relations system has not been erased but it has been blunted. The unions, however, remain unable to project a new voice and contemporary claims that are more than purely defensive, or a new credo. This problem is, of course, one that is shared by many European trade unions. The absence of indigenous unionist thinking and genuinely unionist practice may perhaps create an even greater problem for Greek trade unionism. The differences between the political factions are still one of the basic traditional causes of the instability of the Greek industrial relations system, although to a lesser degree. This is also reflected in the context of the above social dialogue.

Changes and approaches to European policy are, however, proceeding despite the contrasting features within the Greek industrial relations system. It is taking the first firm steps towards an industrial culture, constantly twisting and turning between the dualities and contrasts which it cannot outmanoeuvre and which make up its complexity: institutions and laws which are provided but not always implemented even when the preconditions are fulfilled; the differences between large and small enterprises (where the preconditions are not fulfilled); the considerable scale of the informal labour market, which can only be guessed at – enlarged by the arrival of emigrants of Greek origin and immigrants from Asian and African countries; the difference in treatment between employees in the private sector and in the public sector; the large number of self-employed; the restricted bargaining power of the unions (thus strengthening government incomes policy); and the need to promote them in order to develop the system itself.

It must be added that dynamic changes are likely in the public sector and public administration as a result of reforms aimed at controlling the public deficit and at increasing both the competitiveness and the quality of public services and at improving the flexibility and efficiency of the public sector.

Modernization will be beneficial only if: first, it does not result in the disappearance of all the positive features of the Greek industrial relations system; second, it does not lead to a worsening of pay and conditions, particularly for the low-paid; and third, it does not impair the public function and *raison d'être* of the public utilities and services.

Although the Greek industrial relations system is closely tied to the European Union, there is still room for some choices of its own tailored to the particular nature of the national situation and to modernized social policies not determined exclusively by the rationale of competition. Certain choices that have already been made, such as flexible working time arrangements which benefit the enterprise but ignore the needs of the family (especially children), and privatizations or the introduction of the rationale of the market into the public sector and public administration without any safeguard for general social interests, seem to threaten the fundamental features of Greek industrial relations based on a positive State presence.

Proposals moulded more closely to Greek reality – such as the predominance of small and medium-sized enterprises, the growing extent of the informal labour market, the importance of state intervention for ensuring wider interests, the traditionally high labour mobility and the significance of female labour, which is still invisible – could strengthen the system's authentic and positive characteristics. Having emerged from its geographical isolation, modernized and forming a part of the European Union, it could also serve as a useful example to other Balkan countries with which it has strong historical links – for example, in relation to employee participation within the enterprise and at other levels.

The prospects for the future development of the Greek industrial relations system are dependent, in the main, on whether the social actors adopt, in the context described above, policies which are creative and original rather than purely passive and copied.

Further Reading

Aliprantis, N., *The Legal System and Collective Labour Phenomena*, Athens-Komotini, Sakkoulas, 1984.

Dassios, L., *Labour Procedural Law*, 5 vols. (A/I 1995, A/II 1992, B/I 1983, B/II 1984, B/III), Athens.

European Foundation for the Improvement of Living and Working Conditions, *Collective Bargaining and Equal Opportunities in Greece,* Dublin, European Foundation, 1996.

Karakatsanis, A., *Collective Labour Law,* 3rd edition, Athens-Komotini, Sakkoulas, 1992.

Koukiadis, I., *Labour Law. Individual Employment Relationships*, Thessaloniki, Sakkoulas, 1995.

Koukoules, G., 'Seventy Years of Recent Trade Union History', *Trade Union Review,* 45, pp. 11-28, September 1988.

Kravaritou, Y., *Employee Participation in Greek Companies*, Thessaloniki, Sakkoulas, 1986.

Kravaritou, Y., *Employment and Women's Rights*, Thessaloniki, Sakkoulas, 1991.

Lixouriotis, G., *Collective Labour Agreements: Social Partners in Collective Bargaining*, Athens-Komotini, Sakkoulas, 1992.

Mavrogordatos, G., *Between Pityocampa and Procrustes: Trade Unions in Greece Today*, Athens, Odysseas, 1988.

Spyropoulos, G., *Collaboration of Employers, Employees and the State in Matters of Health, Safety and Working Conditions,* Athens, Health and Safety and Working Conditions Institute, 1995.

Traulos-Tzanetatos, D., *Labour Law at the Crossroads,* Athens, Odysseas, 1990.

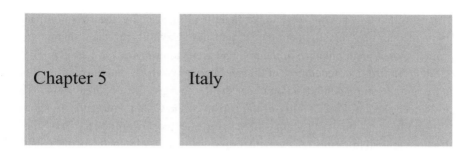

Chapter 5　　Italy

Serafino Negrelli and Tiziano Treu

Historical Background

The history of industrial relations in Italy has been characterized by the delayed development of the process of industrialization, accompanied by a heavy dependence on the state economy. But during the period immediately following the Second World War, the experience of the 20-year Fascist regime (1922-1943) also left its mark. Such an adverse climate helps to explain why in Italy the pluralist model (not only in industrial relations), the trade union organizations and collective bargaining remained weak up till the 1960s. Although the first form of employee representation at workplace level recognized by Italian employers, the *commissione interna* or works committee, had formally come into being as early as 1906 with the company agreement signed between FIOM (the metalworkers' union) and the Itala company of Turin (the original Fiat company), it was not until the Buozzi-Mazzini Agreement of 2 September 1943, between the single unified trade union confederation at that time (CGIL) and the industrial employers' association (Confindustria), that this important form of representation was re-established, initially with extensive bargaining powers but subsequently possessing only the function of monitoring and implementing the outcome of negotiations. And it was not until after the 'hot autumn' of 1969 that the new employee representation formula of 'workers' delegates', forming a *consiglio di fabbrica* or workers' council within each workplace, received recognition as rank-and-file union bodies with powers including the competence to conclude collective agreements.

The rebuilt trade unions were subsequently influenced by the two political movements, the socialist-communist and the Catholic-christian democrat, which gained predominance in the political arena after the fall of Fascism. The CGIL (General Confederation of Italian Workers), which was created as the unitary trade union confederation under the Rome Agreement of June 1944 and expressed the anti-Fascist unity of the parties of the CLN (National Liberation Committee), soon split into three separate confederations: first the Catholic-christian democrat element broke away in 1948 to form the CISL (Italian Confederation of Workers' Unions), and then in 1950 the republican and social democrat elements broke away to form the UIL (Union of Italian Workers). Since then the CGIL has remained dominated by the communists, although retaining a significant socialist faction. This ideological cleavage and attendant dependence of the unions on the political system was to be a permanent feature of the actors in the Italian industrial relations system. However, the divisions did not prevent the development of a pluralist model, characterized by the very high levels of conflict and unionization that were reached in the late 1960s and early 1970s.

There has been very little direct legislative regulation of trade unions and collective bargaining. Although Article 39 of the Constitution not only establishes the right to organize collectively but also provides for the registration of trade unions and employers' associations as a prerequisite for their possession of legal personality and the capacity to conclude collective agreements that are generally binding, ie, covering all employees in the bargaining unit concerned, no legislation has ever been enacted to implement this second part. And in the case of Article 40 of the Constitution, establishing the right to strike, it was not until 1990 that the first legislation was enacted in the form of Law No. 146 on the right to strike in essential public services. The notable role of Law No. 300 of 1970 (the Workers' Statute) must, nevertheless, be emphasized. However, it is only from the second half of the 1980s onwards, in connection with the issues of labour flexibility and the problems created by the level of conflict and claims on the part of autonomous unions outside the traditional confederations mainly in the education, transport and health sectors, that there has been an increased degree of legislative intervention in industrial relations, sometimes supportive and sometimes regulatory.

Collective bargaining has endured as the prevalent method in the Italian industrial relations system from the immediate post-war years up to the present day. Throughout this entire period, three basic bargaining levels have played a central role: national multi-industry bargaining (*contrattazione interconfederale*), industry-level bargaining (*contrattazione nazionale di categoria*) and company-level bargaining (*contrattazione aziendale*). In addition, a fourth, decentralized, level (the regional or territorial level) has always featured as important during certain historical phases and in certain sectors, such as agriculture, commerce, construction and the small craft trades sector (*artigianato*).

A persistent fundamental feature of the Italian industrial relations system, together with its low degree of institutionalization, has also been the traditional 'bipolarity' of bargaining; at any one time, two of these basic levels have tended to be predominant.

Of the factors possibly associated with the birth and development of these bargaining levels, state intervention can be regarded as of only minor importance (given the exception of bargaining within the public administration, which for a long time was characterized by regulatory features very different from those laid down by general legislation and only recently amended to approximate them to those applying in the private sector, under Legislative Decree No. 29 of 1993 on the 'privatization' of the public employment relationship).

A more important influence as regards developments in the Italian bargaining structure has been exerted by the history and forms of employers' organization. The role of Confindustria (the General Confederation of Italian Industry), which for a long time was the sole central employers' association, reinforced the centralization of the bargaining structure during the immediate post-war period and in the 1950s. With the passage of time this role became weaker, particularly from the l960s onwards. This was not only because of the withdrawal of the state-owned and controlled enterprises from Confindustria in 1957 and their formation into two separate associations (ASAP and Intersind), although these performed an innovatory function as regards the birth and development of 'articulated' or formally decentralized bargaining at enterprise level in the 1960s, and the introduction of information and consultation rights in the 1970s and 1980s. It was also a consequence of the emergence, within Confindustria itself, of specific sectoral employers' federations (in 1971 Federmeccanica for engineering, in 1975 Federtessile for textiles and clothing, in 1984 Federchimica for chemicals and, more recently, the Federazione del Terziario Avanzato for service industries), which have obviously placed the emphasis on national bargaining at industry level.

A complementary role as regards these developments in the bargaining structure has been played, in turn, by the history and forms of trade union organization, with the presence of unions organized either on a territorial basis ('horizontal' structure, ie, grouping together all the workers living in a given geographical area, even though they are employed in different production sectors and have different specific skills, such as the *camere del lavoro* (Chambers of Labour)), or on an industry basis ('vertical' structure, with federations such as that for metalworkers which organize, at national level, all the workers employed in a given production sector even though they do different jobs).

More than all these other factors, however, the major influence on the development of the Italian industrial relations system and its associated bargaining structure has come from the production and occupational system. From the late 1950s onwards, the spread of mass-production methods in industry imposed the general manual worker (*operaio comune*) as a new and predominant category of employee. As a consequence, the union centralization of the immediate post-war period gave way to a degree of autonomy on the part of the industry-based federations (*federazioni di categoria*), which were given recognized powers to negotiate variations in pay autonomously, even though for a long time the dynamic of such industry-level agreements remained less than that deriving from the pay indexation (*scala mobile*, literally 'sliding-scale') mechanism regulated by the National Multi-Industry Agreement of 1945. It was only from the period 1968-1973 onwards that the greater strength of the national industry-level union structures, including peripheral areas, became established over the lesser strength of the horizontal structures. The origin of this process is attributable not only to the spread of mass production and the associated change in the composition of the labour force, but also to economic conditions (trend towards full employment) and political circumstances (new centre-left government coalitions) more favourable to the unions.

However, the enduring existence of industrial dualisms, in terms of both enterprise size and regional disparity (North-South), helps to explain the persistence even in subsequent periods of a bipolar structure and the alternating phases of centralization and decentralization which have continued to mark the history of industrial relations in Italy up to the present day. It is, for example, precisely in relation to the fragmentation of the production system and the widespread presence of small and medium-sized enterprises that the importance of the industry-level agreement is emphasized by all the social actors, in terms of the effects on the labour market (or their labour markets). And it was precisely in consideration of these historical characteristics of the development of Italian capitalism and industrial relations that the reform of the bargaining structure introduced in the National Multi-Industry Agreement of 23 July 1993 was directed at defining a dual level of functioning: national industry-level bargaining for the traditional functions of establishing uniformity in regard to minimum standards for labour protection and pay; and decentralized bargaining (either at company level or at district or provincial level) for the functions of establishing supplementary provisions, flexibility and, above all, innovation as regards components of pay linked to company results in terms of productivity, quality and profitability.

The National Multi-Industry Agreement of 23 July 1993 is the first of the three reforms of the Italian industrial relations system agreed between the social partners during the 1990s. The economic crises and restructuring programmes which affected large Italian enterprises during the 1980s and early 1990s led to major downsizing operations and substantial job losses, a situation aggravated by a context of high unemployment and the inability of the tertiary sector to create new jobs as it had done in the past. In addition, the public sector likewise has no longer been able to absorb, as was traditionally the case, the surplus labour from the private sector, given the consistent levels of the government debt and deficit. In the context of the new economic constraints imposed by European integration, the Agreement of 23 July 1993 therefore represents the first reform aimed at imposing an appropriate incomes policy and at bringing inflation within the Maastricht criteria. A second reform, the radical revision of the pensions system agreed between the social partners and introduced by Law No. 335 of 1995, is aimed at achieving substantial savings in social insurance expenditure. And a third reform, the 'Employment Agreement' (*Patto per il lavoro*) signed by the social partners in September 1996 and implemented through Law No. 196 of 1997, is aimed at shifting employment policy away from the traditional passive forms – such as the Wages Guarantee Fund (*Cassa Integrazione Guadagni*) and early retirement schemes – towards the active forms, such as job creation and training, that have been so limited in Italy in comparison with other countries.

Economic and Social Context

Certain features of the Italian economic and social context have a particular influence on the industrial relations system.

Notable among these is the late economic development and transition of Italy from an agricultural to an industrial society: it was not until 1957, following the accelerated process of post-war reconstruction, that the percentage of the total labour force employed in industry exceeded the agricultural workforce; and in 1981 the service sector overtook both of these.

The industrial relations system and the logic applied by the parties involved are still almost entirely based on models derived from the industrial sector – it seems particularly difficult to establish employment relationships suited to the varied nature of the public and private service sectors. Among the various attempts made in this direction, attention should be drawn to Legislative Decree No. 29 of 1993 on the privatization of the public employment relationship, which is intended to bring employment relationships with the public administration within the purview of the same method of collective bargaining as that which prevails in the private sector. The growing importance of the service sector in the Italian economy has also brought a decline in the traditional level of conflict in manufacturing industry and the emergence of new models of industrial action in the tertiary sector, in which the indicators are higher levels of frequency of occurrence and numbers of participating employees, but shorter periods of duration than in the past. More recently, the Government and the social partners have been proposing a 'Work Statute' (*Statuto dei lavori*) that regulates union relations in the vast and growing world of self-employment.

The economic structure of the labour market is highly fragmented, because of the substantial percentage of small and very small work/production units. Although their proliferation no longer necessarily implies that the economic system is weak, it does represent, and not only in Italy, a critical factor for industrial relations and labour law, both of which have been historically based on large industrial enterprises.

The decline in the average size of work/production units to a level below the threshold at which statutory legislation and collective agreements apply (which differs from country to country) has progressively confined a large part of labour law to the regulation of quantitatively minor sections of private sector employment whereas it was in fact originally intended to cover all such employees.

This confused situation is made even more complex by two other trends in employment: the spread of **self-employment**, which in Italy has reached proportions higher than the average levels in other countries and, according to some, is anomalous in that it indicates work of dubious security and social usefulness; and the emerging **differentiation** of forms of working as compared with the prototype of traditional work under a contract of employment of indefinite duration (such forms include part-time work, fixed-term and temporary employment, work/training contracts, subcontracted work, cooperatives, etc).

Both these trends, by giving rise to differentiation, are contributing to erosion of the traditional rules of labour relations without, however, so far foreshadowing alternative stable models (or indeed any way of regulating employment relationships on an individual basis). This effect is all the more marked since these trends form part of even broader changes in the composition of the labour force, both qualitative and quantitative, which Italy is experiencing along with most other developed countries. These include the above-mentioned trend towards the service sector, with the parallel segmentation of labour markets and changes in job qualifications and skills brought about (in part) by the advent of new technologies; the altered ratios of male to female workers, of age group to age group and of employed to unemployed; and the resulting phenomenon of an irregular supply of labour not entirely governed by demand.

This fragmentation is accompanied by other dualisms which have a powerful influence on the regulation of employment relationships. The North-South divide in Italy, which is manifested in all the social and economic indicators, remains the principal element in the national imbalance; the figures for unemployment, which is still concentrated in the south of the country, are merely the most dramatic evidence of this:

					(%)
		1993	1994	1995	1996
Male:	Centre/North	4.05	5.29	5.66	5.26
	South	16.46	14.79	17.01	17.50
	All Italy	9.17	8.52	9.52	9.42
Female:	Centre/North	9.52	11.47	11.89	11.67
	South	27.66	26.29	29.51	30.50
	All Italy	15.68	15.59	16.77	16.84
Total:	Centre/North	6.17	7.67	8.11	7.80
	South	20.10	18.48	21.06	21.73
	All Italy	11.59	11.10	12.21	12.20

Source: ISTAT

The dualism between the private and public sectors in labour relations is common to all countries, though it has tended to diminish in recent years. But in the Italian system it takes on greater importance, if only because of the size of the public sector. The percentage of the working population employed in the public sector is in the medium-to-high bracket on an international scale, but to this must be added those working in public enterprises, which, although regulated by the norms of private sector labour law, have traditionally played a special role that has sometimes been controversial in relation to private companies in the sphere of industrial relations. The privatization of many state-owned and controlled enterprises in the banking, telecommunications and energy sectors under the IRI and ENI corporations, a process that commenced during the 1990s, will have effects on industrial relations that are difficult to predict at present.

In the 1980s, the separation of employment relationships in the public sector from those in the private sector (only partly corrected by the recognition of collective bargaining in the public sector) led to major inconsistencies, and not only in Italy. It enabled rigid and formalistic methods of labour management to survive, not linked in any way to controls of efficiency or effectiveness and in fact even inimical to them. This is a phenomenon that can also be observed in certain private service sectors, such as banking and insurance, which have traditionally been characterized by rules differing from the system employed in industry in so far as they are not exposed to international competition. In this case also, major changes have occurred during the 1990s with the privatization of the public employment relationship mentioned above, which not only extends the role of collective bargaining but also introduces budgetary restraints and increased discretionary powers for management, creating greater autonomy for union action which in the past had too great a degree of co-responsibility for poor human resource management.

It is not merely by chance that increasing international competition, particularly in Europe, is challenging the separation between these various systems and subjecting to powerful stresses the rules and practices prevailing in the service sectors, to an even greater extent than in the industrial sector. Both the National Multi-Industry Agreement of 23 July 1993 for the private sector and the Legislative Decree of 1993 on the privatization of the public employment relationship open with a chapter on the convergence criteria of the Maastricht Treaty (including inflation, Government debt and deficit), which can be met only by achieving the increased efficiency that these two reform measures seek to develop in both sectors through incomes policy. And the effects were immediately positive. Collectively agreed pay increases were well below the rate of inflation in 1993 (2.7 per cent pay increase as against 4.2 per cent inflation) and in 1994 (1.9 per cent as against 4 per cent). This trend was influenced to a large extent by the stagnation of pay in the public administration (increases of 0.8 per cent in 1993 and 0.4 per cent in 1994), which was also a strong signal that in contrast to past practice the State, as the third party to industrial relations, was for the first time observing the priorities laid down by centralized agreements.

If the economic context presents numerous elements of difficulty and turbulence for industrial relations, the same applies to the socio-political context. The fragility of the structures underlying industrial relations in Italy, such as the trade unions and collective bargaining, the traditionally adversarial nature of the system and its lack of institutionalization are linked among other things with the country's strong ideological and political polarization, not only between the Centre and the Left but within the Left itself (owing to the presence of the largest Communist Party in the Western world). During the 1990s that traditional polarization has lessened considerably, both as a result of international events (the collapse of the Soviet model and the consequent rapid changes in communist parties everywhere, including the Italian Communist Party) and as a result of national events (the bribes scandal (*Tangentopoli*) and the resultant disappearance of the traditional parties of government: the Christian Democrats and the Socialist Party). Thus, 1994 saw the first elections based on the new first-past-the-post system and competition between a centre-right pole (Forza Italia, Alleanza Nazionale and minority Catholic parties) and a centre-left pole (the Ulivo or Olive Tree Party, Democratic Party of the Left, the Catholic Partito Populare, the Communist Reconstruction Party, and others). The traditional ideological divisions of the trade unions, and also of the employers' associations, have in actuality been overcome, but the old names and organizations remain even though all the leaders of the various elements profess support for the processes of unification between the various strands.

Institutional and Legal Framework

The most obvious feature is that the Italian trade union system is still among the least (externally) regulated, if not the most autonomous, of all the developed countries with a market economy. None of the principal institutions which make it up (such as trade union freedom, the trade union as an organization and collective bargaining) is subject to legislative control. Italian trade union law has developed outside any legislative scheme, with a significant shift away from the constitutional model, which, while recognizing trade union institutions as a basic component of a pluralistic society, viewed them in an institutional context 'with roles and functions pre-established by a clearly regulated set of competences'.

This absence of legislative control, underlined by the 'private' status of the unions, has never equated to 'immunity' or total deregulation, as is sometimes claimed polemically. It has rather been a case of weak regulation exercised chiefly over the activities rather than over the actors, with the intensity of this regulation varying at different times.

This situation still persists, despite the fact that the Italian trade union movement, like others in developed countries, has for some time been the subject of 'special' rules and treatment which differentiate it from virtually every other private association. These include the provisions supporting trade union activity within companies contained in the so-called 'Workers' Statute', Law No. 300/1970; the legal measures which were already present in the pre-corporatist phase but proliferated after the Second World War, and which grant the most representative trade unions the power to appoint representatives on public bodies of various kinds, mostly administrative (the CNEL (National Council for Economic Affairs and Labour), the main social security institutions, the employment services, etc); and the recognition of the trade union as one of the parties in the dialogue with government bodies, resulting from the support provided by the Workers' Statute, constitutional case law legitimizing 'economico-political' strikes and the practice of these same government bodies.

From 1976 onwards, the relationship between the social partners and the State has become closer, giving rise to a number of instances of tripartite cooperation mainly aimed at combating the high rate of inflation during this period. This tripartite cooperation took the form, among other things, of legislative intervention to exercise direct control over labour costs (in particular of the pay indexation mechanism) and hence over the collective autonomy of the social partners, which had hitherto been the sole regulator of such matters. This was undoubtedly a departure from the abstentionist model, but has gradually lost significance with the slowing-down in the rate of inflation.

During the 1990s calls came from various quarters for a greater degree of institutionalization of industrial relations in the face of the increasing turbulence of the economic and social scene. However, despite pressure for **legislative** intervention as regards various aspects of industrial relations, such as trade union representation and bargaining, these calls gave prominence, instead, to forms of **negotiated** regulation agreed between the social partners. The only exceptions to this trend were Law No. 146 of 1990 on strikes in essential services, which reduced the importance of self-regulation and gave more scope to the role of legislation, and Law No. 125 of 1991 on forms of positive action to further the equal treatment of men and women in employment. This statute reinforces the available sanctions against discrimination and promotes equal opportunities.

The National Multi-Industry Agreement of 23 July 1993 tends, nevertheless, to confirm the priority in Italy of forms of collective regulation expressed through collective bargaining, a priority which was in fact observed even in the case of the two above-mentioned 1990s Laws and in all the 1970s measures (starting with the Workers' Statute) that are referred to as 'legislative support of unions' (*legislazione di sostegno*) and in the legislation of the 1980s on labour flexibility.

Individual employment relationships, unlike collective ones, have always been subject to strict regulation, either from the State (legislation and case law) or through collective bargaining. The rather generalized protective legislation has been supplemented, usually in the direction of improvement, by collective agreements which act as the effective source of regulation of the employment relationship. This large body of regulation has been strengthened by an increased level of judicial activism, supported after the passing of Law No. 533/1973 by a more efficient organization of case hearings.

A characteristic feature of the Italian system is the strict public control of the labour market, which has traditionally been one of the main preoccupations of the authorities, reflecting the typical imbalances above all of the employment situation. At the heart of this rigid control lies the public employment service, the obligatory recruitment channel, traditionally based on the rule that the employer must send to the employment office a request for the workers he or she wishes to take on, not naming any particular individuals but specifying only the number needed (a rule which was devised in order to allocate job opportunities according to impartial criteria such as how long a person had been on the unemployment register). However, the very rigidity of the system, combined with the inefficiency of local employment offices, has made this rule more and more inadequate; it was at first circumvented unofficially, and then gradually modified by legislation. Eventually, Law No. 223 of 1991 radically modified the public employment service system as laid down by Law No. 204 of 1949, by making it permissible for employers to use the 'recruitment by name procedure' (*chiamata nominativa*) for hiring all employees. Under the new system, the employment office merely records movements in the labour market, and has completely lost its original function of mediation between labour supply and demand. In addition, a 1997 judgment by the Court of Justice of the European Communities, which ruled state monopoly of the job placement function to be unlawful, has encouraged the entry of non-public agencies into this field of activity.

This is one area of labour law which has been partly deregulated. For the rest, the Italian system has been noticeably slow to move in response to demands for deregulation of the provisions that traditionally guarantee employment protection. A few cases of de-legislation have been admitted, but they have been made conditional upon agreement between the collective parties: for instance, the lifting of the ban on night work for women (Article 5, Law No. 903/1977) and relaxation of the traditional legal limits on fixed-term contracts (Law No. 56/1987). Agreement between the parties must sometimes be combined with or supplemented by administrative intervention by the authority which in the final analysis possesses the power of exemption. For example, exemption from the condition of continuous service in cases of transfer of undertaking (new Article 2112 of the Civil Code) and exemption from some public placement regulations entrusted to the regional employment commission (Law No. 140/1981 and now Law No. 56/1987).

The most frequent instances are not a matter of deregulation as such, but rather modification of the legislation or, as it is called, re-regulation, aimed both at simplifying the form of regulation and at making it more adaptable. What is more, in May 1990 the legislators extended protection against unfair dismissal to cover the employees of work/production units employing a workforce of fewer than 15 employees, thus opposing the pressure for deregulation.

This trend towards deregulation and re-regulation is also evident in the 'Employment Agreement' (*Patto per il lavoro*) signed by the social partners in September 1996 and translated into law by Law No. 197 of 1997. This new statute regulates a new form of temporary work, ie, temporary-employment agency work (*lavoro interinale*), which was formerly prohibited in Italy. In addition, however, it:

- amends the legal regime governing fixed-term employment, introducing new exceptions and flexibility;
- provides incentives for the introduction of reduced and more flexible working hours and part-time work, which has been little used in Italy;
- contains provisions on the revival of the apprenticeship system and work/training contracts, forms of hiring which are now among the most popular with Italian employers;
- provides for the reorganization of the vocational training system;
- offers incentives for the realignment of pay with the minimum collectively agreed rates in enterprises in the South;
- introduces 'socially useful work' as a programme whereby unemployed persons and individuals receiving payments from the Wages Guarantee Fund can be given employment in activities of benefit to the general community (workfare); and
- launches a special youth employment scheme providing grants and loans as incentives for the start-up of new enterprises.

One fundamental institution for the regulation of the labour market (some maintain that it is the main one) is the Wages Guarantee Fund, which guarantees a proportion (80 per cent) of earnings to employees in companies and sectors undergoing an economic crisis or in the process of restructuring. The Fund has proved to be a highly effective protective instrument in the legislation assisting companies suffering economic difficulties and those employed by such companies. It has indirectly promoted flexibility of employment in so far as it has favoured sizeable structural adjustments to Italian industry without mass redundancies. In the same way it has created a protective network for the presence and activity of trade unions confronted with company restructuring.

Actors in Industrial Relations

The actors in industrial relations, the trade unions and the employers' organizations, represent the area that is farthest removed from outside regulation.

The fact that these organizations belong to the category of non-recognized associations does not preclude their capacity to act as legal entities, to conclude collective agreements, to call strikes and to be legitimately entitled to act in front of a court. Moreover, this status has helped to keep them free from interference in their internal affairs on the part of the law, which in this case has observed a greater degree of self-restraint than in other aspects of collective relationships.

Trade Unions

The lack of legal rules also extends to trade union representation within the company, where, although the Workers' Statute recognizes a range of rights at workplace level (mass meetings, ballots, provision of a room for union activities, time off, leave of absence and reinforced protection of union officers against employer discrimination), no organizational model has been laid down by law.

The sole requirement for legislative support, here as in the other cases described above, is that representation should relate to trade unions defined as 'most representative' on the basis of a series of indices provided partly by legislation and partly by case law (number of registered members, representation activity, extent of presence geographically and in the various sectors, etc). In this way the concept of 'representativeness' has become the filter for identification of the beneficiaries of special legislative support, in place of the registration that was specified in Article 39 of the Constitution. On the basis of similar preoccupations, Italian legislators have avoided recognizing a general trade union right to bargain (with a reciprocal obligation on the part of employers) on the grounds that a sanction of this kind would have almost inevitably meant providing a legislative definition of bargaining agents and procedures and hence (to a greater or lesser extent) of trade union organization.

A number of amendments to this legal framework ensued from the National Referendum of 11 June 1995 (an institution of direct democracy provided for by the Italian Constitution), which included questions on the total or partial repeal of rules of considerable significance to trade union law. In particular, the consequence of the partial repeal of Article 19 of the Workers' Statute has been that only those unions that are signatories to a collective agreement applied in a given work/production unit may form a plant-level union structure. This outcome has given rise to considerable debate as being quite contrary to the intentions of the supporters of the referendum, who had in fact wished to see an increase in the number of those entitled to enjoy the union rights provided for under Part III of the Workers' Statute.

This climate of non-regulated promotion of trade union activity favoured, after the post-war reconstruction period, a consistent growth of trade unions and collective bargaining that was particularly marked during the years 1968-1978. Total union density fell from 50.8 per cent in 1950 to 28.4 per cent in 1960, but climbed back to 38.4 per cent in 1970 to reach a peak of 49.0 per cent in 1980. By 1990 it had fallen again to 39.3 per cent and to 36.8 per cent in 1996.

The increase in union membership recorded in absolute figures in the 1980s and 1990s was mainly attributable to retired workers, whereas, in terms of economically active employees, combined membership of the three major confederations (CGIL, CISL and UIL) fell from 7,137,555 in 1980 to 5,660,956 in 1993 (–20.7 per cent). In 1993, unionization was high in the agricultural sector (93.7 per cent), moderate in manufacturing industry (41.9 per cent) and non-market services (47 per cent) and still low in market services (22.8 per cent).

However, there has been a trend during the 1990s towards a strengthening of trade unionism outside the three major confederations, with unions that had already been growing in strength in the 1980s. These 'autonomous' unions have an established tradition in Italy. CISNAL, the almost wholly public sector union with a registered membership of more than 2 million, has always been opposed to the three confederations by virtue of its links with the political right. CISAL, the quasi-public sector union with a registered membership of 1.8 million, has in its turn always had its base in a number of sectors such as the railways (FISAFS), education (SNALS) and public employees (FISAFS and SNALS are both affiliates). In 1994, 10 organizations in various sectors formed ISA, a grouping of autonomous unions covering 4 million registered members, with the aim of increasing their bargaining power, developing closer organizational coordination and achieving higher visibility.

The other fairly recent element of trade unionism outside the major confederations is directed more towards a revival of a type of craft or skill-based trade unionism, expressed in the form of *cobas* (rank-and-file committees), sometimes emerging in the wake of protest and dissension within the confederations and exhibiting tendencies towards radicalism and militancy. Although more difficult to quantify, this element has been particularly active in mobilizing increased levels of conflict in the transport sector (COMU uniting train drivers) and the public services.

From the very beginning, the Italian organizational model of a trade union has been based on a combination of **vertical** structures, the industrial federations, and **horizontal** structures, the Chambers of Labour or groupings of unions on a geographical basis, converging at the top into the Confederation.

The presence of a strong horizontal component is no longer merely a sign of weakness, as was originally the case and still is in, for example, the French system; it serves, despite quite a few uncertainties, to promote trade union initiatives in the sphere of economic policies and to allow some control of the freedom to negotiate across the various industrial sectors.

Trade union representation in the workplace, traditionally weak in Italy, was strengthened in the late 1960s, particularly in the industrial sector, by the spread of workers' delegates and workers' councils. This is an organizational model of the 'single union channel' type, comparable with the British system of shop stewards. The developments which took place in the 1980s, resulting from changes in the labour force and difficulties in inter-union relationships, greatly weakened this unitary form of representation.

Consequently, following the progressive crisis in and loss of representativeness of the workers' councils, the new company-level combined trade union body known as the 'unitary workplace union structure' (Rappresentanza Sindacale Unitaria, or RSU) was introduced. These RSUs were created by a CGIL-CISL-UIL framework agreement of 1 March 1991, and were given express recognition under the National Multi-Industry Agreement of 23 July 1993 and concrete form by a subsequent Agreement of December 1993 for manufacturing industry. All these agreements confirm the preference of the Italian trade union movement for the single-channel system of representation, since the RSU is simultaneously both the rank-and-file body of the various unions and the body representing the entire workforce in the individual work/production unit concerned. And the composition of these new structures, which retain all the rights granted by law and collective bargaining to the old RSAs (plant-level union structures identified with the workers' councils), including rights to information and consultation and competence to bargain at company level, emphasizes even more than in the past the characteristics of the single channel of representation: two-thirds of the seats on the RSU are filled by representatives elected by the workforce as a whole, with the remaining third reserved for appointment or election by the unions that are signatories to the relevant industry-wide agreement.

Employers

The organizational model of employers' associations has been historically based, not only in Italy, on that of the trade unions, and it consequently likewise displays the dual vertical and horizontal structure.

The horizontal (geographical) component has traditionally played the leading role, more than in the case of the trade unions, although for different reasons. In fact, only a few sectoral federations within Confindustria (in particular Federmeccanica, Federchimica and Federtessile, the engineering, chemicals and textiles employers' federations mentioned above) engage in autonomous industrial relations activity, and even then under control exercised by the Confederation. In more general terms, the solidity of the employers' organizations, their control over affiliated enterprises and their capacity to take initiatives in industrial relations have never been very marked; to a large extent this reflects the dualisms in Italy's economic system which have already been noted, and the consequent divergence of interests among the various employers' sectors.

In this connection it is significant, and a typically Italian trait, that the employers' organizations are not only divided into the major branches of the economy and sizes of company (Confindustria (industry), Confcommercio (commerce), Confagricoltura (agriculture), Confapi (small and medium-sized enterprises), Confartigianato (artisans), and Coldiretti and Confcoltivatori (small farmers)), but for a time were also differentiated by form of ownership, following the disaffiliation of state-owned and controlled enterprises from Confindustria in 1957, which led to the formation of ASAP (grouping all petrochemical public enterprises) and Intersind (grouping all remaining public enterprises). The re-affiliation of these two public employers' associations within Confindustria in recent years has only partly reduced the fragmented pattern of employer representation, since the other three criteria (sector, size and ideology) have persisted.

The new activism in industrial relations observed on the part of employers from the second half of the 1980s, which to a large extent reflects the crisis in trade union representativeness, appears to be sustained by initiatives from individual employers rather than by the various organizations.

The possibility of establishing non-unionized labour relations is regarded as realistic only in certain areas where there are very small high-tech firms.

Elsewhere, the policy of the employers appears to oscillate between seeking to get the unions involved in 'participatory' relations (as exemplified in the IRI Protocol, and in the case of Zanussi or that of Fiat at Melfi) and making attempts on an 'opportunist' basis to restrict the influence exerted by trade unions and consequently the area covered by collective industrial relations (mainly in small or medium-sized enterprises).

The State

From the second half of the 1970s, an important part was played in Italian industrial relations history by the intervention of the State as a direct participant in the various episodes of social concertation (1977 Agreements on labour costs; Agreement of 22 January 1983; Protocol and Decree of February 1984). Among the common characteristics of these episodes and other European experiments in social concertation was the direct and decisive intervention by the State in using public resources (tax reductions benefiting employees and state-assisted reduction of social security charges benefiting employers; active employment policies) to facilitate the agreement between the social partners which was regarded as necessary to achieve economic stability. Such intervention aimed in particular at encouraging voluntary wage restraint and industrial peace on the part of the trade unions, as well as acceptance of the employers' demands for greater flexibility and increased productivity.

The turmoil of 1984-1985 (engendered by the refusal of the CGIL (General Confederation of Italian Workers) to sign the Agreement of 14 February 1984 with the Government, and the organization by the Italian Communist Party of a referendum on the repeal of the legislation on the pay indexation mechanism) revealed the economic and political difficulties bound up with these experiments in social concertation; in any event, the slowing-down of the rate of inflation made them less urgent, at least in this form.

During the 1990s the need to return to using tripartite centralized agreements in order to reduce the rate of inflation and meet the Maastricht criteria for European economic integration has renewed the importance of the State as the third actor in Italian industrial relations, although with different functions from those in the past. This is because the State no longer has substantial resources to put on the negotiating table to facilitate such agreements. Instead, it invites the social partners to show more restraint with regard to incomes policy in exchange for employment policies and measures to support the production system. This approach is illustrated by the National Multi-Industry Agreement of 23 July 1993 and the 'Employment Agreement' of September 1996.

The same approach is followed in the reform of the pensions system, introduced by Law No. 335/1995 as the fruit of extensive social concertation between the Government and the unions, which was aimed at achieving a saving of some ITL 110 billion over the following decade. The reforms designed to achieve this saving are:

- the application of new calculation criteria (changeover from the earnings-related system, ie, pension calculated on the basis of pay during the last years of employment, to the contributions-based system, ie, pension calculated on the basis of the personal record of contributions paid);
- gradual abolition of the separate 'contribution-years based pensions' (*pensioni di anzianità*);
- harmonizing pension arrangements for public employees (formerly more favourable) and for private sector employees; and
- the development of supplementary pension insurance.

In recent years, the role of the State as employer has become increasingly significant, both because of the quantitative importance of the public sector, as has already been seen, and because of the growing osmosis between the logic and treatment applied in this sector and those applied in the economy as a whole (sanctioned by the recognition of collective bargaining in the public sector, as mentioned earlier, under Legislative Decree No. 29 of 3 February 1993 on the privatization of the public employment relationship).

Among the major innovations introduced by the Decree, special mention should be made of the creation of ARAN (Agenzia per la rappresentanza negoziale delle pubbliche amministrazioni), a body entrusted with the task of representing public administration employers as signatories to framework agreements on public employment and national agreements for the various *comparti* (divisions) within public employment, and also, if they so request, with assisting the employing authorities concerned in decentralized bargaining. Thus, although the Agenzia's activities in negotiating and signing collective agreements are still subject to formal approval by the Government, the 'technical' bargaining role of the State as an actor in industrial relations has now, to all intents and purposes, been separated from the traditional duality of the role of the State as employer.

In short, in the context of changes regarding the various roles of the State as employer in the public administration, Legislative Decree No. 29/1993 establishes a clear separation between the tasks of policy direction, which are entrusted to the organs of Government, and the tasks of financial, technical and administrative management that are entrusted to managers, who are given greater discretionary powers in matters including personnel management. From the legislature's viewpoint, managers in the public administration are required to act in the capacity of employer with respect to the employees of the public authorities, with powers corresponding to those possessed by private sector employers plus a responsibility for the results of the activity carried on by the departments they head and for compliance with the relevant budgetary restraints.

Overall, the public administration has exhibited the rigour demanded both by the National Multi-Industry Agreement of 23 July 1993 and by Legislative Decree No. 29/1993. Much of the merit for the fact that many of the targets regarding inflation and the public deficit were achieved during this period is due to this change in the stance of the State as employer; in contrast to what has happened in the past, the State has been more consistent in adhering to the commitments entered into, in particular in the renewal of collective agreements.

Collective Bargaining

From the very beginning, the cornerstone of the Italian industrial relations system has been collective bargaining. The use (as also the principle) of participatory instruments in the broad sense to resolve individual and collective problems of the employment relationship through 'cooperation' has never been significant.

It is not by chance that Article 46 of the Constitution, which sanctions the right of workers to cooperate in the management of enterprises, is the weakest (or perhaps rather the least meaningful) of the constitutional norms. Only in recent years has interest in forms of collective action other than collective bargaining appeared to be on the increase (see below).

In the private sector collective bargaining is not governed by specific regulations relating to procedures, content and participants. The collective agreement, as such, has acquired a legal identity on the basis of the principles of private law worked out by creative case law. The (substantive) clauses of collective agreements are binding only on the members of the (employers') organizations that are signatories to them (Italy is unique in Europe in this respect).

The legal frailty of the institution was offset by the exceptional development of unionization during the 1960s and 1970s, whereby the general de facto application of collective agreements appeared to be an achievable goal. It has, however, become critical again in a new form with the phase of economic crisis and the profound changes in employment relationships mentioned above.

The low level of institutionalization and the instability of Italian industrial relations are also revealed clearly by the lack of development and weak enforceability of the so-called obligational part of the collective agreement: no-strike clauses and clauses providing for coordination between the various bargaining levels.

It is only recently that there have been signs of a reversal of this trend, with renewed attention being paid to the use of these contractual clauses as instruments for the framing of rules and procedures agreed on between the partners (for example in relation to cooling-off procedures and dispute prevention: see below). The National Multi-Industry Agreement of 23 July 1993 confirms the tendency towards a reinforcement of clauses as instruments of 'functional coordination' between the different bargaining levels, in stipulating that the second level (company-level or, alternatively, district-level bargaining) was to deal only with matters and practices which 'are different from and do not cover' those already dealt with at the first level (national industry-level bargaining) and, in the particular case of pay enhancements, only with payments related exclusively to specific company targets on productivity, quality and profitability.

The complexity of the Italian contractual system and its precarious stability are particularly evident in the bargaining structure. Traditionally, this was divided into several levels not found elsewhere: national multi-industry; industry-wide; company; and sometimes geographical.

The importance of the various levels and their inter-relationships have differed greatly over the years. The role of national multi-industry bargaining was a central one during the post-war reconstruction period, and then again in the years 1975-1985, at a time of rapid inflation, and once more in the 1990s.

This level consequently seems to be characteristic of 'crisis' phases; it has been used mainly to provide basic regulatory standards for the treatment or rights of large sectors of the economy: in the immediate post-war period, for instance, the agreements on collective and individual dismissals and on works committees, and subsequently on the Wages Guarantee Fund and on the pay indexation mechanism. It represents a tendency towards political bargaining with the State, as has occurred in the instances of social concertation mentioned earlier: in this case it also has the function of controlling (particularly pay) bargaining at the lower levels.

The industry-wide agreement has been the fulcrum of the system since the 1950s. It concerns general pay and working conditions, establishing the **standard** arrangements which can then be supplemented at the level of the individual company. During the 1970s it extended its scope to cover qualitative aspects of the administration of the employment relationship (health and safety, workloads, staffing levels, labour mobility, overtime) and of company policy (with the introduction of the rights of trade unions to receive information on and monitor investments, restructuring, etc). Company-level bargaining played a decisive role in the strong growth and innovation of the system between 1968 and 1975: it was decisive in bargaining for economic and regulatory conditions which improved the industry-wide standard conditions and were geared to specific production situations and the individual company's ability to pay, without any precise limit being laid down as to the matters covered. It was not until the 1990s that attempts were first made to prescribe limits in a definitive manner and, as seen earlier, were fully achieved in the National Multi-Industry Agreement of 23 July 1993.

As can be seen, it is a characteristic of the Italian system that there is a tendency towards bipolarism in the structure, ie, the presence of two fundamental levels: in the growth phase, these two levels were industry-wide and company-level bargaining, whereas, in the following decade, the national multi-industry level tended to take over from the industry-wide level as the result of a progressive centralization of the entire system.

In the second half of the 1980s there was a tendency towards a (further) decentralization of bargaining, which has affected the relevance of national multi-industry bargaining and, in the opinion of some commentators, has also diminished the role of industry-wide bargaining. This decentralization reflects the general trends in the economy which are favoured by the new flexible production technologies. It often appears to be encouraged by initiatives on the part of employers.

However, even in this case the push for decentralization has been contained and controlled from the centre. Those same employers' organizations have recognized the lasting importance of the industry-wide collective agreement as a stabilizing element, in particular for the myriad small firms which make up the greater part of the Italian production structure and for which industry-wide bargaining is realistically the only practical system.

With the advent of the 1990s, bipolarity again gave prominence to the central role of national multi-industry bargaining. In 1992 this level even, as in 1983, temporarily blocked decentralized company-level bargaining. Then came the National Multi-Industry Agreement of 23 July 1993, which revolutionized the traditional Italian bargaining structure. This Agreement stipulates that in the future there are to be only two levels, instead of the numerous fragmented levels existing in the past. Above all, however, it establishes the functions, duration and limits of these two levels: industry-wide bargaining at national level, with agreements lasting for four years as regards their normative provisions and two years as regards their pay provisions; and decentralized bargaining (company-level or district-level), with agreements lasting for four years and restricted to matters different from those negotiated at the higher level and, in the case of pay, to components linked exclusively to company performance indicators. To date, the industry-wide and company-level agreements signed since 1993 have demonstrated the validity of this bargaining structure, although the dispute in the metalworking sector over the second two-year pay round revealed new problems in industry-wide pay bargaining at national level during periods of low inflation. Nevertheless, any changes needing to be made to a bargaining structure which, after the first four-year trial period, has proved the most appropriate for the Italian economic system, are expected to amount to no more than minor adjustments.

Participation and Other Forms of Trade Union Activity

Mention has already been made of the relative absence of participatory forms in the Italian industrial relations system. The basic reasons for this lie in the structural characteristics of the system already described, the socio-economic imbalances, the high degree of socio-political conflict and polarization, and the strongly class-based and bargaining-culture nature of the Italian trade union tradition.

For many years after the Second World War, any attempt to establish participatory forms within the enterprise appeared to be incompatible with these characteristics, both to the trade union movement, which would have regarded these forms as a compromise impairing its autonomy, and to the employers, who did not consider them useful for stabilizing employee relations.

The system was different in the public sector (at least, until the advent of Legislative Decree No. 29/1993 on the privatization of the public employment relationship), where there has been a tradition of participation in the form of bilateral bodies or committees combining employees and management. One example was the staff councils of the Ministries, which in various ways controlled the administration and regulation of the employment relationship (from recruitment by open competition, to career paths and disciplinary matters and, on occasion, to the whole area of personnel policy).

These participatory forms are linked both to the tradition of trade unionism in the public sector and to the pattern of the public sector employment relationship, which traditionally excluded contractual regulation. In this way, the activity of these bodies represented in part the functional equivalent of the missing element: bargaining. Article 10 of Legislative Decree No. 29/1993 grants the unions only the right to information on matters that were traditionally the subject of participation but are now entrusted to collective bargaining. Although Article 10 is an innovation in the panorama of Italian industrial relations in that for the first time the right to information is given legal recognition, it must nevertheless be noted that the same Article also allows more scope for the prerogative powers of managers in the public administration; once the 15-day period prescribed for the form of consultation known as *esame congiunto* (joint examination) has expired, they are free to take decisions autonomously.

Participatory forms have also always been present in numerous public institutions – such as schools, hospitals and central and regional government – in many of which there is a legal requirement that in some instances the social partners should have a dominant presence. A similar system is to be found in such diverse political traditions as the socialists and the Catholics, and was warmly welcomed by the various elements of the trade union movement, which evidently regarded participation in public institutions active in social and employment matters as more practicable and less compromising than a similar system within private companies.

From the mid-1970s onwards there has been a gradual change in the traditional approach to trade union relationships within the enterprise.

The first, and most widespread, change comes with the sanctioning of trade unions' rights to information in the main industry-wide collective agreements, as from 1976. Appropriate clauses oblige enterprises (over a certain size) to provide trade union organizations (at territorial or company level according to the case) with information about matters relating to the management of the enterprise: investment programmes, technological innovations, decentralization of production and general impact of restructuring processes on employment and work organization; and sometimes also rights to joint examination of these matters. Information rights are regarded not as being a substitute for collective bargaining but as supplementing it, and useful for its more efficient development in the turbulent context of the 1980s.

Considerations of this kind prompted the CGIL, CISL, UIL confederations and the IRI to sign a Protocol instituting the procedures, rather formalized, for advance information and consultation of the trade union side in the matter of company policies. In exchange for this the confederations agreed to introduce means of preventing and cooling down conflict based on conciliation and quasi-arbitration procedures prior to any direct action either on the part of the company or on that of the trade union. Procedures of this kind are also being included in industry-wide agreements.

Even the National Multi-Industry Agreement of 23 July 1993 was not particularly innovative on the subject of participation. There is only general support, in the part relating to company-level bargaining, for the model of employee participation within the company as it exists so far in Italy. This covers the procedures for information, consultation, monitoring and enforcement or negotiation provided for by law (limited), industry-level agreements, all lower-level collective agreements and current bargaining practice, for the purposes of dealing in a consensual manner with the effects on social aspects, levels of employment and working conditions of technological innovation, restructuring and company reorganization.

Company practices in participatory industrial relations have increased over the course of the 1990s. The case of Zanussi is emblematic. There have been numerous agreements instituting a wide range of participation bodies: a committee to monitor company macro-strategies, with management and union representatives; a joint committee composed of union and company representatives and external experts, with decision-making powers on issues traditionally the subject of collective bargaining (payment by results, work organization, vocational training, the work environment, equal treatment for men and women, etc); and a 'committee of guarantee', with arbitration functions, presided over by an expert in labour law. However, other private and public enterprises are also tending to develop participatory practices and, in contrast to what has been the case in the English-speaking countries, the new initiatives on human resource management and direct company/employee relations are complementary to, rather than an alternative to, these participatory practices.

In the particular case of financial participation, there are signs of the timid emergence in Italy of schemes similar to those found elsewhere, as in the form of profit-sharing in the UK and *intéressement* in France. Once again, it was the National Multi-Industry Agreement of 23 July 1993 that provided for a special legislative arrangement establishing a (limited) percentage reduction of the social security contributions payable on company-level pay enhancements linked to productivity, quality and profitability.

Disputes

One of the traditional features of the Italian system, arising from the factors mentioned above, is its high degree of industrial tension. The level of conflict in Italy has always been one of the highest on the international scene; it is not controlled to any great extent from the institutional point of view, given the lack of procedural rules for settling disputes, and is little influenced by trends in the economic cycle, sometimes proving more sensitive to factors in the political cycle.

There has been widespread use, particularly in the past, of 'anomalous' forms of strike action (brief, intermittent and rotating strikes) adopted by the trade unions to maximize the effects on the organization of the enterprise while minimizing the cost to the workers. This is also explained by the absence from the Italian tradition of the forms of financial protection for strikers, such as fighting funds, that are found in other countries.

Another major feature of the Italian system is the 'economico-political' strike, called in order to press for social and economic reforms from Parliament and Government. Action of this type is in line with the aims of Italian trade unions, which are not solely unionist, and has been endorsed by the Constitutional Court as an expression of political activity by the trade union supplementing the forms of representative democracy.

From the legal standpoint, the Italian system is characterized by a lack of any systematic statutory control of conflict, as demonstrated by the fact that it was not until 1990 that the first law was passed on the right to strike in essential public services (see below). Case law has defined various limits on strikes, on the basis of varyingly explicit indications in the legal system such as general principles of contract law or of the law of torts, particularly in the case of anomalous forms of strike action, or of previously existing bodies of penal and administrative legislation which have been confirmed, even if with substantial amendments, by the Constitutional Court.

It can be said that judges' attitudes have on the whole been relatively tolerant of strikes (though not of lockouts), more than in other countries' systems. It is also significant that the right to strike is recognized as belonging first and foremost to the workers and not to the trade union according to an interpretation traditional both in case law and in legal opinion, as is the case in France: this implies the lawfulness as such of 'wildcat' or unofficial strikes.

Another characteristic feature of the Italian system is that case law, and also prevailing legal opinion, has always rejected the concept of a so-called implicit peace obligation, co-essential with the nature of the collective agreement as a 'peace treaty', which guarantees that the trade unions (if not the workers) will abstain from direct disputes aimed at achieving premature revision of the arrangements agreed on. An obligation of this kind exists only if the parties explicitly undertake such a commitment (ie, a no-strike clause).

But traditionally no-strike clauses are rarely agreed upon; the same is true of clauses providing for cooling-off periods and conciliation or arbitration, and of agreed procedures for dispute prevention. Mediation by the public authorities – such as a minister or a mayor – in labour controversies is widespread but somewhat ad hoc.

Since the late 1970s there has been a trend towards sharp reductions in the indicators of conflict. The average annual number of recorded strikes over the period 1995-1996 (with 1974-1979 in brackets) was 725 (3,185); 1.067 million workers participated in stike activity (7.803 million); and there were 1.242 million days lost (15.46 million).

However, the spread of codes of self-regulation of strikes has been blocked by limits on their **effectiveness** in particular, since they are binding only on the workers represented by the trade unions that adopt them; as a result they are discredited by adversarial behaviour on the part of groups of workers, sometimes very small (but in a key position and therefore capable of causing serious harm to consumers), who are promoting diverse interests and are often far removed from the traditional prototype of employees as represented by the traditional trade union confederations.

Eventually, Law No. 146/1990 attempted the difficult task of reconciling the observance of two rights that are both protected by the Constitution: the right to strike and the right of the citizen as a consumer of essential public services. This was done, firstly, by prioritizing collective agreements as the means of defining minimum levels of services to be maintained in strike situations, after having specified those essential services to which the rules apply (transport, schools, health services, telecommunications, energy and the judicial system) and having imposed a minimum obligation to give 10 days' advance notice of any strike in these sectors; and secondly, by establishing a special *Commissione di garanzia* (Commission of Guarantee on Strikes in Essential Services). This Commission, composed of experts nominated by Parliament, has the task of identifying situations where the minimum levels specified are not properly observed and putting forward proposals when there is disagreement between the parties in defining those minimum levels. However, these proposals are not binding and carry only the force of moral persuasion. The fact that the Commission possesses no binding powers and cannot impose more dissuasive sanctions has been criticized by many as limiting its effectiveness. Nevertheless, it would be wrong to underestimate the effects achieved by the new Law in moderating the level of conflict in critical sectors which, in the 1980s and 1990s, were the particular target of protest by new unions outside the major confederations.

Prospects and Conclusions

Italian industrial relations exhibit a pattern of weakly organized pluralism: this is subject to recurrent tensions which can be ascribed either to external factors, such as economic and political upsets, or to internal factors, above all political divisions within the trade union movement.

External economic factors are exerting strong pressures both through the growing need for labour flexibility and economic competitiveness and through the context of high unemployment, concentrated in the South among young people, and surplus labour in large enterprises which have, however, traditionally been characterized by a very high rate of unionization. In contrast to this, the political context, after a rather difficult transitional period for the role of the unions during the first phase of the changeover to the first-past-the-post system, seems to be considerably improved, with wholehearted support from all the social actors for the model of tripartite concertation that was initiated with the National Multi-Industry Agreement of 23 July 1993.

As regards internal factors, leaving aside traditional ideological divisions, the challenge presented by the autonomous unions and the *cobas* movement (rank-and-file committees) must be regarded as a new and growing element, even though for at least a brief period they did not appear to pose a significant threat to confederation-based representation. However, the legislative provisions on the regulation of strike action (Law No. 146/1990) and the criteria for union representativeness (Legislative Decree No. 396/1997) have helped to reduce that challenge to some degree. And the more innovatory trends, particularly in the case of rules on employee representation in public employment, could well be the subject of the extension to the private sector that is being advocated from many quarters.

The Italian pluralistic system of industrial relations overall still does not reflect all the conditions typical or necessary for evolving towards participatory models (a united trade union movement with strong control by the central trade union and employers' organizations over their rank and file), even though there has recently been progress along the road to other essential conditions such as governments that are pro-labour and stable, and a public administration capable of guaranteeing the attainment of the objectives of political change.

Problems continue to be caused by the lack of institutionalization of the rules governing these attempts: trade union participation practices (in companies, in institutions, and in the management of economic policy) have not been translated into established rules which can be relied on to any extent and which would serve to consolidate the processes; they remain almost totally informal.

However, the 1990s have seen the paradoxical emergence of a significant reinforcement of the participatory model, mainly in large enterprises, with a simultaneous major decline in unionization in these same enterprises resulting from job losses due to restructuring; changing occupational trends in favour of medium to highly skilled young workers who show little inclination to join a union; and new managerial initiatives towards direct relations between the enterprise and its employees which, although not developed as an alternative to collective industrial relations, nevertheless tend to some extent to erode employees' traditional loyalty to their unions.

At the micro level, this balance between human resource management and industrial relations, or between the individual dimension and collective labour relations, presents the most important challenge facing the Italian system and the development of the participatory model at the decentralized company level.

At the macro level, the 1990s have witnessed the construction of the Italian 'social pact' based on an exchange between incomes policy (Agreement of 23 July 1993) and an active employment policy (1996 'Employment Agreement'), in a context of cutbacks in social security expenditure, particularly as regards pensions insurance (1995 reform of the pensions system). The chances of success for this social pact are linked primarily to its capacity to adjust to ongoing changes in the economic, political and social climate. Examples such as the effects of low inflation on industry-level pay bargaining, or the pressures exerted on the various actors in industrial relations by the call made by the Communist Reconstruction Party for the introduction of a statutory 35-hour working week, provide sufficient illustration.

Apart from these adjustments with respect to the external context, the Italian industrial relations system is also under pressure to adjust internally. Among such changes, the most significant is related to the greater degree of balance between centralization and decentralization that was introduced by the National Multi-Industry Agreement of 23 July 1993, with the resultant need for the exercise of more control by the central actors of industrial relations both over the collective bargaining structure and within the ambit of the unions and employers' organizations themselves. But these possible developments remain subordinate to the final factor that is essential to reinforce the participatory model of industrial relations in Italy in the immediate future: trade union unity.

Further Reading

Accornero, A., *La parabola del sindacato,* Bologna, Il Mulino, 1992.

Baglioni, G. and Milani, R. (eds.), *La contrattazione collettiva nelle aziende industriali in Italia*, Milan, Angeli, 1990.

Bordogna, L., *Pluralismo senza mercato. Rappresentanza e conflitto nel settore pubblico,* Milan, Angeli, 1994.

Brunetta, R., Cella, G.P., Treu, T. and Urbani, G. (eds.), *Il conflitto e le relazioni di lavoro negli anni '90,* CNR-Progetto strategico, 5 vols, Turin, Giappichelli, 1992.

Cella, G.P. and Treu, T. (eds.), *Relazioni industriali,* Bologna, Il Mulino, 1997.

CESOS, *Le relazioni sindacali in Italia*, Annual Reports 1981-1995, Rome, Edizioni Lavoro, various years.

Giugni, G. (ed.), *Lo Statuto dei lavoratori. Commentario,* Milan, Giuffrè, 1979.

Ichino, P., *Il lavoro e il mercato,* Milan, Mondadori, 1996.

Negrelli, S., *La società dentro l'impresa. L'evoluzione dal modello normativo al modello partecipativo nelle imprese italiane*, Milan, Angeli, 1991.

Negrelli, S. and Santi, E., 'Industrial Relations in Italy', in G. Baglioni and C. Crouch (eds.), *European Industrial Relations. The Challenge of Flexibility*, London, Sage, 1990.

Regini, M., *I dilemmi del sindacato,* Bologna, Il Mulino, 1981.

Reyneri, E., *Sociologia del mercato del lavoro*, Bologna, Il Mulino, 1996.

Treu, T. (ed.), *Sindacato e magistratura nei conflitti di lavoro,* Bologna, Il Mulino, 1975.

Treu, T. (ed.), *Le relazioni sindacali nel pubblico impiego,* Rome, Edizioni Lavoro, 1988.

Zan, S., *Organizzazione e rappresentanza,* Florence, La Nuova Italia, 1992.

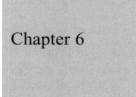

Chapter 6   The Netherlands

Paul van der Heijden

Historical Background

The Dutch economy has undergone fundamental changes since the end of the Second World War. The immediate post-war period was marked by the need for reconstruction of the productive infrastructure and a revival of industrialization, with US Marshall aid playing an important part. Consumption was for a number of years constrained by an accepted strategy of austerity. One of the forms in which this national acquiescence was embodied was the *geleide loonpolitiek,* ie, the centrally directed pay policy controlled by the Government, which lasted until the 1960s. Under this policy, restrictions on pay increases were maintained through annual pay rounds at national level. Another example of the austerity strategy was the initially slow development of the national social security system. Before the war, social security had been confined to limited forms of employee insurance against such eventualities as accidents at work, illness and invalidity (old age). During the war, at the request of the Government-in-exile in London, the Van Rhijn Royal Commission drew up a new blueprint for post-war social security in the Netherlands, inspired by the British Beveridge Plan. Along with the establishment of statutory unemployment insurance, this blueprint also contained proposals for the introduction of forms of national insurance for groups in society who up till then had not been covered by social security, such as the elderly, widows and orphans, disabled people and the self-employed. Except for statutory unemployment insurance, however, it was not until the late 1950s that more progress was made towards developing the Dutch social security system as envisaged by Van Rhijn. Between 1957 and

1967 a number of major laws were passed on old age pensions, survivors' pensions (for widows and orphans), sickness benefits, disablement benefits, medical expenses and social assistance.

The Netherlands was one of the original group of countries to participate in the process of European integration, having signed the European Coal and Steel Community (ECSC) Treaty in 1951 and the Treaty of Rome and Euratom Treaty in 1957.

There followed a gradual shift of focus both on the part of the Government and on the part of employers and unions away from the reconstruction of the productive system towards greater scope for consumer spending. This was sustained, as everywhere else in Europe, by a successful Keynesian socio-economic policy. Annual growth rates in national income of around 5 per cent (or more) were not unusual. This prosperous economic growth also heralded the end of the centrally controlled pay policy by the early 1960s.

Until the first oil crisis in 1973, apart from the usual cyclical fluctuations, economic growth continued to make almost uninterrupted progress. Up to that point, the post-war Dutch industrial relations system can be summed up in the following three basic features:

a)   a dominant role played by central government;

b)   a high degree of centralization in decision-making and collective bargaining; and

c)   reliance on inter-organizational consultation.

Economic and Social Context

In a sense, the year 1973 may be seen as a turning point, the year when the first cracks in the Keynesian policy began to show. Dutch industry was heavily dependent on energy-intensive sectors, such as chemicals, in which the oil crisis brought substantial cost increases. Another associated impact was the steep rise in unemployment, which trebled between 1970 and 1980. The second oil shock in 1978 made matters still worse. National output and profits declined further, while unemployment continued to soar. Stagflation (simultaneously rising inflation and unemployment) became a new feature of the Dutch economy. An added serious consequence was the increase in the Government's budget deficit, which between 1975 and 1982 rose from 4.3 to 10.7 per cent of GDP. At the same time, growth in GDP came to a virtual standstill.

During the 1980s the situation gradually improved as a result of positive developments in the international economic climate, but also through the effects of a pay restraint policy pursued by the social partners and of government cuts in public spending. High unemployment persisted, however. The large increase in the number of long-term unemployed (people remaining unemployed for longer than a year) was particularly disturbing.

The new jobs created in the improving economy of the 1980s were mainly taken by women. While women's (especially married women's) labour force participation had been among the lowest in Europe, social and cultural changes in the 1980s contributed to a significant increase in the number of women seeking work. One consequence was that groups who lost jobs in the 1970s did not benefit from the economic improvement until the late 1980s.

Between 1987 and 1997, the Dutch economically active population (ie, people in the 15-64 age group who are on the labour market, including both those in jobs (working more than 12 hours a week) and those without jobs) increased from 6,592,000 to 7,360,000. In 1995, of the total number of those in work (6,596,000) 4,067,000 were men and 2,529,000 were women. In the same year total registered unemployment was 464,000, with men accounting for 260,000 and women for 204,000. In 1996 and 1997 this unemployment rate, which in 1995 represented 7 per cent of the economically active population, dropped further to 6.6 per cent (as against the figure of 9.7 per cent in 1985).

OECD figures indicate that, at the end of the 1980s, unemployment in the Netherlands was above the OECD average, and in Europe above that of Germany and the UK but below that of France. By 1997, however, the Netherlands scored far better within the European Union; its unemployment rate of 6.6 per cent placed it at the bottom of the list of Member States with the highest unemployment (Belgium 9.9 per cent, Denmark 10 per cent, Germany 10 per cent and Sweden 9.7 per cent).

The strong growth in employment during recent years has to a large extent been associated with a high proportion of part-time jobs (defined as work involving less than the normal working hours of 40 or 38 hours per week). At present, part-time jobs represent 35 per cent of all jobs in the Netherlands. This is by far the highest figure in Europe (the EU average is 14 per cent). In the Netherlands, part-time work is predominantly 'women's work': 67 per cent of all part-timers are women. It accounts for a substantial proportion of the influx of women into the labour market. In 1981, 30 per cent of women aged 15-64 engaged in gainful employment outside the home, whereas by 1995 the figure had reached 42 per cent.

Particular problems confronting the Dutch labour market in 1997 are:

a)   absorption and training of new young workers/ageing of the population;

b)   the very large number of people classified as suffering from employment disability;

c)   the link between education and training and the labour market;

d)   the situation of women;

e)   early retirement; and

f)   the position of ethnic minorities.

Ageing workforce: it is forecast that between 1994 and 2010 the economically active population will increase by 8 per cent. Its composition is, however, changing significantly in that the proportion of young workers is growing rapidly while on average the working population is becoming older. This will create pressures in the labour market for those sectors where large numbers of young workers are employed (retail distribution, hotel and catering industry).

Employment disability: in 1967 the Disablement Benefits Act (WAO) was introduced in the Netherlands. Since the introduction of this Act, the number of people in receipt of disability benefits has confounded all expectations by soaring from a few hundred thousand to around 830,000 by 1997. To place this high figure in perspective, it may be noted that the rise in the number of people classified as disabled has been accompanied since 1983 by a growth in employment. As a rule, women are slightly more likely than men to become beneficiaries under the employee disability insurance scheme. Another factor to be noted is that the educational level of beneficiaries is markedly lower than that of people in employment. The most common categories of disability are problems with the motor apparatus, heart and vascular diseases and psychological disorders. The likelihood of becoming classified as disabled is highest in agriculture, the construction sector and manufacturing (non-metal) industry, and lowest in commercial services, the transport sector and the metalworking industry. Those most likely to return to work are the younger age groups, men and the more highly qualified.

Training: overall, the problems regarding the relationship between education and training and the labour market are centred on the following three points:

i) people with a vocational qualification are in a better position in the labour market than those with general education and training;

ii) the position of women in the labour market is more disadvantaged than that of men with the same level of education and training; and

iii) those who have no secondary education qualifications are in a poor position in the labour market. In general, the likelihood of unemployment decreases with rising levels of education and training.

Women on the labour market: between 1975 and 1995 the activity rate of women rose from 32 to 42 per cent, bringing it up to a level comparable with that in countries such as Belgium, the Federal Republic of Germany and France. Nevertheless, it still lags behind the level for men. Female unemployment is also high in comparison with that for men (around three times as high in the 35-44 age group). Other aspects, some of them already mentioned, are that: the growth in employment among women has chiefly been in the form of part-time work; women are more likely than men to become beneficiaries under the WAO employee disability insurance scheme, and are less likely to return to work subsequently; and women are over-represented in low-grade jobs.

Early retirement: during past years early retirement was popular as a route for older employees to leave employment. Approximately 50 per cent of private sector firms operate an early retirement scheme, and the various areas of the public sector and semi-public sector also have early retirement arrangements of their own; the average retirement age is around 60. Between 1977 and 1995 the number of people taking early retirement rose steadily from 3,000 to 152,000 per annum. Since then, however, employers' enthusiasm for early retirement has waned. Some collective agreements now fix retirement ages which are higher than 60, and there is growing talk of the introduction of flexible retirement ages for older employees. In the public sector, provision for flexible retirement was introduced in 1997 (from the age of 55 onwards).

Ethnic minorities: ethnic minorities in the Netherlands have a higher rate of unemployment than that of native Dutch citizens, reaching an average of around 40 per cent. Leaving aside immigrants from the Mediterranean countries, this group consists predominantly of people from Surinam and the Netherlands Antilles. Since the lifting of the Iron Curtain, it has also included immigrants originating from Central and East European countries.

To sum up so far, it can be said that the late 1980s and early 1990s saw a marked recovery in the Dutch labour market. That recovery became consolidated in the mid-1990s, with relatively low unemployment (within the EU context), a rising activity rate and a decline in the number of people classified as disabled under the Disablement Benefits Act.

Over the past few decades there has been a shift in employment away from agriculture into industry and subsequently from industry into the service sector. Whereas in 1930 some 20 per cent of the economically active population were still employed in agriculture and 26 per cent in industry, by 1997 these figures had fallen to approximately 4 per cent and 16 per cent respectively. Over the same period, the proportion employed in commerce and services rose from around 34 to 75 per cent. In the years to come the figures for the agricultural and industrial sectors are at best likely to remain stable.

By European standards, the collective burden of taxation and social security charges as a percentage of national income is high in the Netherlands. The reasons for this are a high level of expenditure on social security, an activity rate which is still too low in comparison with the labour forces of other European countries, an extensive system of government subsidies in areas such as housing, education and health care, and a large national debt (80 per cent of GDP in 1996, with a falling trend). For many years now, government policy has been directed at reducing this burden. One of the instruments used has been pay restraint, or reduction of labour costs (given that there is some linkage between market-sector pay levels and social security benefits).

Between 1970 and 1997, annual spending on social security soared from NLG 18.8 billion to 132.8 billion, ie, approximately one third of national income. The ratio of the number of economically inactive individuals to the number of workers is unfavourable: in 1996, for every 100 workers there were 81.4 benefit dependants (as against 83.2 in 1993). There was also a slight decrease in the rate of social security expenditure (*sociale zekerheidsquote*), a figure expressing the volume of social security costs as a proportion of GDP: this was 19 per cent in 1993 and 16.8 per cent in 1996. The main reasons for the low activity rate among those under 60 are involuntary unemployment, illness and classification as disabled.

The Government has been attempting to reduce the volume of benefit dependants by pursuing an active labour market policy and introducing changes in social security legislation. First, as from 1 January 1987, the social security system was split into two parts (unemployment and incapacity for work). Further major changes at the beginning of the 1990s were followed by the introduction, in 1996, of a radical measure overturning the statutory provisions on illness and invalidity. Employees who are absent from work through illness are now protected by a mixture of private and public provision. As from 1 March 1996, following a change to the Civil Code, employers are liable under private law to continue paying such employees at least 70 per cent of their normal pay for up to 52 weeks (after which the pre-existing public disability benefit provisions come into effect). Employers are thus faced with the choice of either covering this sick pay through a private system of insurance or simply carrying the financial risk.

The income trend over the period 1970-1996 shows that, when viewed strictly in these terms, the Netherlands is becoming steadily 'poorer'. However, this is a consequence of the reduction in working hours and the increase in part-time work. Greater affluence is being converted into leisure time. The percentage of people who feel that they have difficulty in making ends meet decreased between 1970 and 1996.

The amount of the statutory minimum wage and of the benefits associated with it has been the subject of an intensive social policy debate for a number of years. There is a proposal to reduce its level, in order to allow more room for differentiation at the bottom of the wage structure. One of the reasons why this is considered necessary is the fact that there is a large surplus of low-skilled workers in the Dutch labour market: there is a view that the labour they can provide is not worth the minimum wage. In anticipation of any such future reduction, the fact that the minimum wage has been frozen for several years now means that as pay levels rise a relative decrease is occurring automatically.

When we consider the implications of all this for the industrial relations system, the following comments can be made.

- The three traditional features of the system that were mentioned earlier under the heading 'historical background' – namely the dominant role of central government, centralization and reliance on consultation – have come under considerable pressure. Although the role of central government, including the attendant centralized decision-making mechanisms, can still be described as important, it has gradually become more distanced. This is reflected in elements such as the decision to opt for an 'active' labour market policy, in which the social partners may be presumed to play a key part. Another example is offered by the fundamental changes that have taken place in statutory social security provisions. Here too, the Government is involving the parties immediately affected (employers and employees) more directly than in the recent past. The most striking example is the 1996 'privatization' of sickness benefit. This means, in addition, that the enterprise level has become more important in Dutch industrial relations.
- The scale of unemployment and the number of workers classified as disabled remain a cause for concern. Particular attention will need to be paid to the problem of the weaker groups in the labour market such as women, disabled people and ethnic minorities. There will, for example, be more need than in the past for the establishment in collective agreements of quotas for such groups to help their integration into the enterprise's workforce.

Institutional and Legal Framework

Labour and social security legislation has a tradition dating back some 100 years in the Netherlands. The history of legislation in this field began in 1874 with the introduction of the first act to impose restrictions on child labour (known as the 'Kinderwet Van Houten'), and thereafter the legislation gradually developed up to the present day. In addition to the emergence of a range of laws on health and safety, employee protection and social security, the legislative regulation of collective agreements was a significant historical milestone. The first legislative basis of the collective agreement took shape in 1907, in the Civil Code, and was then supplemented by specific enactments in 1927 and 1937. From the start, the collective agreement has formed an important feature of the Dutch industrial relations system, which was organized along corporatist lines. This corporatism was inherent in the 'pillarized' structure or segmentation of Dutch society that prevailed in the early years of this century, the main pillars (*zuilen*) being the Protestants with their doctrine of sovereignty in the personal sphere, the Catholics with their doctrine concerning subsidiarity, and the social democrats. After the Second World War, however, for a long time the collective agreement faded into the background with the advent of comprehensive new labour and social security legislation.

It is customary to divide post-war developments in Dutch industrial relations into four periods: 1945-1964; 1964-1974; 1974-1982; and 1982 up to the present day.

The period 1945-1964 was the era of the centrally controlled pay policy (*geleide loonpolitiek*). This was based on a high degree of consensus between organized employers and employees and the Government. The leading actor in this form of centralized control was a Board of Government Mediators (College van Rijksbemiddelaars). It was during this period that the principal institutions of the Dutch industrial relations system were set up. The first of these, the Labour Foundation (Stichting van de Arbeid), founded in exile in 1944, was legally established in 1945. As a forum for cooperation between organized employers and employees at national level, this body had an important part to play in the implementation of the centralized pay policy. Another significant development in this context was the introduction of the Extraordinary Decree on Labour Relations (BBA), whose provisions included the requirement for prior approval of collective agreements and the protection of employees against dismissal. This was followed in 1950 by the creation of the Social and Economic Council (SER), a body of tripartite composition, which was initially the top-level institution in the public-law organization of business and industry, and whose main function quickly became that of advisory body to the Government on socio-economic policy and its implementation. The Council is made up of equal numbers of employers' representatives, trade union representatives and independent experts appointed by the Crown. The success of the pay policy pursued at that time is largely attributable to the high degree of consensus between the three parties involved.

During the second period, 1964-1974, this consensus was subjected to severe pressure. The strong economic growth of the time, together with the tightly constrained labour market, was largely responsible for this. There was a clear call for a less rigid policy on wage formation. In 1970, the provisions of the 1945 Extraordinary Decree on centralized wage control were replaced by those of the Wage Formation Act. Despite the crumbling away of national consensus, in 1972 the parties concluded a central agreement for 1973 which included provisions on the maximum cost-of-living adjustment of pay.

The next period, 1974-1982, saw government efforts to cope as well as possible with the consequences of the two oil shocks (1973 and 1978). In 1974 the Enabling Act was passed as an attempt by the Government to revert to a centrally controlled pay policy. Under this Act, a number of decrees were issued imposing annual pay measures. Around 1980 the growth in unemployment accelerated, and this revival of the centralized pay policy came to an end.

In 1982 the employers' confederations and trade union confederations, within the Labour Foundation, agreed on central recommendations favouring genuine collective bargaining on pay and conditions at industry and enterprise level. These recommendations can be identified as a new turning point in industrial relations: a changeover to decentralization. Further agreements were reached within the Labour Foundation in 1984 and 1986 covering, in addition to wage formation, measures to tackle unemployment, training for unemployed people, vocational training, etc. Attention thus shifted from the expenditure side to the production side of the economy. The rapidly growing popularity of the demand economy in the UK and the USA and the failure of the Keynesian intervention policy were unquestionably also contributing factors.

In the development of labour law in the post-war period, a marked discontinuity in the process is discernible at the point where the Keynesian government policy was transformed into a policy of deregulation and self-regulation. This transformation occurred around 1980. For example, closer examination reveals that over the period 1970-1990 the labour law field saw the introduction of some 50 laws on a variety of subjects in the areas of wage formation, termination of employment, participation, equal treatment, working conditions and job placement. Prior to 1980, the emphasis was on the creation of the major enactments; in the period following this, however, the emphasis was mainly on corrective legislation. From that point, legislative development lost its clear sense of direction and purpose, and the legislative machine, which initially functioned so successfully, exhibited instead a marked degree of hesitancy.

The consequences of the trend towards self-regulation included the introduction in 1991 (and subsequent amendment in 1997) of a new Employment Services

Act, which removed responsibility for the management of the job placement process from central government and placed it in the hands of the social partners. This involved a remodelling of the Employment Service network into a new, independent organization. Similar self-regulating structures already existed for the day-to-day management of much of social security.

Lastly, some comment is called for on the subject of the individual contract of employment. This has been regulated in the Netherlands since 1907, in the Civil Code. A revised version was introduced in 1997, in which Article 7:610 defines the individual contract of employment as a contract whereby one party, the employee, undertakes to perform work subject to the authority of the other party, the employer, in return for pay and during specified times. The contract implies a number of obligations for both employer and employee which extend beyond pay alone (equal treatment for men and women, paid annual holidays, health and safety, the general qualities of good employer practice, an obligation on the employee to obey the employer's instructions, restraint of trade and competition, the law on termination of employment, and so on). A notable feature in the Netherlands as regards the termination of employment has been the existing public-law requirement for prior official authorization of both dismissal and resignation.

The law on termination of employment was amended in May 1998. Following a long period of debate, Parliament passed an important new law, the Flexibility and Security Act. Although the system of prior authorization has been maintained, the prohibition of termination is now restricted to the employer's side of the contract: from January 1999, only the employer wishing to dismiss an employee will need to obtain such official authorization. Other features of this amendment of the law on termination include a tightening of specific bans on dismissal (during parental leave, men versus women, native Dutch employees versus other employees, etc), shorter periods of notice and greater flexibility as regards the renewal of fixed-term contracts.

An extensive body of case law has accumulated in respect of the contract of employment. This subsection of labour law is primarily judge-made law. Unlike other countries, the Netherlands has no special system of courts or judges for dealing with labour matters. Disputes relating to a contract of employment come under the jurisdiction of the first-instance ordinary courts, with the possibility in principle of appeal to a higher court. As regards flexible employment relationships (work through temporary-employment agencies, homeworking, freelance work, etc), the substantial case law that had accumulated was written into the statute book in 1997.

To sum up, it may be said that since around 1980 the Dutch industrial relations system, following a period of thoroughgoing juridification, has exhibited a tendency towards deregulation or self-regulation. As a consequence, the central level is losing importance in favour of the industry level and the individual enterprise. Compared with the first 20 years after the Liberation, industrial relations have, in a sense, swung from centralized control by the Government towards decentralized freedom for the social partners.

Actors in Industrial Relations

Despite the current marked trend towards decentralization, the parties that operate at national level in the industrial relations system are still of considerable importance: the employers' confederations, the trade union confederations and central government. Collective relations between these parties mainly took shape immediately after the Second World War. The trade union movement in particular, through its support for the national policy of reconstruction, gained recognition as a national partner in central consultation (*overleg*). The Government also explicitly established itself as one of the parties involved.

The first trade unions and employers' associations originated in the last quarter of the nineteenth century.

Trade Unions

The process of union formation led to the setting up in 1906 of the socialist Netherlands Federation of Trade Unions (NVV), in 1909 of the Protestant Christian Trade Union Federation (CNV) and in 1925 of the Roman Catholic Workers' Federation (RKWV), which was later to become the Catholic Workers' Movement (KAB) and then, in 1964, the Catholic Federation of Dutch Trade Unions (NKV). In 1976 the NVV and the NKV merged to form the Dutch Trade Union Federation (FNV), the process being formally completed in 1982. In the meantime, the Federation of Managerial and Professional Staff Unions (MHP) was formed in 1974. A new fourth confederation of (semi-)public employee unions, the General Federation of Trade Unions (AVC), was then formed in 1990 and was duly granted official recognition by the Social and Economic Council, though in 1998 it merged with FNV. The FNV, CNV and

MHP therefore now constitute the three formally recognized trade union confederations at central level in the Netherlands. In addition to the unions affiliated to these confederations, there are also numerous non-affiliated unions (*categorale bonden*), mostly composed of employees belonging to particular occupations (airline pilots, technicians, nursing staff, etc). Whereas in 1980 unionization among Dutch employees was still 39 per cent, by 1997 this figure had dropped to 28 per cent. The FNV has the most members (around 1.4 million, including 100,000 it acquired from its merger with AVC); this is followed by the CNV with some 300,000 members and the MHP with around 250,000.

Employers

On the **employers' side**, there are now three central employers' confederations, representing the following groups: large employers in industry, commerce and the service sector; the small-firms sector; and agriculture and horticulture. They cooperate with each other through the Council of Central Employers' Organizations (RCO) and, like trade union confederations, have seats on the Social and Economic Council and the Labour Foundation. The largest is the new Confederation of Netherlands Industries and Employers (VNO-NCW), which was formed on 1 March 1995 as a result of the amalgamation of the Federation of Dutch Enterprises (VNO) and the Dutch Christian Federation of Employers (NCW), and represents approximately 150 sectoral employers' associations and their 65,000 member enterprises.

Government

The **government side** signifies in particular, with respect to industrial relations, the Minister for Social Affairs and Employment; this Ministry covers the important fields of pay, social security, employment, participation and working conditions. The Ministers for Economic Affairs, for Finance, for Health, Welfare and Sport and for Home Affairs are also important. The Minister for Home Affairs is responsible for policy on pay and conditions for government personnel.

Independent 'crown members' appointed by central government to watch over the public interest (*algemeen belang*) and representatives of the trade union confederations and employers' confederations meet regularly in the tripartite Social and Economic Council. The Council advises the Government not only on socio-economic policy but also, for example, on social security, labour market policy and employee participation. There is also the bipartite Labour

Foundation, in which the Government is not represented. In addition, the three parties try, albeit with varying success, to reach agreement annually at central level on pay policy and other important aspects of social policy. In recent years, for example, much energy has been devoted to ways of reducing the high level of sickness absenteeism and the number of workers receiving disability benefit.

At enterprise level, the first important element is the system of institutionalized employee participation. The original Works Councils Act dates from 1950, and has been substantially broadened in successive amendments in 1971, 1979, 1982, 1990 and 1997. The Act confers on Dutch employees a right to prior consultation, a right to information and a right of consent. The right of consent (*instemmingsrecht*) applies to any measures contemplated by the employer on job evaluation, health and safety at work, employee appraisal, hiring and promotion, complaints procedures, pension schemes, working hours, shift work, profit-sharing, etc, provided that there is no collective agreement with the unions on the subjects concerned. If the works council does not consent, then management may appeal to the first-instance ordinary court (see above).

The right to prior consultation (*adviesrecht*) applies to major economic decisions (investments, mergers, hiving-off parts of the enterprise and so on) and organizational decisions (reorganization, division of management, etc). In legal terms, works councils do not possess the capacity to negotiate with the employer on the establishment of pay and conditions in collective agreements: this falls within the domain of the collective bargaining rights of the particular unions concerned.

Workplace-level union structures do exist in a number of sectors. This structure (*bedrijvenwerk*), as an organized union branch at individual workplace level, mostly performs a communication and support function for, on the one hand, the union executive officer (*vakbondsbestuurder*) who conducts formal bargaining with the employer and, on the other hand, the group of local union activists (*vakbondskader*) who have seats on the works council. However, in terms of the real-life situation, in enterprises where only a few union members are employed the works council is increasingly assuming the function of negotiating with management on pay and conditions.

In larger enterprises in particular, the philosophy that sees employees as human capital has received considerable attention in recent years. Personnel policy in such enterprises has gradually evolved towards human resource management. In

156

the context of this style of management, employees are participating to a growing extent through practices such as direct consultation on work and working conditions, autonomous work groups and quality circles. In the enterprises concerned, human resource management is adding an extra dimension to labour relations.

Lastly, note should be taken of a new form of employee participation which has recently emerged and may be regarded as supplementing the formal institutionalized participation regulated in the Works Councils Act. It consists in the conclusion of informal works agreements (*ondernemingsovereenkomsten*) between the works council and management. Such local agreements are concluded for a variety of reasons, very commonly relating to matters such as reorganization, mergers, etc.

Collective Bargaining

Collective bargaining assumed a prominent position in the Dutch industrial relations system from the early days. The first legislation in this area came into being in 1907 through contract of employment law as set out in the Civil Code, and this was followed in 1927 by the Collective Agreements Act and in 1937 by the Extension of Collective Agreements Act, which enabled collectively agreed provisions to be declared generally applicable.

Until recently, the most important level at which collective agreements were concluded in the Netherlands was the industry (sectoral) level. In the past few years the enterprise level has also become more important, although this has to be seen in relative terms as regards the number of employees covered: despite the fact that the total of some 900 agreements registered with the authorities in 1996 comprised 700 company agreements and 200 industry-level agreements, the company agreements concerned covered approximately 600,000 employees whereas the industry-level agreements covered a total of 2,700,000 employees. Comparison with the figures for 1983 (593 company agreements covering 400,000 employees and 190 industry-level agreements covering 2,500,000 employees) therefore reveals a slight trend in favour of company agreements.

Not all employees are covered by a collective agreement; average coverage for all employees in the market sector and the semi-public sector is 80 per cent.

Collective agreements constitute the outcome of collective bargaining between individual employers or employers' associations and trade unions. They may

157

cover any number of workers and are usually concluded for either one or two years. They establish mainly primary terms and conditions of employment (pay, working hours, holiday allowances, etc) and secondary terms and conditions (promotion and career development, physical working conditions, training schemes, etc).

In recent years there has been a tendency for the range of topics covered by agreements to become wider. Nowadays, for example, their content may include arrangements for a 36-hour week, ways of reducing sickness absenteeism and the number of workers classified as eligible for disability benefit, the improvement of poor working conditions, employment quotas for weaker groups in the labour market, such as women, ethnic minorities and disabled people, and continuing education for employees.

Also, in the context of the flexibilization and deregulation of the national economy, a debate has recently been sparked off on the possible abolition of the official procedure for the extension of collective agreements. Under the 1937 Act mentioned above, this authority to render an agreement (or part of it) binding on all employers in the particular industry concerned is vested in the Minister for Social Affairs and Employment and up till now, at the request of the social partners, it has been used very frequently. Opponents of the procedure argue that this policy instrument hinders the operation of the national economy to an excessive degree, whereas its supporters hold that abolition of the procedure would lead to wage competition between enterprises because of possible underbidding. The instrument's regulating function would be lost, leaving open the prospect of a sharp increase in industrial conflict and strikes.

The annual bargaining procedure commences in the autumn, when the Government specifies at national level the pay bargaining range affordable for the coming year, determined mainly on the basis of price movements and labour productivity. The Government attempts to reach central agreements with the social partners for this purpose. However, as already indicated, in recent years such agreements have occurred only rarely (1982, 1987 and 1989). Because of the continuing process of decentralization, it is not expected that further detailed central agreements on pay will be concluded between Government and the social partners. Tripartite meetings still take place but they focus on issues like training, part-time work and parental leave.

Bargaining then starts in the various sectors and in individual enterprises. Sectors and enterprises that are important pay leaders are the metalworking industry, the electrical engineering industry, the construction industry, Philips, Unilever, Shell and the AKZO chemicals multinational.

Collective agreements in the semi-public sector – which covers government-funded but legally independent entities – differ somewhat from those in the market sector. The freedom of employers in this sector to negotiate is largely dependent on the pay bargaining range allowed them by the Government each year, which means that the principle of free collective bargaining is possible only on a restricted basis. There are approximately 65 agreements in force in the sector, applying to some 530,000 employees. The major ones are the hospitals agreement (covering 170,000 employees), the welfare sector agreement (135,000 employees), the old people's homes agreement (70,000 employees) and the Dutch Railways agreement (27,000 employees). From 1986, pay trends in the semi-public sector were based on the recently abolished Act on Pay Adjustment in the Semi-Public Sector (WAGGS).

For public servants in the government sector in the strict sense (ie, 'civil servants'), the settlement of pay and conditions again differs from that in the market sector. Up till now, pay trends for public servants have broadly followed those in the market sector. Prior to 1959 uniform pay increases were dictated by the centrally controlled pay policy. After 1959, there was a changeover to a 'trend' policy, based on a kind of weighted average of collectively agreed rates of pay in the market sector. From the mid-1970s, the need for cuts in government spending became clear. One consequence was a stricter pay policy in respect of public servants. Thus, their salaries were lowered by 3 per cent in 1983 and then as good as frozen from 1985. However, since 1987 there has been a return to a rising trend more or less equal to that in the market sector. In addition, since the beginning of the 1980s there has been a proposal to introduce a wholly independent pay policy for public servants which would resemble the market sector in terms of procedures. In preparation for this, the existing system of central settlement of pay and conditions has now been changed fundamentally by being decentralized into a total of eight sectors: central government, provinces, local government, polder-board districts, education, police, judiciary and defence. As part of the same process, the Works Councils Act has also been made applicable to public servants (1995) and their special social security arrangements are to be abolished and replaced by the ordinary system applicable to private sector employees.

Since 1984 the General Public Service Regulations (ARAR) have made provision for arbitration for public servants in the event of disputes. As a result, in the same year a special Advisory and Arbitration Committee (AAC) was set up in this sector.

Lastly, it should be noted that no formal system of arbitration as yet exists in the market sector. It takes place only on an ad hoc basis where the parties concerned so wish.

Participation and Employee Representation at the Workplace

Traditionally, in the Netherlands, there has been little form of union presence at workplace level. Before and immediately after the Second World War, the phenomenon of the informal workplace union representatives (*vertrouwenslieden*) still existed in a few sectors like shipbuilding, but in the subsequent period union activity at workplace level almost entirely disappeared from the scene. The recognized trade union movement attached all strategic importance to influence acquired at national level (in the Social and Economic Council and the Labour Foundation). It was not until the mid-1960s that the then Industriebond NVV (a merger of unions in metal and electrical engineering, chemicals, textiles, clothing and leather, mining and miscellaneous industries) made a serious attempt to introduce a union structure at workplace level (*bedrijvenwerk*). This met with only limited success, owing to the fact that in the meantime the works council had gained a recognized position within many enterprises. In such enterprises, union activists gave priority to participating in the works council over helping to make the union workplace structure effective. Despite the trend towards decentralization in Dutch industrial relations (and although workplace-level union structures do exist in a relatively high proportion of enterprises where union density is above 35 per cent), this situation has not basically changed up to the present day. On the contrary, works councils (on which non-union members may also have seats) are coming to play a growing role in aspects of the determination of pay and conditions. This is proving to be at the expense of the influence of the union executive officers who conduct company-level negotiations with management.

In a strictly formal sense, however, works councils are still unable to engage in the determination of pay and conditions since they do not possess the capacity to conclude collective agreements. The growing popularity of informal works agreements between works councils and employers mentioned above shows that the existing legal infrastructure is too restrictive to cater for the real-life situation.

Within the enterprise, the works council is management's main counterpart on the employee side. Works councils have actually been set up in 92 per cent of large enterprises (100 or more employees) and in 87 per cent of smaller enterprises (50 to 99 employees).

Before 1998, works councils in smaller companies (35 to 99 employees) were limited in functions and powers compared with those in companies with 100 or more employees. In 1998, the Works Councils Act was amended and the distinction abolished. Works councils are now mandatory in enterprises with 50 or more employees, and there are no more distinctions between their functions and powers. So, under the terms of the Works Councils Act, management is required to provide the works council with general information about the enterprise as well as, on an annual basis, information on financial and employment-related issues. In addition, the works council has a right of prior consultation with respect to the appointment and dismissal of managers and to major decisions relating to financial, economic, technical and organizational issues. It also has the right to promote enforcement of statutory and collectively agreed matters, equal opportunities and consultation over working methods. Finally, it has the right to consent over measures in the field of labour relations and personnel policy. Apart from all this, the works council also has a series of further rights by virtue of acts of Parliament, such as the Working Conditions Act, the Notification of Redundancy Act and the Civil Code (which grants it rights of investigation).

Although enterprises with only 10 to 49 employees may also set up a works council, it is not mandatory. Employers in such enterprises are, however, required to give their employees the opportunity to meet at least twice a year to discuss the general position of the enterprise. At these meetings, the employees concerned have the right of prior consultation by the employer on decisions relating to employment and pay and conditions.

In addition to such representative consultation through the works council, various direct forms of consultation and participation also exist in many enterprises. The most widespread is direct employee consultation on work (*werkoverleg*): in 1985 it existed in 43 per cent of enterprises with 100 or more employees and in 20 per cent of those with 20-99 employees. It may be described as a systematic and regulated form of consultation between the head of the establishment and the workforce, which enables employees to have a voice in and exert influence on decision-making relating specifically to work and physical working conditions. Other less widespread practices include workers' self-management in some (mostly smaller) enterprises, work structuring, autonomous work groups and quality circles. An attempt has also been made to give employees collective rights of control over the enterprise's capital in the form of statutory collective employee share ownership (*vermogensaanwasdeling,* or VAD), but this failed.

Recently, there have also been economic reasons for the growing significance of employment factors in the context of human resource management, mainly in larger enterprises in the core sectors of the economy (the motor vehicle industry, chemicals industry, metal industry and electronics industry). In these enterprises new production concepts are quite often introduced which demand considerable involvement and motivation of employees. Giving importance to the labour factor in such ways is a feature of systems such as total quality management (TQM). Although it is not known exactly how many employees and enterprises this applies to, it may nevertheless be assumed that in the near future the TQM trend will gain ground, and this will provide both challenges and opportunities for existing forms of employee participation as regulated by the Works Councils Act.

Disputes

In comparison with other European countries, the Netherlands has traditionally enjoyed a high degree of industrial peace with relatively few strikes. According to the available literature in the field of industrial relations, the contributing factors tend to be as follows:

a) organizational stability, ie, recognition of the trade union movement as a partner in government consultation at national level and acceptance of bargaining procedures by all the parties concerned;

b) the absence of leadership disputes and internal conflict, ie, a united trade union movement with a highly centralized structure;

c) stable relations between employers and employees, ie, acceptance by both sides of bargaining structures, and hence their consolidation;

d) the effective political representation of labour, ie, the existence of a social democratic party which also promotes employees' interests; and

e)   an active State, ie, a State that is both a major employer and fulfils a central role in socio-economic planning.

Although the factors mentioned do apply to a significant degree to a country like the Netherlands, there are also specifically Dutch factors involved. One such example is the negative view of industrial disputes held by many Dutch employees.

Scrutiny of the strike statistics for the past decade shows that the number of recorded disputes fluctuated between 11 (1980), 45 (1985), 29 (1990) and 14 (1995). The total number of available working days per 1,000 employees lost reached an absolute peak in 1995 at 691.5 (compared with 55.4 in 1980 and 206 in 1990). Between 1980 and 1985 the average number of employees involved in a given dispute was approximately 25,000 and in 1995 it was 55,000. The year 1996 was notable in that it involved a long-term dispute in the construction industry.

Compared with other West European countries, the Netherlands shows a low rate of working days lost through strikes: 15, 8 and 8 days per 1,000 employees in 1992, 1993 and 1994 respectively (as against 60, 18 and 7 in the Federal Republic of Germany).

It is relevant to mention that no statute exists in the Netherlands on the right to strike, either for private sector employees or for public servants. A right to strike exists by virtue of the 1961 European Social Charter, which grants workers this right in the context of the right to bargain collectively. In individual cases application is often made to the courts for a decision on a particular strike. For this purpose the courts take their cue from the Supreme Court, which in 1986 ruled that decisions relating to the right to strike in the Netherlands should be based on the 1961 European Social Charter in conjunction with the national law of torts. The presumption thereby adopted is that it is lawful to strike in the context of collective negotiations on terms and conditions of employment, provided that certain procedural rules are properly observed and that excessive harm is not caused to the life of the community at large (public transport, refuse collection, postal service, etc).

The majority of strikes relate to disputes over employees' pay and conditions. In addition to these, in recent years there have also been a number of disputes with a political tinge to them. In particular, disputes between public servants and the Minister for Home Affairs and also disputes in the semi-public sector have more than once embodied an attempt to influence parliamentary decision-making.

During the 1980s the major disputes in the Netherlands occurred primarily outside the market sector: in 1982 a strike in the education sector; in 1983 strikes by public servants and railway workers; and at the end of the 1980s strikes by nursing staff and care workers and, again, railway workers. The explanation for this lies in the policy of cuts in public spending, which had already been applied for some years and had resulted in the pay of employees in the public sector and semi-public sector dropping markedly behind that of employees in the private sector, despite the fact that a generalized policy of pay restraint for all employees had also been implemented.

The fact that arbitration exists only on a limited basis in the Netherlands has already been mentioned above. As yet, formal provision for arbitration relates solely to disputes involving public servants.

Prospects and Conclusions

Since the mid-1980s there have been important changes in the industrial relations system. The Government has to a large extent distanced itself from the industrial relations scene, and the position of the unions has become much weaker than it formerly was while that of the employers has simultaneously become stronger. The three traditional features of the Dutch system that were described under the section on 'historical background' above are not as pronounced as they were. We shall re-examine them briefly here.

The first feature mentioned was the dominant role of central government. This has certainly lessened considerably as a result of the distancing process already noted. However, the Government's influence still cannot be disregarded entirely. Although the era of the centrally controlled pay policy has been left far behind, government policy on the national economy still acts as a framework for pay bargaining. What it amounts to is the requirement for the exercise of self-discipline on the part of employers and unions.

However, the role of central government has become more obvious in relation to the development of labour law. A proportion of labour law is now more influenced by the economy – for example, flexibility in employment relationships is regulated under the terms of the Flexibility and Security Act (1998). Furthermore, labour law, particularly in the field of health and safety at work, is increasingly covered at European level. This supranational level is likely to assume ever greater significance in the future.

The second traditional feature of the system that we mentioned was the high degree of centralization of decision-making and collective bargaining. This too has eroded considerably over past years. Again as a result of the Government's withdrawal, with the need for deregulation, self-regulation and flexibilization of the economy, the industry level and the individual enterprise level have gradually assumed greater significance. One recent example of the move towards self-regulation is the change from public to private protection in the case of sickness benefit. However, despite such developments, in comparison with, say, the British industrial relations system the Dutch system is still highly regulated and centralized. At the lower levels also, the parties still accept an indicative framework that is agreed at central level. Whether this will continue to be the case is uncertain. For example, the current debate on the possible abolition of the extension procedure for collective agreements may, in the long run, actually lead to its abolition. This would have far-reaching implications for the lower levels of the industrial relations system.

Another development at the lower levels of the system is the growing importance of non-statutory rules, such as those laid down in the internal work rules of individual enterprises, staff manuals and informal local agreements. In an increasing number of cases it is not the union that is involved here, but the works council.

The third feature mentioned was reliance on inter-organizational consultation. The altered balance of power between the parties in the system means that this too has become much less important, at least at central level. By contrast, the industry level has become more prominent in this respect.

This overview demonstrates that a marked change has occurred in the nature of the Dutch industrial relations system. It has become less distinctly structured, and it is now less possible to predict what it will look like in the future. The important questions that remain open include the following.

a)   What degree of government distancing from the system is justified before this starts to imply fundamental prejudice to the protection of employees?

b)   Will the trade union movement succeed in continuing to be the appropriate countervailing power in dealings with the employers?

c)   How much scope will further European integration leave for a distinctively national industrial relations system in the Netherlands?

Whatever the answers, one thing that seems certain is that the process of decentralization witnessed over recent years is irreversible as regards the increased prominence of the individual enterprise as a level of operation. This development alone is enough to warrant the statement that the Dutch industrial relations system has been turned on its head.

Further Reading

Albeda, W. and Dercksen, W., *Arbeidsverhoudingen in Nederland (Industrial Relations in the Netherlands,* Alphen aan de Rijn, Samsom, 1994.

Bakels, H.L., *Schets van het Nederlandse arbeidsrecht (Outline of Dutch Labour Law)*, Deventer, Kluwer, 1997.

van Drimmelen, W. and van Hulst, N., *Loonvorming en loonpolitiek in Nederland (Wage Formation and Wage Policy in the Netherlands)*, Groningen, Wolters-Noordhof, 1987.

Jaspers, A.Ph.C.M. and Riphagen, J., *Schets van het sociaal zekerheidsrecht (Outline of Social Security Law)*, Deventer, Kluwer, 1991.

Metze, M., *De staat van Nederland op weg naar 2000 (The State of the Netherlands on its Way to the Year 2000)*, Nijmegen, SUN, 1996.

Noordam, F., *Inleiding sociale zekerheidsrecht (Introduction to Social Security Law)*, Deventer, Kluwer, 1997.

Pennings, F. (ed.), *Flexibilisatie van het sociaal recht (Flexibilization of social law)* Deventer, Kluwer, 1996.

Reynaerts, W.H.J. and Nagelkerke, A.G., *Arbeidsverhoudingen in theorie en praktijk (Industrial Relations in Theory and Practice)*, Leiden, Stenfert-Kroese, 1986.

Rood, M.G., *Introductie in het sociaal recht (Introduction to Labour Law)*, Arnhem, Gouda Quint, 1996.

Smitskam, C.J., *Flexibele arbeidsrelaties (Flexible Labour Relations)*, Deventer, Kluwer, 1989.

Smitskam, C.J. (ed.), *Flexibele arbeidsrelaties (Flexible Labour Relations)* (loose leaf), Deventer, Kluwer.

Sociale Nota (Social policy document), Cabinet 1995, 1996, 1997.

Visser, J. and Hemerijck, A., *A Dutch Miracle, Job Growth, Welfare Reform and Corporatism in the Netherlands,* Amsterdam, Amsterdam University Press, 1997.

Windmuller, J.P., de Galan, C. and van Zweeden, A.F., *Arbeidsverhoudingen in Nederland (Industrial Relations in the Netherlands)*, Zutphen, Het Spectrum BV, 1990.

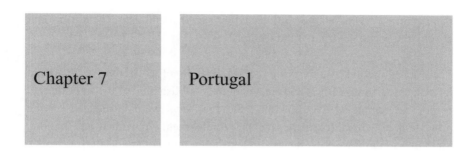

Chapter 7 — Portugal

*Mário Pinto, Pedro Furtado Martins and
António Nunes de Carvalho*

Historical Background

The current Portuguese industrial relations system was profoundly influenced by the political, economic and social changes that occurred after the revolution of 1974, although its present configuration is also the result of earlier historical developments dating back to the start of industrialization. In general, this process of development followed the same course as in other EU countries, but with a number of characteristics peculiar to Portugal deriving, essentially, from two factors: first, the slow pace of industrialization (the primary sector, which in 1900 represented over 65 per cent of employment, still accounted for over 49 per cent in 1950); and second, the fact that for almost fifty years (1926-1974) the country was ruled by an authoritarian corporatist regime in which the State took over and controlled the entire industrial relations system.

The evolution of the Portuguese system can be divided into four broad periods.

The first period (1834-1891) was the era of the rise of liberalism, characterized by a break with the structures of the old regime and the affirmation of the principles of liberal individualism, but also by the start of industrialization, the emergence of the 'social question' and the first workers' movements. This era saw the abolition of the mediaeval corporations and the prohibition of 'classist' or collective occupational interest associations (1834) and of strikes and lockouts (1852). It was mainly from the 1870s onwards that the first workers' collective actions took place, with numerous strikes and forms of protest manifesting workers' claims, influenced by socialist and anarchistic ideas and also by the social doctrine of the Church.

The second period begins with the legalization of collective occupational interest associations (1891) and ends with the establishment of the authoritarian corporatist regime (1926). In 1891, the first laws were introduced on the protection of labour (regulation of the employment of women and minors, limitation of daily working hours and legislation on health and safety at work). With the establishment of the Republic (1910), the right to strike and the right to impose a lockout were recognized. The economic and social situation did not alter significantly, and workers remained subject to extremely difficult conditions. The trade union movement gained considerable momentum (with a substantial growth in unionization and numerous strikes, many of them successful) and in 1919 the first Portuguese trade union confederation was formed: the General Confederation of Labour (CGT). However, starting from around 1910 the divisions between anarchists and socialists became more pronounced, particularly after the First World War, and led to the progressive weakening of the union movement. In addition, during this period collective bargaining was almost non-existent. Meanwhile the political scene was one of enormous instability, against the backdrop of the deep-seated hostility of the political authorities towards the Church. There were successive changes of government, attempts to seize power by force and social disturbances.

In 1926 the military seized power, marking the start of the third period, which was to last until the revolution of 1974 and was characterized by the corporatist dictatorship headed by Salazar from 1933 to 1968.

Very shortly afterwards, in 1927, the legislation on strikes and lockouts was repealed, but it was mainly after the adoption in 1933 of a new constitution and the National Labour Statute (*Estatuto do Trabalho Nacional*) that the foundations of the corporatist regime were put in place, within the framework of what was called the 'New State' and defined as 'social-corporatist, anti-liberal and anti-democratic'. This state corporatism was based on the principle of cooperation and on the rejection of class struggle, with the subjection of capital and labour to the national interest. The former 'classist' occupational interest associations were disbanded and replaced by a system of corporatist organization: the trade unions and the employers' associations (the latter were called *grémios*, or guilds) became national in nature, in a system of monopoly representation for each category, and were controlled by the State.

In 1947 the first legal regime of collective bargaining was introduced, but the non-existence of a right to strike and the political control of the unions and of the actual content of collective agreements (which were subject to government approval) meant that its relevance was limited in practice, except during the final years of the regime. But important developments did take place early on with regard to individual employment relationships and social legislation. The first general regulation of the contract of employment was adopted in 1934; it was subsequently amended in 1967 and 1969, and parts of the latter system are still in force today. This period also witnessed the first rules on protection against accidents at work (1936) and the progressive extension of social welfare.

On the economic level, although the system incorporated private ownership and the rationale of the market, it was strictly controlled by the State, closed to the outside world and dependent on the protected markets and raw materials to which its colonial territories gave it access. Living standards remained fairly difficult mainly up to the years following the Second World War, but then underwent a distinct improvement which was brought about by an economic situation favouring employment and also benefiting from massive emigration to other European countries, and which continued uninterrupted until the first oil crisis in the 1970s.

From the late 1960s, with the death of Salazar, there was an attempt to liberalize and modernize the regime. The trade union movement entered a new phase, with elections for various primary unions enabling them to be taken over by new leaders, many of them opponents of the regime. Some unions gained considerable bargaining strength, particularly in the tertiary sector (banking, insurance and office staff). Thus, collective bargaining was given a fresh momentum and was also revitalized by the adoption in 1969 of a new law on bargaining, despite the fact that the constraints on free bargaining remained in place, especially government control of the content of agreements, the ban on strikes and the compulsory use of peaceful means of settling industrial disputes. There was also progressive liberalization and modernization on the economic front. Nevertheless, political tensions, fuelled by the colonial war and growing discontent within the armed forces, and by the international isolation of the regime, eventually led to a retrogression in the opening-up process and to its subsequent collapse.

The fourth period begins with the military coup of April 1974 and divides into two phases: the revolutionary phase (1974-1975) and the democratic phase (from 1976 to the present day).

The early months after the fall of the former regime saw a movement of political radicalization, with the progressive takeover of the apparatus of the State by leftist factions mainly linked to the Communist Party. There was also a climate of increased agitation in industrial relations, with an upsurge in strikes, the occupation of enterprises accompanied by the expulsion of their former owners, the enforced removal or departure of managements and the occupation of land estates in the south of the country. The trade union structures inherited from the old regime failed to contain this movement entirely, and new workplace representative bodies began to emerge: the *comissões de trabalhadores* (workers' commissions). All the major sectors of the economy were nationalized and a regime of union monopoly, ie, a single-union system, was imposed by law with the legal recognition of one central trade union confederation, namely CGTP-Intersindical.

Starting from November 1975, and in particular after the adoption of the new Constitution of 1976, the process of normalization began, with the progressive removal of the military from political institutions and the consolidation of the democratic parties. The level of social and industrial conflict declined, accompanied by a move towards the normalization of industrial relations. There was a transition towards a regime of freedom to organize, with the emergence of a second trade union confederation, the General Workers' Union (UGT). In the years immediately following this, the prevailing climate was one of marked tension between the two union confederations, expressing the conflict between the respective models of trade unionism that they advocated: the trade unionism of political and ideological conflict represented by the CGTP (with links to the Communist Party) and the reformist trade unionism represented by the UGT (linked to the Socialist Party and the Social Democratic Party). This dualism of the central union confederations was matched by a corresponding dualism of trade union stances which came to mark the entire evolution of the subsystem of employment and union relations, leading to the progressive affirmation of a reformist model whose most recent expression was the institutionalization of the concept and practice of 'social concertation'.

Collective bargaining became generalized, albeit slowly, given the weight of state intervention in the regulation of labour relations, as was also the case in the economy as a whole. During this phase, and after an increase in real earnings won by the claims culture of the revolutionary phase, there was a significant deterioration in economic conditions. Inflation reached very high values, as did the public debt, unemployment rose and there was a marked decline in investment and productivity. It was not until the end of the 1980s that the economic crisis began to lessen and the institutionalization of an economic system incorporating a market rationale, with private ownership and economic initiative, became consolidated.

Economic and Social Context

Portugal is a small open economy and has been a member of the European Communities since 1986. Even before its accession, however, it had close economic links with the European economy: as a member country of EFTA, two-thirds of its foreign trade was with European countries. In addition, mainly starting from the 1960s, there was large-scale emigration to European countries, particularly France. Lastly, the bulk (more than half) of foreign investment originates from European countries.

Between 1966 and 1973 real GDP recorded an average growth of nearly 7.5 per cent, followed by 3.39 per cent over the period 1974-1979 and 2.75 per cent over the period 1980-1991. The time span since the end of the 1960s has included two phases of regression, during the revolutionary period of 1974-1975 and the period of austerity measures in 1983-1984. In recent years, between 1991 and 1995, the average annual variation in GDP has been lower (around 1.4 per cent) owing to the occurrence of a new crisis cycle in 1993 (with a negative variation of –1.1 per cent) and 1994 (increase of barely 0.7 per cent). In 1996, the trend showed a return towards an improvement in the macroeconomic indicators, with a growth in GDP of 2.5 per cent at the end of the first half of 1996 compared with the previous 12 months.

The respective contributions to GDP of the primary, secondary and tertiary sectors are 10, 40 and 50 per cent.

In the industrial sector, light industry predominates and is the strongest exporting element. In 1991 exports of clothing, footwear and textiles together accounted for some 43 per cent of the total. During the same year, some 75.2 per cent of exports went to EU Member States and 9.7 per cent to EFTA countries. In the case of imports, 71.9 per cent originated from EU Member States.

Exports are strongest in hides and footwear (33.3 per cent), machinery (14.6 per cent), wood, cork and paper (12.5 per cent), textiles and clothing (9.7 per cent) and farm produce and foodstuffs (8.9 per cent). Consumer goods represent 19.5 per cent of imports, as against 34.6 per cent for capital goods and 37 per cent for intermediate products.

The State plays a major role in the economy. As mentioned earlier, this role was considerably enlarged during the revolutionary period of 1974-1975, which saw a sweeping wave of nationalizations. Between the months of March and June in 1975 the banks, insurance companies, iron and steel industry, shipbuilding, heavy engineering, land, air and sea transport, petrochemicals, cement and fertilizer industries were nationalized. During the same period these sectors were closed to private enterprise, creating state monopolies. And in the agricultural sector, land belonging to large estates was occupied by organized groups, followed by legal expropriation. This trend was given concrete expression in the Constitution of 1976, whose original text sanctioned the process of nationalization and even went as far as acknowledging the non-existence of compensation. In addition, this constitutional text regarded the nationalizations carried out since 25 April 1975 as irreversible victories for the workers.

As recently as 1986 the sector under direct state ownership still represented 15 per cent of GDP, controlling 17.5 per cent of investment. The percentage of indirect state holdings was far greater.

Mainly owing to lack of incentive, the majority of the state-controlled enterprises had begun to incur losses, necessitating support by the banking sector (itself state-owned), which, in its turn, started to sustain losses.

This situation has been changing, initially with the sale of indirect state holdings and the opening-up of the financial sector to private enterprise. Subsequently, and in particular after the second revision of the Constitution in 1989, a programme of selling-off nationalized enterprises commenced and this reprivatization continued in succeeding years.

With a total population of 9.37 million, the economically active population of mainland Portugal amounts to approximately 4.6 million, representing a participation rate of 48.8 per cent.

The distribution of the employed population by economic sector shows a clear predominance of the tertiary sector, which in 1995 accounted for 56.3 per cent of the employed population as against 32.2 per cent in the secondary sector (with the emphasis on manufacturing industry) and 11.3 per cent in the primary sector (chiefly concentrated in agriculture). The general trend in recent years is towards a small but continuous increase in the predominance of tertiary sector employment.

Over the past five years both the economically active population and the participation rate have remained relatively stable, with a slight increase overall from 48.5 per cent in 1992 to 48.8 per cent in 1996 (a rise from 41.4 to 42.6 per cent in the female participation rate over the same period, and a decrease from 56.3 to 55.6 per cent in the male rate). The most significant change is in the distribution between those working on another's account (essentially, employees) and those working on their own account (essentially, the self-employed), with a decrease in the former from 3.22 million in 1992 to 3.03 million in 1996, and an increase in the latter from 1.04 million to 1.15 million over the same period. It should, however, be noted that, although no official figures are available, the widely held view is that many instances where work is ostensibly performed on a self-employed basis correspond, in reality, to situations of employment as an employee, ie, 'disguised' contracts of employment (*contratos de trabalho dissimulados*).

Among employees the traditional model of employment prevails, consisting in full-time work under a contract of employment of indefinite duration. In 1995, 2.7 million employees had contracts of indefinite duration, whilst 336,000 were on fixed-term contracts. Unemployment as recorded in the last quarter of 1996 stood overall at 7.2 per cent, with a predominance of women (8.1 per cent in contrast with 6.4 per cent for men). Long-term unemployment has risen more than short-term unemployment, and the same is true of adult unemployment (those aged over 25) as compared with unemployment among young people. Despite the rise since the beginning of 1993, the trend is towards a stabilization of unemployment.

Institutional and Legal Framework

As mentioned earlier, following the revolution of 1974 the regime of state corporatism and political authoritarianism fell and the way was opened up for Portugal to make the transition to democracy. Unfortunately, however, the immediate process of institutionalization of a democracy was traumatized by dogmatic and authoritarian tendencies which imposed a leitmotiv of antagonistic conflict in political life during the revolutionary period of 1974-1975, until the establishment of the constitutional model of 1976. This ideological and political background was gradually shifted aside and can nowadays be said to have been totally superseded, particularly following the 1982 and 1986 amendments of the Constitution, which brought about the definitive institutionalization of a pluralist democracy in a reformist context.

A parallel evolution took place in the subsystem of employment and trade union relations. Trade union freedom was restored following the coup of 25 April 1974. However, growing communist influence over the political authorities and society meant that the Trade Union Act of 1975 perpetuated the unitary or monopolist principle, ie, the system of single unions. Subsequently, the struggle for establishment of the principle of union pluralism accompanied a battle against communist influence itself, culminating in the enshrinement of the principles of trade union freedom and union pluralism in the Constitution of 1976.

In 1978, on the basis of these constitutional principles a second central trade union confederation was created: the General Workers' Union (UGT). Its formation ended the monopoly of the General Confederation of Portuguese Workers (CGTP, also known as Intersindical) which had existed in practice since 1974. This marked the opening of a new period characterized by the existence of two central union confederations and a corresponding dualism of trade union stances: the reformist trade unionism of UGT, and the conflict-based trade unionism encompassing ideological antagonism of the model preferred by CGTP. As stated above, this dualist aspect marked the entire evolution of the subsystem of employment and trade union relations in Portugal, ending in the progressive affirmation of a reformist model whose most recent expression was the institutionalization of the concept and practice of social concertation.

A characteristic feature of the present-day industrial relations system in Portugal lies in the importance that has come to be assumed by social concertation.

The year 1984 saw the creation of the Council for Social Concertation (CPCS), a tripartite body made up of representatives of the Government, the central trade union organizations and the central employers' organizations, with formal powers to examine and issue opinions on socio-economic measures and policies. The CPCS was replaced by the present Economic and Social Council (CES), whose formal establishment in the 1989 revision of the Constitution – as a 'body for consultation and social concertation in the field of economic and social policies' – represented the institutionalization of social concertation in the Portuguese subsystem of employment and trade union relations.

The principal manifestation of social concertation has been the conclusion of various tripartite agreements or social contracts, notably the following: the agreements on incomes policy for the years 1987, 1988 and 1992; the 1990 Economic and Social Agreements, which also included an agreement on incomes policy for 1991; the 1991 Agreement on Vocational Training Policy; the 1991 Agreement on Health and Safety at Work; and, under the auspices of the new CES, the 1996 Agreement on Short-Term Concertation and the 1997 Agreement on Strategic Concertation. These last two social contracts, like the 1990 Agreement (all of them signed by the Government, the three employers' confederations and the UGT), are notable in covering a very wide range of issues, including undertakings by the parties in diverse areas such as employment, the regulation of labour relations, competitiveness, the reform of social protection, the restructuring of the fiscal system and prices and incomes policies.

In terms of the employment and trade union relations subsystem, the establishment of social concertation, both in its institutional expression and, above all, in its effective implementation, completes the process of opting for a model that encompasses a reformist conception and political co-management between unions, employers' associations and governments, and at the same time signals the final rejection of the practice of ideological antagonism that marked the revolutionary period immediately following the revolution of 1974.

As mentioned earlier, state intervention, which runs through the whole of the Portuguese industrial relations system, takes place largely through direct statutory regulation. Thus, the degree of juridification of employment relations is extremely high, with reaction to political vicissitudes and economic circumstances resulting in an immense corpus of legislation. At the same time, however, because legislative intervention has taken place on this basis as and when required, superimposed enactments have resulted in a labour law which is 'alluvial' in nature and difficult to deal with. Furthermore, both the fact that the Constitution imposes a relatively wide-ranging and detailed set of principles and the fact that the adoption of labour legislation requires a sustained effort of concertation in the political and social fields make it difficult to achieve any real change to the coordinates of the legal system. The consequence is, as a counterpoint to the high degree of juridification of the system, an excessive rigidity of the legal framework.

Thus, the scope for adapting the regulatory system to the profound changes taking place in the production structure is limited. As a result of all this, we find a broad area of dysfunction between the legal framework on the one hand and the labour market and actual economic and social reality on the other.

The 1976 Constitution imposes numerous tasks on the State in the sphere of changes to employment relations and production units as regards the cultural, technical and vocational training of workers, social welfare and the organization of time off and leisure time, etc. It also charges the State with the obligation to pursue policies of full employment and to preclude all forms of discrimination on grounds of race, sex or age.

In the area of employment, state action in recent years has given priority to reducing unemployment and opening up the labour market to young first-time job-seekers. To this end, various incentives have been provided for the creation of jobs for young people entering employment for the first time.

Another area of state intervention, also linked to underlying employment problems, is the rescue of enterprises that are suffering economic difficulties. A variety of measures designed to avoid the closure of production units have been adopted.

In the field of vocational training, measures have been taken to restore technical and vocational education and training, which were practically eliminated at the time of the revolutionary period of 1974-1975.

In addition, in the field of vocational training in general, the State has been able to benefit from the opportunities opened up by accession to the European Communities, in the form of resources made available through the European Social Fund.

As regards the regulatory framework of individual employment relationships, some of its most pronounced characteristics have already been mentioned: high degree of juridification, alluvial structure and rigidity.

The extreme regulation of employment relationships dates back to the period of the corporatist regime. In Portugal, this took the form of a state corporatism in which the direct regulation of employment relationships was imposed exhaustively, leaving little or nothing to the parties themselves. The approach adopted in the period which followed the revolution of 25 April 1974 maintained this legalistic aspect, using legal instruments to impose the changes considered necessary. The promulgation of the 1976 Constitution, which was aimed at defining a whole series of principles on labour-related matters and guaranteeing the legal situation of workers and their representatives in scrupulous detail, reinforced this tendency. This was because the provision of a generous range of social rights inevitably multiplied the ordinary legislative interventions associated with their regulation.

Curiously, in a system marked by exaggerated regulation of employment relationships, intervention by the legislators has rarely been directed at overall reform, either of a particular area or in general.

Scattered legislation (*legislação avulsa*) has consequently multiplied, corresponding to interventions made on separate occasions as the need arose. A typical example is the subject of working time, whose regulation has been divided between the 1969 Contract of Employment Act, the 1971 Working Hours Act, the 1976 Annual Holidays, Public Holidays and Absence from Work Act and the 1983 Overtime Act: in 1991 and 1996 various further amendments were made to these individual statutes. However, under the terms of Law 12/96, a statutory working week of 40 hours was introduced from 1 December 1997, though actual working time is often below this.

The rigidity of the system is caused by the sheer proliferation of legal enactments, meaning that in the majority of situations provisions are enshrined in formal terms. Added to this is the fact that in many cases the matters concerned are ones which, in accordance with the Constitution, fall within the competence of the Assembly of the Republic. Bearing in mind that only since 1989 has the constitutional system seen a situation in which one political party has an absolute majority, it is easy to appreciate the difficulty involved in the enactment by the Assembly of legislation that introduces profound changes in the industrial relations system. Lastly, the rules governing the participation of employees' representative organizations in the formulation of labour legislation have introduced some measure of practical difficulty in the enactment of more controversial provisions.

Two further aspects may be added to this list of characteristics of the Portuguese labour law system: proceduralization of the exercise of certain of the employer's powers (eg, disciplinary power), and 'guaranteeism'. The latter merits one or two comments. As a rule, Portuguese law allows exemption from its provisions by collective agreement only in cases where the changes to be agreed are more favourable to workers (and in some instances they may not be changed even to make them more favourable). Hence the fact that in most instances agreements are not overtly innovatory, but confine themselves to filling the gaps left to them by the law. Furthermore, the rigidity of the system and the existence of a legislative 'hard core' inherited from the 1975 period, and bearing the stamp of extreme protectionism in favour of the workers, give Portuguese law a strongly 'guaranteeist' emphasis (to the benefit, obviously, of employees). All this naturally combines to centre the system around the law and the vicissitudes of the legislative process.

This prominence of the law inevitably tends to strengthen the role of the courts and the administrative bodies responsible for supervising compliance with legal rules. In connection with the latter, the fundamental role of the Labour Inspectorate-General must be stressed, as the body responsible for ensuring the· observance of labour laws.

As regards the courts, it should be noted that labour disputes represent a significant proportion of the legal actions brought before them (more than 20 per cent). However, given the lengthy delays in the process (which for cases referred to the appeal courts and then on to the Supreme Court of Justice may take several years), forms of extrajudicial settlement are frequently used. In this context, special significance is assumed by what might be termed the 'test case', ie, a legal action brought by an employee (generally a union representative) regarding issues which apply to a large number of other employees, as a way of obtaining a decision which pressurizes the employer to accept the settlement being claimed: after losing one case, the employer may expect to lose others and is often compelled to agree to a claim in order to avoid legal costs.

Until the overthrow of the corporatist system, labour law did not exist as a separate discipline in academic law faculties because it had been integrated under corporatist law. As a result, legal precedents, particularly decisions by the higher courts, play a role that in practice is frequently greater than is the case in other branches of the law.

Actors in Industrial Relations

There are two characteristics specific to the case of Portugal which must be mentioned in relation to the protagonists in the industrial relations system

First, in terms of employee representation, alongside trade unionism there is the phenomenon of the workers' commissions (*comissões de trabalhadores*). Whereas the unions correspond to a means of voluntary representation, exercising the right to bargain and the authority to call strikes, the primary responsibility assigned to the workers' commissions, which are formed for each enterprise on a basis of institutionalized representation (they represent the entire workforce in the enterprise), takes the form of the scrutiny and monitoring of management (*controlo de gestão*). The importance of these commissions was crucial during the post-revolutionary period, which saw an explosion of numerous forms of organic expression of employees' interests. The main purpose in establishing the legal framework of the workers' commissions (although this came relatively late – the relevant Act was not passed until 1979) was to restore some degree of order to this type of representation. However, the relevance of intervention by the workers' commissions is greatly reduced nowadays as a result of developments which led, in practice, to the legally recognized functions of these bodies being frequently exercised instead by the unions.

Secondly, as regards the employers' side, some lack of activity on the part of the organizations concerned must be emphasized. The employers' confederations actually feature as a combined pressure group with political influence, and as actors of social concertation also influencing the direct participants in concertation processes, chiefly at the level of centralized social concertation. At the level of concrete sectoral bargaining, the intervention of the employers' associations makes itself felt mainly in those economic sectors where small firms predominate (eg, the retail trade).

Trade Unions

As defined in Portuguese law, the *sindicato* (trade union) is a permanent association of employees formed for the purpose of defending the social and employment-related interests of its members. In Portugal, the term *associação sindical* is reserved for organizations that defend employees' interests (trade union organization), and, in addition to the primary unions (*sindicatos*), includes second-level organizations such as associations of trade unions (either *federações,* ie, industry-based federations covering a particular sector of activity or industry, or *uniões,* ie, regional federations) and also third-level organizations (confederations). They are collective persons under private law which are governed by special statutory regulations but to which the regulation of private-law associations may be applied on a supplementary basis. As already mentioned, the Portuguese trade union system is characterized by trade union freedom and union pluralism, and includes two union confederations: CGTP-Intersindical, founded in 1975, and UGT, created in 1978.

The Constitution also lays down that the unions shall govern themselves in accordance with the principles of independence (from political and economic power, employers and religious denominations) and democratic internal organization and management. As far as the first of these principles is concerned, it must be acknowledged that it has been grossly violated, given the close relations in some instances between unions and political parties, and the common occurrence of one and the same individual combining the functions of union officer and senior official in a political organization (despite an express legal prohibition). As regards the guarantee of internal democracy, the Constitution specifies detailed provisions, enlarging on a wide range of stipulations contained in the Trade Union Act (expressly guaranteeing the participation rights of a union's members, the right to elect and be elected as union officers, voting by secret ballot, the duty to facilitate effective exercise of the right to vote, etc). In addition to this, the Constitution guarantees the right to form political factions within unions (*direito de tendência*).

In terms of organization, it is possible to distinguish two main patterns: first, a grouping of small unions which unite to form national federations for particular sectors of activity; and second, large industrial or service sector unions which are not grouped into second-level organizations. In the former case, these federations act through sectoral agreements and combine to form territorially based groupings and, ultimately, a confederation. In the second case, there are some regional federations, particularly in the tertiary sector, almost always corresponding to models inherited from the corporatist period; in the main, however, there are simply large unions, regional or national, which do not fit easily into the other organizational structure described. Each of these patterns corresponds, in turn, to the model chosen by each of the union confederations: the first to CGTP-Intersindical and the second to UGT. No reliable studies at all have been made of the representativeness of the central union confederations, or of the other types of trade union organization. Indeed, there are not even any credible up-to-date figures on union density in Portugal.

CGTP has more member unions, although the actual number of employees represented is thought to be not much larger than that for UGT. The smaller number of unions affiliated to the latter is also due to the inherited model of a grouping of large industrial and service sector unions. The fact that CGTP represents not more than 25 per cent of the total number of unions in existence, and UGT 20 per cent, underlines the significant proportion of independent unions (ie, not affiliated to either confederation).

Employers

On the employers' side, the dismantling of the corporatist system following the revolution of 1974 saw the emergence of new employer organization models. To some extent, however, it was likewise under the influence of the corporatist organizational model that three new confederations emerged: the Confederation of Portuguese Farmers (CAP), the Confederation of Portuguese Commerce (CCP) and the Confederation of Portuguese Industry (CIP). CAP groups together federations roughly corresponding to the major agricultural areas of Portugal, composed in their turn of regional associations, cooperatives and specialist associations. CCP represents associations, some of them united in federations. CIP represents sectoral and regional associations, in some cases also grouped into sectoral federations. Figures reveal that in 1994 there was a total of 368 employers' associations with a total 211,285 members.

The State

In addition to intervention by way of legislation, to which reference has already been made above, state intervention in the industrial relations system also takes the form of support for collective bargaining and the promotion of social concertation.

Despite its strong presence in economic activity, the State features directly as an employer only in the case of public administration, which stands apart from the rules of labour law since it is governed by special regulations of a statutory nature (although since 1989, in particular, there have been legislative moves to approximate regulations for the public service to private-law employment relationships). The entire state enterprise sector is governed by labour law (or more or less hybrid systems), with each enterprise enjoying a notable degree of autonomy (the State exercises only a tutelary capacity).

The specialist departments of the Ministry of Employment and Social Security (nowadays renamed the Ministry of Training and Employment) play an important role in providing attendant services during disputes and technical support for collective bargaining, although this intervention takes place on a supplementary basis, ie, as a back-up procedure for use when the parties have not agreed on specific arrangements.

Collective Bargaining

In Portugal, as in most other European countries, collective agreements are a source of labour law having the legal character of collective contracts binding on both parties. The number of collective agreements concluded every year is relatively large. It exceeds 400, although only a few dozen of these can be regarded as new agreements or as full-scale revisions of existing agreements.

The majority of these instruments correspond to occupational or industrial sectors, the number of company agreements being relatively small. Most of the latter are concluded in public enterprises, the reason being that, until 1992, the law favoured autonomy of the bargaining process in these enterprises.

The rarity of company-level bargaining can be explained both by a tradition of industry-level bargaining and by a degree of reluctance on the part of employers, which is the result of brief experience of bargaining and the extremism of some unions in the post-revolutionary period. Public enterprises constitute a special case from this point of view as well, since in many instances they represent an entire sector, their managements are frequently acting in line with state policy, and they tolerate unions whose activity has proved effective. However, practical implementation of the process of privatization is likely to bring about a number of changes in this area.

Also, there are no rules which impose a specified bargaining level. The level is chosen freely by the parties, and the law confines itself to stipulating that any vertical agreements that are concluded automatically prevail over pre-existing horizontal agreements. Hence, the Portuguese system does not accommodate articulated (linked multi-level) bargaining. This means that company-level agreements need to be comprehensive in content, which makes their negotiation more difficult.

On the employers' side, the capacity to conclude collective agreements is possessed both by individual employers and by their representative associations. On the employees' side, exercise of the right to bargain is subject to a union monopoly (primary unions, second-level and third-level organizations). Curiously, although the law permits the conclusion of agreements by the confederations, this has so far never occurred.

In theory, agreements apply exclusively to those employees who are members of the unions that have signed them. Nevertheless, the tendency is for all employees to be covered by instruments of collective labour regulation. This is because it is regular practice for the Ministry of Employment to extend, by formal directive, the applicability of agreements to employees within the bargaining unit who are not members of the signatory unions. Hence the high rate of coverage of all workers classed as employees: in 1994, 98.4 per cent of employees were covered by instruments of collective labour regulation, a figure which includes those covered as a result of these extension directives.

In terms of content, collective agreements are, generally speaking, very conservative. Beyond matters that are typically regulated through collective bargaining (definition of grading systems, pay determination, regulation of career progression and mobility mechanisms), agreements in many instances confine themselves to summarizing the multiple scattered legislation, functioning in practice as employment manuals. Little progress has been made, however, in terms of the institutionalization of mechanisms of employee participation in the introduction of new technology or in taking more important company decisions.

Note should also be taken of a tendency to include in agreements a type of clause that refers the definition of rules on certain matters (eg, career progression) to 'derived' bargaining. The standing of such 'derived' regulations is not clear, although they function de facto as authentic agreements and tend to be regarded as such by the parties. Sometimes, these regulations (which are not published officially, nor deposited with the Ministry of Employment) deal with matters which the law excludes from the scope of the parties (this is the case, for example, with supplementary social security benefits).

Once in force, rules in collective agreements which define terms and conditions of employment become incorporated into individual contracts of employment, in cases where they are more favourable to employees and therefore carry judicial guarantee. Although there is general acceptance of the traditional distinction between clauses in collective agreements that have normative force and those that have obligational force (a distinction that is to some extent

183

included in the Collective Labour Relations Act), the courts tend to treat all clauses as possessing the same force: that of legal rules.

Employee Representation at the Workplace

As mentioned above, employee representation lies both with the unions and with the workers' commissions. However, whereas the unions pursue their activity beyond the bounds of the enterprise, but are restricted to the occupational category represented, the activity of the workers' commissions is confined to the context of the enterprise but extended to all of the enterprise's employees. Thus, one case constitutes an associatively based form of representation through an organization that is typically external to the enterprise (the union), and the other an institutional form of representation of the enterprise's entire workforce. This disparity is also clearly reflected in the difference between the procedures for appointing workplace union representatives (election, by simple majority, within the workplace union branch, with only those employees who are members of the union concerned entitled to vote) and members of the workers' commissions (voting based on electoral lists, with proportional representation on the commission, and all employees in the enterprise entitled to vote).

This dual channel of representation simultaneously implies a division of powers. Thus, while the union representatives within the enterprise (in the shape of the workplace representatives elected from among the enterprise's unionized employees) administer the application of agreements and defend those whom they represent, the workers' commission centralizes powers regarding rights to information and the monitoring of the management of the enterprise (*controlo de gestão,* ie, scrutiny and monitoring of management). Symptomatically, the authority to call a strike lies with the union, thereby linking exercise of the right to bargain with the right to take direct action (*autotutela*).

The list of matters concerning which the workers' commissions are granted the right to be provided with information is wide-ranging, encompassing all major acts of management and the entire area of unilateral definition of terms and conditions of employment, including the approval of works rules. They are also afforded participation in disciplinary procedures involving dismissal and in the procedure for collective dismissal.

As emphasized above, however, this special attention from the legislators is nowadays no longer justified in practice. Union influence has tended to extend into the areas formally entrusted to the workers' commissions, as employees' enthusiasm for and participation within the commissions have declined. Increasingly, the situation occurs where trade union delegates combine this function with that of member of a workers' commission.

Experience in Portugal regarding the institutionalization of a continuous dialogue between management and employee representatives is limited. Employers in general adopt a defensive attitude partly because the legal affirmation of employees' participation and bargaining rights coincided in time with a revolutionary phase during which employee action was strongly politicized and ideologically driven.

Disputes Procedures

The difference between disputes of rights and disputes of interest is clear from Portuguese legislation. Disputes of rights, because they concern the interpretation or application of an existing source (legally recognized as such), are susceptible to referral to the competent jurisdiction. For this purpose the law provides, inclusively, a special procedure which may culminate in an *assento* (a ruling by the Supreme Court of Justice, carrying generalized mandatory force, on how the contractual provisions in question are to be interpreted). Disputes of interest, which involve the formation of new legal positions or changes to existing ones, are dealt with in the first place through the autonomous will of the parties (possibly with the assistance of specialist government services) and in the second place through compulsory arbitration or administrative regulation.

For the peaceful settlement of collective disputes, the law makes provision for three procedures in which the element of third-party intervention plays a successively stronger role: conciliation (in which this intervention is confined to encouraging the parties to negotiate), mediation (which involves the possibility of working out a recommendation to be proposed to the parties) and arbitration (which culminates in a decision (arbitration award) that is imposed on the parties). As a rule these procedures are voluntary, and the alternative of direct and immediate recourse to forms of industrial action is lawful.

Portuguese law is notable in two ways with respect to industrial action: its generous recognition of the right to strike and its prohibition of the lockout. Both rules are, furthermore, constitutionally established. In addition, the radical nature of this abandonment of the theory of equal bargaining power extends to the point of the lockout being formally deemed an indictable offence.

The unions have a virtual monopoly of strikes (the one exception being that, in enterprises where there is no adequate union representation, the decision to strike may be taken by a mass meeting of employees). Despite the existence of the Strike Act of 1977, in both case law and the literature the legal regulation of strikes is fairly fluid, with numerous problems arising in practice. The Strike Act omits to define a strike, thereby giving rise to enormous controversy. Also, although the performance of essential services is subject to legal regulation (to which significant changes were made at the end of 1992), the original version gave rise to heated disputes regarding the interpretation of these rules, which were frequently violated. Lastly, the wording of the constitutional precept guaranteeing the right to strike (where it states that workers themselves shall possess exclusive competence to define the scope of the interests to be pursued through strike action, which the law may not restrict) fuels endless debate regarding the admissibility of political strikes and secondary or sympathy strikes. Practice, in its turn, is bound to raise new questions. This happened in 1985 and 1986 and again in 1988 with the first general strikes ever organized in Portugal, called simultaneously by the two union confederations.

Nowadays, the most widely used form of industrial action in Portugal corresponds to the legal concept of what is customarily referred to as a *greve clássica*, a strike in the strict sense of a concerted total cessation of work by employees, as opposed to forms of disruptive action short of a strike consisting in a defective rendering of the work performance due. The sole exceptions, which are rare, are mostly cases of industrial action involving an overtime ban, where employees continue to work normally but refuse to work outside normal working hours. A very common form of action (representing around half of the total instances of industrial action recorded) consists in token stoppages, where advance warning is given of threatened strike action but the strike action never actually materializes. In 1995 there were 324 such token stoppages, 315 strikes, 26 demonstrations and 23 other forms of industrial action recorded, a total of 688 forms of action.

The effectiveness of strike action would appear to be limited, since in 1995 some 80 per cent of the claims put forward by unions in the course of strikes were totally rejected by employers. About 14 per cent were partly accepted and only 6 per cent wholly accepted.

Prospects

The present era is, for various reasons, one of transition. Both because of the far-reaching reforms taking place on the institutional and political fronts (with rules and restrictions dating from the post-revolutionary period being replaced), and because of changes entailed by full accession to the European Union (particularly as regards modernization of the production sector and increasing business competitiveness), further changes ahead are inevitable. Some of these can be foreseen relatively clearly.

Labour legislation will, necessarily, have to be made to correspond more closely to reality. Neither rules that were determined in accordance with the industrial paradigm and doctrine current in the late 1960s nor laws adopted during the revolutionary period or in reaction to its consequences are appropriate to an economy which is evolving at an accelerated rate. Hence, as seen above, the widening gap between labour law and actual practice.

Consequently, significant changes in the legal framework of industrial relations may be anticipated. Some have already taken place. For instance, over the last few years measures have been adopted that may be regarded as forming part of the process of reform, in areas such as working time; the employment relationship of professional and managerial staff occupying positions of special trust; termination of the contract of employment; and multi-skilling or functional mobility.

This legislative reform will, in part, govern the pace and progress of the modernization of a substantial proportion of enterprises. Such modernization, due to be accomplished as from 1993, is certain to cause a rise in the level of unemployment (already making itself felt) and a further increase in the growing use of precarious forms of employment relationships. And the requirements of the new industrial paradigm will inevitably imply profound changes in the pattern of employment relations.

On the collective level, two phenomena are noteworthy. Firstly, the possibility of growing convergence between the two union confederations. Signs of this convergence may be detected in the positions now being adopted, while the collapse of the regimes in the East and the stances assumed by the more influential trade unionists and communists in CGTP suggest that relations between them will become easier. Secondly, there is a declared intention to make collective bargaining more flexible, for instance with respect to the duration of agreements. This measure, allied with the imperatives of modernization and the growing need for an increasingly trained and well-qualified workforce, will encourage the qualitative enrichment of collective bargaining.

Conclusions

In general terms, the characteristics of the Portuguese industrial relations system may be said to divide into two broad opposing tendencies. On the one hand, it is a system which incorporates the principles of the freedom of the social partners to organize and act collectively and the principle of collective autonomy, supported by generous recognition of the right to strike. On the other hand, there is also strong state intervention, not only in the form of direct statutory regulation but also as regards the relative dependence which the activity of the social partners exhibits towards the State.

The system also has two other distinctive features. The first concerns the links between the trade union movement and the political parties with their corresponding political stances, which has contributed significantly to a number of difficulties in relations between the two major trade union confederations and between them and the various governments. The second concerns the institutionalization of 'social concertation' and the vitality it has displayed in practice in recent years.

This latter aspect also points to a further conclusion: that the Portuguese industrial relations system appears to have opted decisively for a reformist model incorporating social concertation and the inherent involvement of the social partners in the co-management of the system.

Further Reading

Acórdãos Doutrinais do Supremo Tribunal Administrativo, Rio do Mouro, Simões Correia Editores Lda (monthly journal).

Barretto, J., 'Portugal: Industrial Relations Under Democracy' in A. Ferner and R. Hyman (eds.), *Industrial Relations in the New Europe*, Oxford, Blackwell, 1992, pp. 445-481.

Colectânea de Jurisprudência, Coimbra, Associação Sindical dos Juizes Portugueses (quarterly journal).

Cordeiro, A. Menezes, *Manual de Direito do Trabalho,* Coimbra, Almedina, 1990.

Fernandes, Monteiro, *Direito do Trabalho,* 10th edition, Coimbra, Almedina, 1998.

Instituto Nacional de Estatística, Av. António José de Almeida, 1708 LISBOA CODEX (source of statistics).

Neves, J.C. Das, *The Portuguese Economy – A Picture in Figures,* Lisbon, Universidade Católica Portuguesa, 1994.

Pinto, M., *Direito do Trabalho,* Lisbon, Universidade Católica Portuguesa, 1996.

Pinto, M., Martins, P.F. and Carvalho, A. Nunes de, *Comentário às Leis do Trabalho – Vol. I – Regime Jurídico do Contrato Individual de Trabalho* (annotated legislation), Lisbon, Lex, 1994.

Relatórios e Análises – Departamento de Estatística do Ministério para a Qualificação e o Emprego, Praça de Londres, nº 2, 1091 LISBOA CODEX (source of statistics).

Veiga, A. Da Motta, *Lições de Direito do Trabalho,* 6th edition, Lisbon, Universidade Lusíada, 1995.

Xavier, B. Lobo, *Curso de Direito do Trabalho,* 2nd edition, Lisbon, Verbo, 1993.

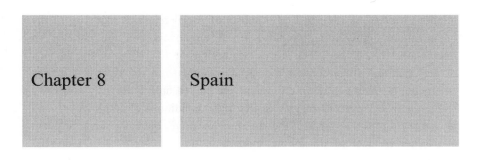

Antonio Martín Valverde

Historical and Economic Background

The development of Spain's economy in the early stages of the process of industrialization was characterized by various closely interrelated features. One of these features was protectionism, which enabled industries to become established and expand in the domestic market. A second feature was strong intervention by the authorities, normally with the aim of selectively promoting economic activities of certain kinds and occasionally (as in the early years of the Second Republic) with the idea of responding to popular demands. Another salient characteristic of Spain's economy over this period was the very marked influence of political factors or events, such as the instability of government institutions, the succession of different regimes each intent on emphasizing its differences from its predecessors, and the necessity of coping with episodes of war and the resultant need for reconstruction.

The outcome of this combination of factors was an economic system of 'corporatist capitalism', not at all conducive to innovation and growth, in which the various actors clung stubbornly to their ideological positions and to the protection of their particular interests. All this largely accounts for the delay in industrialization in Spain compared with most other West European countries, a delay that can be illustrated by a single figure: as recently as 1950, half of Spain's working population were still employed in agriculture.

Although the gap has narrowed greatly over the last 50 years, this delay in industrialization has had a major influence on various aspects of the industrial relations system, in the sense of a subset of social relations made up of the organizations representing employees and employers and the patterns of interaction between them. The most obvious signs of this influence are: the lack of any tradition of structured industrial relations and the relatively recent emergence of such a system; the minor role played until latterly by collective bargaining as a means of regulating terms and conditions of employment; and the considerable importance of the 'agrarian question', both as a social problem and as an element of the labour market, in the development of industrial relations.

In contrast to the slow pace of the earlier period, since the 1960s Spain's economy has undergone rapid and profound change. Three very different phases can be distinguished in this period of accelerated modernization: the phase of expansion (1960-1973), during which annual GDP growth rates of around 7 per cent were reached; the phase of serious economic recession (1974-1982), largely coinciding with the years of political transition, which was marked chiefly by a fall in employment and in the participation rate; and the present phase covering, in succession, an interval of recovery in economic activity and employment (1985-1991), further serious recession (1992-93) and, since 1995, signs of the start of renewed expansion.

Underlying the differing features of these separate phases, a common trend is discernible throughout the period, namely the integration of Spain's economy into the international context. From the policy of isolationism and 'inward' growth which was pursued from the start of industrialization and taken to its extreme in the autarky of the early years of the Franco regime, the movement of events led, via various stages of progressive opening-up to the outside world, to Spain's accession to the European Communities in 1986, the full application of Community law since 1992 (the year marking the end of the transitional period provided for in the Treaty of Accession) and, in recent years, the prominence of policy on European convergence as the central axis of economic and social policy.

A brief description of those aspects of Spain's economic structure that are most relevant from the industrial relations point of view must mention, firstly, the wide diversity of the industrial sector, with production geared chiefly to covering the various elements of domestic demand. Secondly, as in the whole of Europe, many areas of industry (iron and steel, shipbuilding, textiles, automobiles, household electrical appliances, etc) have been profoundly affected by the economic crisis, which resulted in the disappearance of many companies and in certain industries necessitated the adoption of conversion plans in the face of excess capacity and organizational deficiencies.

Another facet of the industrial structure that should be included in this description is the highly capital-intensive nature of its production processes, which accounts for the sector's limitations as a source of job creation. As will be seen later, this feature of Spain's industry is discernible even in periods of strong economic growth, when the growth rate has to exceed relatively high levels in order to produce a net creation of employment.

As a result of the process of urbanization and the development of tourism, the construction sector saw a spectacular upsurge in the 1960s and early 1970s, becoming the main sector to absorb the surplus manpower no longer needed in agriculture. After suffering seriously from the impact of the economic crisis, the construction sector has again enjoyed a strong upturn in recent years, chiefly thanks to public infrastructure projects. From the standpoint of industrial relations, this sector is marked by a sharp division into small and large enterprises, often linked together by a widespread network of subcontracting.

The contribution of the service sector to GDP has been around 50 per cent since the 1960s, having risen dramatically to almost 60 per cent in the 1980s. As in other countries, this is a particularly mixed sector of Spain's economy, combining both long-established and new service activities, with a marked move away from the former towards the latter in the last few decades. Other relevant features of the service sector in Spain are the importance of activities connected with tourism and the strong growth, since the period of political transition, in public services. At present, the proportion represented by public employment in the service sector as a whole is around 30 per cent. In absolute figures, public servants employed in the central and Autonomous Community administrations number over 1 million; when the employees of public enterprises and institutions and the public servants in the municipal authorities are added, this gives an approximate total of 2.2 million employed in the public sector.

During the period of modernization that began in 1960, agriculture has acted as the source of supply of the manpower and capital needed for urban economic development. At present, its share of GDP is under 6 per cent. But this decrease, and the shift in resources, must not be interpreted solely as evidence of the agricultural sector's decline: rather, it demonstrates the strong growth of the other sectors. And agriculture too has modernized during this period, in terms both of mechanization and of products and cultivation methods. In any case, for reasons that will be seen later, the importance of Spain's primary sector in the industrial relations system is greater than its contribution to the economy as a whole would suggest.

Social Context

These changes in Spain's economic structure have been correspondingly reflected (although with certain distortions) in the labour market and in the make-up of the working population. First of all, there has been a drastic fall in the agricultural labour force as a proportion of the total working population, which by 1988 was already under 15 per cent, and since 1994 has been approximately 10 per cent. The percentages of the working population employed in the other sectors are at present 30 per cent in the secondary sector (with 21 per cent employed in manufacturing industry and 9 per cent in construction) and 60 per cent in the service sector.

Despite all indications, however, this decline in the agricultural labour force does not in fact represent a process of rural exodus; this is demonstrated by the fact that there has been a steady loss of employment in agriculture since more or less the middle of the century, independently of fluctuations in the economic cycle. It must also be borne in mind that one third of those working in agriculture are self-employed, mostly concentrated in the southern regions of Spain. In these regions the primary sector still plays an important part in the course of labour relations.

Employment trends in the secondary and tertiary sectors have, on the other hand, been governed to a greater or lesser degree by fluctuations in the economic cycle. In the service sector, which as stated above has undergone a spectacular increase over the past 15 years from a share of 40 per cent of total employment to 60 per cent, the rate of job creation has been higher during periods of economic growth and has stagnated or declined slightly during periods of recession. Manufacturing industry and construction are far more vulnerable to fluctuations in the economic cycle, and this pattern has meant drastic job losses up till 1985, similarly substantial job creation during the period 1985-1991, and a further serious decline in 1992-1993 which slowed and then halted over the following two years.

For the whole of the working population in the various sectors of the economy, the distribution between employees and the self-employed fluctuates around figures of 70 per cent employees and 30 per cent self-employed. The trend in recent years was for a proportionally larger increase in the number of self-employed, owing to the difficulty of finding a job during the years when the economic crisis was worsening. This trend appears to have halted and even reversed in the late 1980s, with a slowing-down in the number of self-employed workers establishing new enterprises or setting up forms of association (cooperatives, workers' limited companies, etc).

Apart from the impact on the sectoral make-up of the working population, the changes in Spain's structure of production have markedly altered the occupational structure, generating at the same time substantial occupational mobility of the labour force. This mobility, manifested in the form of retraining, has been associated in some cases with a change of job or employment and in others with the introduction of new production or work-organization techniques, which, even in the context of the same occupation or job, have profoundly changed the scope and content of the tasks performed. A useful indicator of this change is the increase over the course of the 1980s in the number of workers with intermediate qualifications (100 per cent increase) and higher qualifications (50 per cent increase).

It must, nevertheless, be acknowledged that the labour market is suffering from a serious mismatch between the skills of the available labour force and the demands of the production system, calling for major reform of the institution that provides basic and further training.

One of the principal factors that must be singled out when analysing the economic context of industrial relations in Spain is the incapacity of the production system to provide employment for the entire available labour force. This phenomenon, which is a constant factor underlying the whole course of modern-day developments, has manifested itself in various ways. The first of these is emigration, which has gone on incessantly since the late 1800s and reached a particularly high level, in the form of emigration to other Community countries, at the very stage of economic expansion that started in the 1960s. In round figures, this enormous emigrant flow, paradoxically coinciding with the years of strong growth in industry and the service sector, amounted to 1 million workers.

The other manifestation of the chronic incapacity of Spain's economy to utilize the whole of its manpower resources is the level of unemployment resulting from the economic crisis. The stagnation of production activity and the return of emigrants together raised this figure in 1985 to 21 per cent of the economically active population (some 3 million workers), revealing the full magnitude of this imbalance in employment. The renewed period of recession in the early 1990s brought an even further increase in the number of unemployed, which at the end of 1995, according to the National Institute of Statistics' Survey of the Working Population (the most 'pessimistic' source), was close on 3.6 million, representing 23 per cent of the economically active population. However, the same official figures recorded a substantial decrease in unemployment of two percentage points in the years 1996 and 1997.

In considering the unemployment figures in Spain, various other figures should also be taken into account, some serving to worsen the diagnosis of the situation, and others to improve it. The factors that worsen it include, in particular, the low participation rate of the section of Spain's population who are of working age (49 per cent in 1995). Here too, the explanation for this figure, which is certainly below the European average, is the incapacity of the production structure to create employment, which discourages many potential members of the working population, particularly women, from entering the labour market.

It should be noted, nevertheless, that the delayed participation of female labour in economic activity outside the home has recently seen a spectacular rise: after passing the 30 per cent mark in 1986, the participation rate of women reached 32.8 per cent at the end of 1988 and was already over 36 per cent by the end of 1995.

Other figures which adversely affect the diagnosis of unemployment in Spain, but which at the same time are showing signs of an underlying improvement, are those for youth unemployment (individuals aged 16-24) and long-term unemployment (unemployment lasting for more than a year). There is a clear downward trend in youth unemployment (44 per cent in 1985, 38.8 per cent at the end of 1988 and 35 per cent at the end of 1992), and a similar trend is apparent in the figures for long-term unemployment: 64 per cent at the end of 1987, 61 per cent at the end of 1988 and 57 per cent at the end of 1994.

Among the factors indicating that the real scale of unemployment in Spain is less serious than might appear, mention should be made of the widespread and, in the author's view, well-founded belief that the official figures are overestimated. The reasoning on which this belief is based can be summarized as follows: the unemployment figures as 'recorded' or declared in official surveys take no account whatever (in the case of unemployment registered with the employment offices) or presumably very little account (in the case of unemployment reported in the quarterly Surveys of the Working Population) of undeclared employment in the hidden or informal economy.

An assessment of the recent employment trends must also include, on the positive side, the change of direction in external migration flows. Not only has Spain ceased to be a country of massive emigration, but since the 1980s it has been transformed into a country of immigration. This is a new phenomenon in the history of contemporary Spain, which denotes both a certain capacity to absorb labour and a trend towards a selective internal demand for employment. Two significant figures give an idea of this inward migration flow: the number of authorized immigrants at the beginning of 1990 (close on 70,000) and the number of authorized immigrants in the campaign conducted for this purpose in 1991, which was just over 110,000.

A final comment that should be made about the economic context of industrial relations in Spain concerns the geographical imbalance in the production structure. As regards employment, this imbalance is reflected in the high figures for migration within Spain. The overall level of unemployment thus conceals a very unequal distribution of surplus manpower among the various regions of the country: the surplus is very high in the agricultural regions of southern and western Spain but is (or was, until the recent economic crisis) lower in the north, where heavy industry is concentrated, and in the east, where there have been major centres of industries producing consumer goods since the early 1800s.

Institutional and Legal Framework

During the second half of the 1970s, Spain witnessed the start of two processes of legal change which profoundly altered the shape of industrial relations. The first of these changes, which was essentially political, was brought about by the transition from General Franco's dictatorship to the present parliamentary monarchy. The second occurred in the context of the national economy, and was closely linked to the economic crises and changes that have been described above. The purpose of this latter process was to achieve greater flexibility in the deployment and management of human resources within the enterprise.

The basic outlines of the change in industrial relations generated by the political transition are laid down in the 1978 Constitution, which recognizes the 'right to organize collectively', the 'right to bargain collectively', the 'right to strike' and 'freedom of enterprise in the context of a market economy'. As is immediately evident, the adoption of the Constitution affected virtually every aspect of the legal framework of industrial relations, as examined below.

The first aspect affected was the status or legal position of the social partners or their representative bodies. The recognition of freedom of association immediately triggered the open, unrestricted activity of the trade unions and workers' 'coalitions', which had previously existed in a precarious world where they were semi-clandestine organizations subject to intermittent repression. It also implied the extinction of the old regime's official Trade Union Organization (Organización Sindical) or 'Vertical Union', characterized by the compulsory inclusion of both employers and workers in a complex network of corporatist bodies controlled by the State.

A second aspect of the legal framework which was affected by the reform launched in 1976 was intervention by the authorities in industrial relations. Overall, the State's role in this area of society has significantly diminished since 1976, as regards both regulatory and administrative intervention. The essential reason for this withdrawal by the authorities lies in the greater scope for freedom of action formally granted to the industrial relations organizations in the new legal and political context. As regards administrative intervention, account must also be taken of another reform concerning industrial relations: the transfer of many of the powers of intervention to the decentralized authorities of the regions or 'Autonomous Communities'.

Finally, the change in the legal framework of industrial relations has itself influenced two significant aspects of bilateral relations between the social partners. One of these is the scope of collective bargaining on terms and conditions of employment, which is much broader and more clearly defined than before. The other concerns the available means of defending labour interests, with workers and trade unions being given the 'conventional' weapons of self-help (in particular, the right to strike) of which they had been deprived under the old political regime.

This process of political change is now virtually completed, and there are signs that the forward thrust of industrial relations may soon be characterized not, as hitherto, by the creation and implementation of 'legal machinery' but by the activities of negotiation and participation which are the proper features of a working industrial relations system. The legal decisions taken in 1986 on the distribution of the *patrimonio sindical acumulado* (the assets accumulated by the official Organización Sindical during the Franco period) and the repayment of the *patrimonio sindical histórico* (assets seized from workers' unions in 1939) seem to symbolize the end of this period of change in the legal framework of labour relations.

The second process of change in the legal framework of industrial relations in Spain has been driven, as stated above, by economic considerations. These include demands for efficiency (productivity, profitability, competitiveness) that derive from the opening-up of Spain's economy to international competition and have been especially pressing since the 1980s. As has been pointed out on more than one occasion, it was in the 1980s that the demands of the fight for markets spread from the traditional areas of prices and marketing into those of internal company organization and labour costs, areas which today are still covered by a greater degree of protection.

One of the most salient features of this process of legal change is its gradual nature. The trend towards labour flexibility actually began as early as in Decree-Law No. 17/1977 on Labour Relations, one of the key provisions of the political transition, and Law No. 8/1980, which contained the initial version of the Workers' Statute. A further move towards labour flexibility came with the extensive reform of labour legislation in 1984, which affected all forms of employment contract and financial protection against unemployment. There were also steps in the direction of flexibility in the recent labour legislation reform of 1994, completed in 1997, even though not always along the same lines as those followed in 1984.

The most important repercussions of the reform of labour legislation that took place in 1984 were a change in the structure of employment by type of contract and an increase in the provision of financial assistance for unemployed persons. Since its implementation, the great majority of all contracts of employment concluded have fallen into the category of temporary or fixed-term contracts. This new phenomenon in hiring practices has radically transformed the basis of employment relationships or the structure of employment by type of contract. The most recent official Surveys of the Working Population show that, from a situation in the early 1980s where temporary contracts represented only approximately 10 per cent of all contracts of employment, employees on temporary contracts now constitute over a third of all employees, while the proportion of those employed under permanent contracts has decreased correspondingly to around 65 per cent.

The increase in the coverage of financial protection against unemployment was also significant. In round figures, provision rose from protection for one third of the unemployed population to two-thirds. This rising trend, with the resultant increase in expenditure on unemployment, seems to have reached a turning point in 1992, the year which saw the introduction of a more restrictive legislative approach, whose effect on the proportion of unemployed people receiving financial assistance is already discernible.

It is uncertain whether, viewed overall, the effects of the labour legislation reform that followed in 1994 will be greater than those of the reform of 1984. It can, however, be said at the outset that it is more extensive in its material scope. In terms of principles or tendencies, the implications of this major legal reform may be summarized as follows:

1) a lifting of the public monopoly of job placement, through the legalization of temporary employment agencies and non-profit-making private employment agencies;
2) revision of the legal regime governing temporary or fixed-term contracts, lowering the economic barriers to forms of training contract to promote entry into working life and restricting the cases in which temporary contracts are permitted;
3) establishment (subject to certain restrictions) of the principle of internal mobility within the enterprise, a principle that broadens the scope of the employer's discretionary powers as regards human resource management;
4) a modest relaxation of the rules governing both individual and collective dismissal, with the aim of reducing litigation costs and payments awarded; and
5) a transfer of greater regulatory powers from the law to collective bargaining, and a tendency towards the decentralization of bargaining.

In the labour reform of April 1997, a number of these tendencies have been moderated in some cases and maintained in others. First, it goes one step further in making the rules on dismissals required by the enterprise's economic needs more flexible. Secondly, it continues the process of restructuring collective bargaining. And lastly, it focuses more strongly than the 1994 reform on adopting measures to create stable employment and promote the hiring of employees under permanent contracts. Its main objective is to reduce the high proportion of temporary workers in the working population which has resulted from the relaxation of the restrictions on fixed-term contracts introduced in 1984.

Formation of the Spanish Industrial Relations System

As has just been stated, the years 1976-1986 saw not only a fundamental change in the laws governing labour relations but also the formation of an industrial relations system. Beginning with a situation in which the trade unions were fragmented and there were huge gaps not covered by employers' associations, this period saw the gradual consolidation of a definite structure of representation, which now enables us to identify the social partners without any great difficulty. As regards the interaction of these representative bodies, both with each other and with the authorities, certain rules governing relations emerged during this period and have, with a few exceptions and reservations, made it possible to achieve some acceptable results as regards industrial peace and the reconciling of interests.

The particular shape of these elements of Spain's industrial relations system today has obviously not emerged purely by chance but is the result of the combined effect of various factors. One of these is the **historical** factor, which includes both the influence of the rules and traditions of the past and the ability of established interest groups to survive. A second factor was, and still is, **political** – the inclination of political institutions (parliaments, governments, public administrations, parties, etc) to influence the structure of representation in industrial relations by selectively promoting certain trade unions or employers' associations. To these we can add a third factor which is an **economic** one: the coincidence of the formation of the industrial relations system with the crises and changes in production and trade following the 1973 rise in oil prices.

Historical influences did not mean that the ways open to political institutions for influencing elements of the industrial relations system were limitless, but they were nonetheless very great. In point of fact, the trade union and employers' organizations that existed when the transition to democracy began were of sufficient importance to ensure that account was taken of them, but they were not strong enough to resist the power of political forces to shape and promote a particular system. Similarly, the traditions and practices of the social partners could not be openly suppressed or opposed, yet they were not well-rooted enough to withstand a planned operation to reform and modernize many aspects of them.

Political institutions have taken full advantage of this relative malleability of the various elements of the industrial relations system during its recent formation to point them in a certain direction. Opportunities to exercise this influence have not been lacking and have included, in particular, the transformation of labour law mentioned in the preceding section. Certainly, legislative regulation of the independent trade unions and labour rights serves the primary function of 'democratizing' labour relations. But it could also serve an implicit secondary function of shaping the industrial relations system in a certain way. This, as we shall have a chance of demonstrating later, is what has actually happened.

As for the influence of the economic factor, it is anticipated here that the crises and changes in the production structure and trade since 1973 have been reflected first and foremost in the attitudes and behaviour of the parties involved in industrial relations and also, though less strikingly or directly, in the actual structure of representation.

Of all the economic processes and events over this period, those with the greatest impact in the field that concerns us here have unquestionably been the steep decline in employment and corresponding increase in the number of unemployed people which occurred up till 1985. This climate of economic emergency and the simultaneous reconstruction of the industrial relations system, which provided an impetus in the same direction, prepared the psychological ground for the successive tripartite agreements reached through social concertation which feature frequently in the period concerned. In those agreements, moderation of the claims put forward by employees' representatives in collective bargaining was met, in exchange, with a social and economic policy agreed between the Government and the trade union and employers' organizations themselves. This point will be examined in more detail below.

The epoch of moderation on the part of employees' representatives ended, significantly, when signs were perceived of growth in the economic cycle in the second half of the 1980s. And it is no less significant that, in 1994, there was a return to moderation and the 'social dialogue', echoing, with the natural delay corresponding to the interval between the occurrence of a social phenomenon and general awareness of it, the serious crisis of the previous two years.

Actors in Industrial Relations

Industrialization and economic growth during the period 1960-1975 were accompanied, in the sphere of industrial relations, by the appearance and spread of sources of independent trade union activity, concentrated first in enterprises and workplaces and then spreading to cover wider areas. These sources of activity acquired their first official coverage in the 'bodies to promote labour harmony' in workplaces that were set up by legislation under Franco and called *jurados de empresa* (works councils), bodies which included representatives elected by the workers. Soon afterwards, *enlaces sindicales* (official workplace representatives), who were also elected by the enterprise workforce and whose function was, on paper, to serve as a go-between or intermediary for the official Vertical Union or Organización Sindical with the rank and file of workers, were utilized towards the same end of developing trade union activity in the real sense.

From the decentralized level of enterprises and workplaces, the representatives elected by the workers could move on to perform functions within the Vertical Union itself, in bodies officially responsible for reconciling the interests of employers and workers at sectoral and regional level. From the second half of the 1960s, full advantage was taken of this opportunity by the sources of trade union activity just mentioned, so that, during the final years of Franco's rule, it was often they who controlled the peripheral sections of the official Organización Sindical.

This trade union movement which emerged in the 1960s was, despite its inclusion in official representative bodies, clearly a form of political dissidence with the established regime. Its main protagonists were the *comisiones obreras* (workers' commissions), which were strongly influenced by the Communist Party but also included other opposition factions. Supporters of this policy of making use of available representative channels likewise included a trade union organization also founded in the 1960s and called Unión Sindical Obrera (USO: Workers' Trade Unionist Confederation). At the time, however, this strategy of infiltration was opposed, for one reason or another, by the trade union bodies that had been broken up at the end of the Civil War, ie, the Unión General de

Trabajadores (UGT: General Workers' Confederation), which was affiliated to the Socialist Party, the anarchistic Confederación Nacional del Trabajo (CNT: National Confederation of Labour) and Solidaridad de Trabajadores Vascos (ELA-STV: Basque Workers' Solidarity), a trade union exponent of Basque nationalism. Following a long period of inactivity, these trade union organizations too began to show signs of life in enterprises and workplaces during the final years of Franco's rule.

Although the Franco dictatorship did not substantially change its initial stance, the trade union front of opposition to the regime did, in those final years, enjoy a degree of tolerance because of its capacity to resist and also, to some extent, as a result of the attempts made at assimilation by the official Organización Sindical. Such tolerance was, at all events, a precarious state of affairs, alternating with or interrupted by relatively frequent periods of repression. This ambiguous situation of semi-clandestine activity, now tolerated and now repressed by the political powers, lasted until 1976, the year that marked the beginning of the period of political transition and saw the first steps being taken towards abolishing the official Organización Sindical and the announcement of the legalization of independent trade unions. These first steps were followed in 1977 by actual legal recognition of freedom of association and the right to strike, and the continued dismantling of the Vertical Union. As already stated, this process of legal change culminated in and was consolidated by the adoption of the 1978 Constitution.

The development of the system of employer and employee representation during the years of political transition was marked not only by these legislative events but also by the expansion of the trade union movement's membership figures and organizations and the appearance of employers' associations. These two movements, representing different interests, were to follow different paths. The employers' associations subsequently opted for joining forces in a single organization: the Confederación Española de Organizaciones Empresariales (CEOE: Spanish Confederation of Employers' Organizations), which was founded in 1977 by the merging of various employers' confederations set up shortly before. The expansion of the trade union movement, on the other hand, followed the opposite path, with its various elements representing different ideological stances and occupational sectors dispersing to form separate organizations. The trade union structure resulting from this proliferation of organizations had a somewhat disjointed appearance in which it was possible to distinguish three distinct 'strata' of trade unions: the 'historical' unions, which dated back to before the Civil War and had re-emerged during the last years of Franco's rule; the trade unions founded in the 1960s on the basis of union activity in workplaces; and the newly formed trade unions, some affiliated to equally new political parties, others created with the more limited aim of protecting workers in their particular sectors.

When the period of political transition came to an end with the adoption of the Constitution and the launching of constitutional bodies, the process of formation of the system of industrial relations representation was not even nearing completion. For several years, this area of society remained fluid and saw a rapid succession of events. On the employers' side, the most important development was undoubtedly the consolidation of the CEOE as the employers' mouthpiece at national level. A milestone in this process of consolidation was when, in 1980, the most widely established employers' association among small and medium-sized enterprises, the Confederación Española de la Pequeña y Mediana Empresa (CEPYME: Spanish Confederation of Small and Medium-Sized Enterprises), joined the CEOE.

On the trade union side, the most remarkable event over the past few years has been the clarification of the landscape of representation, with the take-off of two national confederations (UGT: General Workers' Confederation; and CC.OO: Trade-Union Confederation of Workers' Commissions), which won clear majorities in the 1980 elections of workers' representatives in enterprises and saw their positions confirmed in the 1982 and 1986 elections. Since 1988 these two confederations have formed a coordinated front, apart from occasional episodes of disagreement when elections are being held, producing a situation that may be referred to as unity of action. The successive 'union elections' of 1990 and 1994 did not alter this basic situation, although in the last election the respective positions of the major confederations were reversed, with UGT losing its leading position to CC.OO.

This national dominance of two confederations, which tends to be projected on to each and every regional district by the mechanism of the 'extension of representativeness' to the bodies included in each district, has led to the coining of the term 'bi-unionism' to describe the structure of the trade union movement in Spain. If we are to use this term, it would in fact be more accurate to speak of 'imperfect bi-unionism', since there are other trade union organizations which, although clearly minority groups in the system of industrial relations representation as a whole, are dominant in certain regions (eg, ELA-STV in the

Basque Country and CIG (Galician Trade Union Interconfederation) in Galicia) or specific occupational sectors (eg, USO, the Workers' Trade Unionist Confederation, and CSIF-CSI in the public sector).

Another notable trend in the more recent history of the system is the stagnation in the growth of the unions following the brief period of expansion during the political transition in Spain. The most important manifestations of this phenomenon are: the low density of unionization, which, according to the calculations that appear to be the most accurate, is less than 15 per cent of the working population; the restriction of trade union representation to the traditional working class core and its failure, with rare exceptions, to cross the barrier into new labour sectors (technical specialists, middle-management staff, skilled services, office staff, etc); and, lastly, the financial inability of the trade unions to cover their own everyday running costs.

The framework of industrial relations representation as described in broad outline here has been shaped by various factors, some intrinsic and some extraneous to the organization and strategy of the trade unions and employers' associations. These factors will be analysed later. It does, however, seem appropriate to draw attention here to one internal factor to complete the description of the formative process of industrial relations representation in Spain. The fact is that a large number of regional and sectoral trade union bodies were set up under the impetus of the respective confederations, with a view to the rapid reconstruction of the trade union movement. A similar phenomenon, though limited to regional bodies, also occurred within the CEOE. This contribution of the confederations to the founding of the representative organizations which constitute their membership has been reflected, as might have been expected, in the centralization of representation and in the initial vigour of the trade union movement, a period of expansion that coincided, and not by chance, with the recruitment by the national confederations of the activist members and officials they needed to establish themselves at regional level.

Employee Representation at the Workplace

The tradition of employee self-help in enterprises and workplaces, which was orchestrated in the second phase of Franco's rule by making use of the channels offered by works councils and official workplace representatives, was not only maintained but became much stronger in the years of political transition, when the foundations of a new legal framework for industrial relations were being laid. With respect to the institutions representing employees at enterprise level, this reorganization signified the disappearance of official workplace representatives as a result of the abolition of the official Organización Sindical for which, on paper, they were supposed to serve as a go-between, and the conversion of works councils into 'workers' committees' (*comités de empresa*) or 'workers' delegates' (*delegados de personal*). The change of title was not, in this case, merely cosmetic: it was accompanied by a significant change in content. Workers' committees and workers' delegates were designed to represent and defend the interests of employees and thus consisted only of members belonging to the various groups of workers. By contrast, the former works councils, in accordance with their institutional duty to seek the common interest of the enterprise, had been of mixed composition, including representatives of the employer as well as of the workers.

As happened in many other areas of labour law, the regulations issued on workers' committees and workers' delegates during the period of political transition formed the basis of the corresponding legislation passed after the Constitution had been adopted. Thus, the Estatuto de los Trabajadores (Workers' Statute) of 1980 maintained and still maintains the broad lines of the aforementioned regulations on employee representative bodies: appointment of workers' delegates in small enterprises and workers' committees in large and medium-sized enterprises; workers' delegates to be elected by the workers and workers' committees to consist of members elected by the various occupational groups; and responsibility of these representatives to protect the interests of the entire enterprise workforce.

Among the many functions and powers of these unitary bodies representing an enterprise's entire workforce, the Workers' Statute establishes the right to disclosure of information on the enterprise's financial situation, expenditure and financial results; the right to consultation should the enterprise reduce or terminate its activities or introduce or modify systems of work organization, etc; the power to monitor the employer's compliance with labour regulations; and, what is truly extraordinary, collective bargaining at enterprise or workplace level.

This authority to conduct collective bargaining extends not only to taking practical decisions jointly with the enterprise's management, but also to the concluding of actual collective agreements at enterprise level, that is, agreements of a broader and more systematic nature, formalized in writing, to regulate employment and working conditions. On paper, the authority of workers' committees and workers' delegates to negotiate such company agreements clashes with an equivalent bargaining power granted contractually to those trade unions which are firmly established in the enterprise. In practice, however, this collective bargaining power has in most cases been assumed by the unitary representative bodies and not by trade union representatives in the strict sense.

The tradition of collective representation at enterprise level, together with the important functions assigned to these representative bodies within enterprises by the Workers' Statute, could have given rise to a structure of representation in which industry-wide and national multi-industry levels were reserved for trade unions, while unitary representative bodies were responsible at enterprise level. However, this hypothetical situation in which one might witness the emergence of two separate systems to represent workers (on the one hand the trade unions and, on the other, unitary representative bodies within enterprises) has not materialized. On the contrary, the two forms of representation have become so closely linked that they might rightly be considered facets of a single system of representation. The factors connecting the two are various. One is the strong presence of the trade unions on workers' committees and among workers' delegates. Another is the major role attributed to the trade unions in the procedure for electing these representatives. A third is acknowledgement of the right of trade unions to set up their own representative bodies in workplaces, bodies that are connected organizationally with workers' committees when the trade unions concerned are well established in the enterprise.

Collective Bargaining

As mentioned earlier, the second phase of the Franco regime saw a certain trend towards the kind of industrial relations practices prevailing in industrialized democracies. The signs of this about-turn are perceptible, though with very marked differences, both in representative bodies and in collective bargaining practices. In the case of representative bodies, this trend was a result of the emergence of workers' 'coalitions' which ended by forming a trade union movement of considerable strength.

In the case of collective action, the classification of 'workers' strikes' as a crime of sedition (1944 Penal Code) and the notion that the labour authorities had exclusive power to regulate employment and working conditions (1942 Labour

Regulations Act) were superseded, in a remarkable change of approach, by recognition of the collective agreement as a means of improving the workers' situation (1958 Collective Agreements Act). As a result of this legal recognition, the law also subsequently accepted the calling of collective labour disputes (Decree of 1962) and the decriminalization of strikes themselves (1965 reform of the Penal Code).

The step which Franco's legislators refused to take in relation to this aspect of collective labour relations was to legalize strikes. Although it ceased to be a crime as from 1965, the collective cessation of work continued to be considered an illegal act in civil breach of the contract of employment and, possibly, an offence against 'public order'. As a breach of or failure to comply with the contract of employment it was punishable by the employer, and penalties could include dismissal in the case of 'active participation' in strike action. As a public order offence it was punishable by fines imposed by the authorities.

The structure and process of collective bargaining which emerged during the second phase of Franco's rule had some very peculiar features because of the singular nature of the legal and political framework within which they developed. The main peculiarity of the collective bargaining process was, as we have already indicated, the existence of legislation which discouraged strikes and other direct forms of collective industrial action. This did not mean that situations of open industrial conflict did not arise, but rather that they were accompanied by additional problems and tensions and quite frequently became political and social conflicts too.

As regards the structure of collective bargaining during this period, the essential factor to be borne in mind is the existence at the time of two completely separate and unconnected forms of collective agreement: the company agreement (negotiated by the works councils) and the industry-wide agreement (negotiated within the official Organización Sindical by 'social' and 'economic' representative bodies). Gradually, the forward thrust of collective bargaining was tending to reserve the company agreement for work/production units of a certain size, and to adapt the distribution of industry-wide bargaining units to the organizational structure of the peripheral administration of the Organización Sindical. These two paths of development led, in the early days of political transition, to a bargaining structure consisting of two separate elements: company agreements and industry-wide agreements, the latter being very highly fragmented and scattered.

The structure of collective bargaining today owes much to this historical inheritance. One resultant aspect is the division of negotiation between company agreements and industry-wide agreements, which together cover three-quarters of all employees. Another is the separation or lack of coordination of these two types of agreement, each covering different segments or parts of work/production units. A third aspect is the fragmentation of industry-wide bargaining units, though negotiation practice over the past few years has taken a few steps towards redefining the scope of agreements and incorporating provincial agreements into national agreements.

Without losing sight of these persistent features, it should be noted that the current structure of collective bargaining in Spain is marked by some significant innovations. Probably the major innovation is the appearance and consolidation of national multi-industry agreements negotiated by the most representative trade unions and employers' associations at national level.

These 'summit' agreements have had two fundamental objectives. The first, which in the past few years has receded in step with the crisis in social concertation, was to regulate certain issues covered by collective bargaining at industry-wide or enterprise level, as a centralized means of dealing with the consequences of economic crises. The second objective has been to respond to specific issues such as workers' participation in public enterprises (1986), continuing training (1992, 1996), departure from Labour Ordinances or Regulations dating back to the earlier regime (1994, 1995 and 1997), the extrajudicial settlement of labour disputes (1996) and the collective bargaining structure (1997).

Another notable feature of the structure of collective bargaining in Spain is the existence of two classes of agreement, depending on their range of applicability: the agreement with *erga omnes* force, which has general applicability to all members of the occupational group and not just members of the contracting organizations; and the agreement with limited applicability, which, in principle, covers only the employers and workers directly represented in the negotiating unit as a result of their membership of the contracting associations. Obviously, for a collective agreement to have *erga omnes* force, certain requirements regarding official recognition and procedure must be met, as laid down in the 1980 Workers' Statute; if these requirements are not met, the agreement is classed as an agreement of limited applicability, governed not by the Workers' Statute but by the general legislation covering representation and contracting, and is called an 'extra-statutory' agreement.

Today, the industrial relations scene appears to be dominated by generally applicable collective agreements, usually signed by committees and delegates at enterprise level and jointly by the major trade unions at industry-wide level. We cannot, however, ignore the fact that a change in the composition or strategy of trade union or employers' representative bodies would lead to a substantial increase, more or less overnight, in the number and significance of extra-statutory agreements. A breakdown in the policy of joint action normally observed in this area by the two major trade union bodies would be enough to give rise to such a situation, at least as regards industry-wide agreements. In point of fact, at the level of national multi-industry agreements, there has been an alternation of generally applicable agreements and agreements of limited applicability because of differences in trade union policy followed with respect to these agreements by the major confederations, the UGT and CC.OO.

The combination of elements of change and continuity that can be observed in the current structure of collective bargaining in Spain can also be detected in the other component of the negotiation sytem, ie, the process of drawing up and renewing agreements. The most outstanding difference from the previous situation here is undoubtedly recognition of the right to strike, which has eliminated the complication of labour disputes and episodes of repression, a complication that frequently arose during the final years of Franco's rule.

However, in addition to the change in the collective bargaining process brought about by recognition of the right to strike, a significant persistent feature should also be pointed out: the considerable effort that has to be devoted to negotiation, an effort that is certainly out of proportion to the absolute and relative numbers covered by agreements. There are two main reasons for this unwieldy negotiating machinery. The first is the custom of renewing agreements annually; this practice is beginning to die out but is still followed in many cases. The other reason is the lack of any connection or coordination between industry-wide and company agreements, which means that many aspects which could be negotiated just once at industry-wide level have to be discussed in every enterprise. To put this disadvantage into perspective, however, it should be pointed out that legislation and bargaining practice have established a number of mechanisms to alleviate the problem. These include the role that certain company agreements play as a model for others, the rule of temporarily retaining the substantive content of the previous agreement when it is impossible to conclude a new agreement, and the continuing validity of the statutory industry-wide regulations from the previous regime, which are maintained to supplement any regulatory areas not covered by collectively negotiated provisions.

Disputes

The history of industrial relations in Spain, particularly in the period prior to 1936, contains few instances of negotiation or compromise between unions and employers; rather, it features numerous examples of strategies of outright imposition or resistance from the two sides. In a situation of this nature, the stances adopted by the social partners each reflect a mirror image of the other. On the employers' side, the stance is one of totally dominating labour relations, turning the contract of employment into a contract of acceptance and, in the event of a dispute, refusing to make any concessions and continuing to resist until the outcome is either victory or defeat. On the unions' side, likewise, the stance is one of rejecting all idea of compromise between offers and counter-offers, preferring to use 'direct action' as a means of dictating employment and working conditions unilaterally. In Spain, these intransigent attitudes have been inspired or reinforced by an ideological view of industrial conflict, widespread in the traditional labour movement, whereby strikes are regarded as a kind of 'revolutionary training ground', or even as the means of bringing about social revolution or the overthrow of a hostile political regime.

These attitudes and strategies promoted a spasmodic pattern of industrial conflict, usually occurring in a climate of strong tension and public unrest, with prolonged and bitter disputes alternating with equally lengthy lulls and periods of inaction. The difficulty of institutionalizing and regulating strikes and labour disputes in the industrial relations system has been due in no small measure to the lack of an adequate legal channel for them during almost the whole of this period of history.

From 1975 onwards, partly as a result of the changed attitudes of the social partners and partly as a result of the changes in the legal framework, industrial conflict in Spain lost the insurrectional or all-out confrontational ingredients that had so often accompanied it up to 1936, and also the identity of being a struggle against the political regime which was a feature of labour disputes during the second phase of Franco's rule. Nevertheless, labour disputes have not entirely lost their political slant, even though their characteristics and significance may have changed.

The fact is that, with strikes legalized under the labour law system, industrial conflict in recent years has taken the shape that might be expected in the context of a trade union movement which has a small membership and scarce financial resources and is strongly inclined towards representation on public bodies: strikes are brief (and often intermittent); they are usually accompanied by demonstrations or actions to attract the attention of public opinion; and they call more or less explicitly for support or mediation from the labour administration or the political authorities. With industrial conflict taking this shape, it is hardly surprising that it is labour disputes in the public sector that have become particularly important, especially in the public transport sector where strikes have the greatest impact.

In so far as the strategic approach to industrial disputes adopted both by the unions and by the employers pays particular attention to their impact on public opinion and, thereby, on the political process, it may be said that industrial conflict in Spain has a political slant. On the part of the workers, strikes and other forms of industrial action are used both as a financial weapon against the employers and as a political weapon against the public authorities. For their part, the employers or relevant public authorities gear their reaction to concentrating on winning over public opinion because of the harm caused by industrial action affecting essential public services or the general body of consumers.

The political significance of industrial disputes in Spain is also underlined by the fact that, during the years of the formation of the industrial relations system, collective bargaining usually seems to have taken place in a context of social concertation, with the more or less explicit participation of the Government. Up to 1986, these negotiations based on social concertation had varying results, but never led to mobilization of the workers; if they failed, the price in terms of conflict was paid in added difficulties for the collective bargaining process at industry-wide and company level. The crisis in social concertation that erupted in 1987 and 1988 had a very different outcome, and the unions' protest against the Government's economic policy culminated in a resounding episode of industrial conflict: the general strike of 14 December 1988.

The repercussions of that strike on Spain's industrial relations system can already be assessed to some degree. In general terms it can be said that it emphatically marked the end of the system's formative period and of the climate of consensus that accompanied it, initiating a new phase in which the pattern and relationships between Government, parties and unions were beginning to change. From a broader perspective, the 1988 general strike did not result in a complete split between the Socialist Government and the trade union movement as a whole, even though it created major difficulties in their mutual relationships which also became more strained and turbulent than in earlier periods. Significant episodes in these difficult relationships include the 'bilateral' negotiation (excluding the employers' associations) of the 1991 law on union monitoring of contracts of employment; the similarly bilateral negotiation of a draft law on strikes which failed in 1993 just before the final hurdle of parliamentary approval; and the resounding union protests, also expressed in the form of general strikes, against the Decree-Law on cutbacks in unemployment benefits and the formulation of the measures constituting the labour legislation reform of 1994.

Two other features of industrial conflict in Spain should be mentioned in this general account. One is the limited role of the lockout, which under current legislation may be used by employers only in specific circumstances to protect property and people on the work premises; the purpose of this was to put a stop to the spiral of confrontational action and resistance that was mentioned earlier. The other feature is the infrequent use up till now of special independent means of settling labour disputes, such as conciliation, mediation and voluntary arbitration. There is, on the other hand, a long tradition of settling collective 'disputes of rights', for example over the interpretation or application of existing regulations, through the courts. However, there have been signs in recent collective agreements on the matter in various Autonomous Communities that this lack of development of non-jurisdictional means of dispute resolution (clearly influenced by the interventionist tradition) is being overcome. The conclusion at national level in January 1996 of the Agreement on Extrajudicial Dispute Settlement confirms this trend.

State Intervention in Industrial Relations

The ideologies and practices of the social partners (tending on the one side towards 'direct action' and 'social revolution' and on the other towards the 'iron hand' and authoritarianism) did not create an atmosphere propitious to the regulation of labour relations by collective bargaining. In this context, the growing presence of the State made itself felt on two major counts: the passing of protective legislation, with ad hoc mechanisms to ensure its application, and the setting up of a network of corporatist bodies whose members were representatives of the employers' and employees' organizations, chaired by a public official. These bodies were known as joint committees (*comités paritarios*) under Primo de Rivera's dictatorship (1923-1929) and joint councils (*jurados mixtos*) under the Second Republic (1931-1936).

The central role of the State in Spanish industrial relations, which, as we have seen, has persisted despite a succession of political regimes of differing tendencies, reached its peak during the first phase of Franco's rule when the Government, via the Ministry of Labour, took exclusive responsibility for the industry-wide regulation of terms and conditions of employment (the regulations issued were called 'Labour Ordinances' or 'Labour Regulations') and exercised strict control over certain decisions taken by enterprises in connection with staff management, such as the adoption of company rules, changes in employment relationships and dismissals. All this was in addition to the Ministry's power over the official union, the Organización Sindical, in that it controlled its structure and appointed its officials, and its general regulatory powers, which were virtually unrestricted.

The introduction of 'collective agreements', which, in industrial relations, marks the beginning of the second phase of Franco's rule, signified the opening up of certain areas to the collective autonomy of occupational groups. But the prevailing trend was still heavy state intervention. The Ministry of Labour retained its power to regulate employment conditions at industry-wide level, reducing the function of the collective agreement to one of merely improving on the statutory conditions. Legal regulations governed the settlement of disputes, the courts were to hear any cases deriving from the interpretation of collective agreements and, to complete the picture, it must be borne in mind that the higher organs of the State were used with great frequency in the early 1970s to intervene in labour affairs.

However, the period of political transition to democracy saw the beginning of a gradual reduction of administrative intervention in industrial relations and of legislative and official intervention in the regulation of minimum employment conditions. Thus, the power to regulate labour relations at industry-wide level was used only in exceptional cases, although the body of Labour Regulations and Ordinances which had accumulated during the previous regime remained in place, and served to supplement collective agreements, up till the recent labour legislation reforms of 1994 and1997. Similarly, opportunities for the State to regulate employment conditions from the substantive point of view were virtually reserved for the legislators, who used them with restraint. Intervention by the labour authorities in collective labour relations was confined to defining the minimum level of service to be maintained in the event of strikes in essential public services, seeking settlements of collective labour disputes and provisionally controlling the legality of collective agreements.

Yet the recent withdrawal of the State from certain aspects of industrial relations did not imply the disappearance of its central role in this area of society. The labour authorities still have significant powers over labour relations within enterprises, such as authorizing collective dismissals caused by economic difficulties, or general changes in working conditions. Secondly, recourse to the courts is still very frequent in labour relations and influences important issues. Thirdly and most importantly, the suppression of public intervention in some areas has been partly offset by the appearance of intervention of a different kind. This includes social concertation and the promotion of a selective and centralized framework of employee and employer representation.

Since the late 1970s and early 1980s, social concertation, or the joint definition by the Government and the major trade union and employers' confederations of the broad lines of collective bargaining and important aspects of economic and social policy, has enabled the Government to shape the content of collective bargaining to remain within limits that are compatible with its economic objectives. The forerunner to this series of agreements based on social concertation was the 1977 Moncloa Pact, although this was actually a political pact between political factions rather than a true social contract. This preliminary political pact, which included practical compromises as regards pay restraint, was followed by other social contracts or pacts based on social concertation in the true sense, sometimes taking the form of tripartite agreements between the Government, trade unions and employers' organizations (1981), sometimes national multi-industry agreements between representative trade union and employers' confederations (1980, 1983) and sometimes a combination of the two (1984). In addition to this legal role, the Government has always participated fully in initiating and drafting these agreements.

The concessions granted in return for the pay restraint and industrial peace sought by the Government via social contracts have been of various kinds. One has been the influence exerted by the trade unions and employers' associations over labour legislation, which is clearly perceptible in the Workers' Statute and the Trade Union Freedom Act (1985), which allowed the establishment of trade union branches within enterprises. Another is their participation in determining economic and social policy, hard evidence of which can be seen in the consultations preceding the submission to Parliament of draft state budgets and the passing of regulations governing employment policy. A third is the right granted to the most representative trade unions and employers' associations to be represented on the constituent bodies of the social administration and part of the economic administration.

The State's principal means of promoting such a framework of representation have been the granting by law of 'special status' to the most representative unions, and the legislators' choice of certain criteria of representativeness with a view to producing precisely the effects of selection and centralization. By virtue of their special status, the most representative unions have succeeded in securing the main advantages and powers granted by law to the trade unions, ranging from the negotiation of statutory collective agreements to a preferential entitlement to funds from the *patrimonio sindical acumulado*. As a result of all this, in certain sectors and occupations, designation as 'most representative' has become a condition of survival in the trade union market. By virtue of the criteria of representativeness chosen by the legislators, unions that are members of the major national confederations have automatic access to this special status, while those that are not confederated or are not members of other confederations must have won over 10 per cent of places on the unitary representative bodies in the sector or district in question.

Prospects and Conclusions

Now that we have analysed the development and elements of the industrial relations system in Spain, it may be appropriate in this final section to attempt to give a general description of the system, summarizing its salient features. These are, in the author's opinion:

1) the rapid, state-assisted creation, at the end of the Franco regime, of the various elements of the system: representative bodies, bargaining practices and intervention by the authorities;

2) the fact that being a 'voters' trade unionism' rather than a 'members' trade unionism' naturally governs the activities of the unions in relation to the workers; and

3) the interconnection of action by the State (labour legislation, management of public social services) and by the employers' and employees' organizations (collective negotiation of conditions of employment), the most conspicuous illustration of which is social concertation, though it is also reflected in other aspects.

These three features may be supplemented by a fourth: the relative weakness of the representative function performed by the unions and employers' associations at industry-wide level, which are restricted from above by the significant powers of the national confederations and from below by the tradition of the enterprise as the centre of negotiating activity.

The rapid formation of the industrial relations system was made possible by re-establishing institutions and organizations dating from previous political regimes on to new legal bases of freedom of association and the autonomy of the social partners. Inevitably, the bodies representing employers and workers played a very important role in this process, having to undertake the task of both reconciling interests and constructing or reconstructing their own organizational structures. We must not, however, forget the strategic intervention by the State in the development of the industrial relations system, establishing ground rules which facilitated the rapid creation of the system and implementing a clearly selective policy on representation. By 1997, after numerous 'union elections' and continuing collective bargaining, the system was certainly well established, though there were some worrying signs of bureaucratization.

One of the reasons for the rapid formation of the industrial relations system in Spain (and, within the system, of the framework of representation) was, as stated earlier, the repeatedly good results won by the major confederations in the elections of workers' delegates and workers' committees. But the function of 'union elections' in the system as a whole extends beyond this contribution to clarifying the trade union scenario. These elections have also made it possible to build a strong, stable bridge between the trade unions and the unitary bodies representing the entire workforce within enterprises and workplaces. Yet another function of these elections has perhaps been even more important: that of legitimizing the position of some unions whose broad institutional powers contrast with their small memberships.

In seeking a name for a trade union situation such as that described here, the one that seems to be the most appropriate is 'voters' trade unionism', since this underlines the significance of electoral results in the union context, and at the same time suggests the blurring or disappearance of the importance of union membership. This replacement of a 'members' trade unionism' by a 'voters' trade unionism' is also reflected in two other important elements of the labour relations system: the generalized applicability of collective agreements irrespective of union membership, and the restrictions on union security arrangements (the closed shop, collective bargaining levy, etc). Irrespective of the primary purpose they fulfil, these regulations have had the secondary effect of inhibiting two of the main incentives for individual union membership: pressure from the union side through collective bargaining and the worker's interest in the financial returns of union membership. With a legal framework of this kind, the motives for union membership are reduced (in the absence of any real pressure from the peer group, which is effective only in highly unionized work environments) to ideological affinity or the actual holding of representative office. It is therefore not surprising that, in Spain, only officials, activists and workforce representatives within enterprises tend to be trade union members.

The assistance provided by the State to help the industrial relations organizations rapidly to re-establish themselves carried the more or less explicit price of their collaboration in consolidating the new democratic regime and seeking a way out of the economic crisis. With the coming to power of a Socialist Government, this trading of assistance and collaboration between the State and the main employers' and employees' organizations turned into an exchange of influences in their respective areas of activity. The State has conceded financial advantages and participation in its decisions on social and economic matters; the representative bodies have until now consented, with varying degrees of difficulty, to bring their approach into line with the Government's economic objectives.

Nobody can guarantee that this relationship of 'political' exchange between the State and the industrial relations organizations will last in the medium or long term. There are, however, strong objective reasons in favour of its continuation, including the historical tradition of representation on public bodies, the advantages of industrial peace and the financially weak position of the unions. That is probably why social dialogue and social concertation on specific issues have been maintained up till now, without any special difficulties, with the centre-right Government that was formed after the 1996 election.

One last feature which can be pointed out in this description of Spain's industrial relations system is the relative insignificance of the industry-wide level of collective bargaining, whose field of action seems to be squeezed between national agreements based on social concertation and the mass of company-level agreements. The reasons for this relative lack of bargaining activity at industry-wide level have included, in particular, the absence of any connection or coordination between industry-wide agreements and company-level agreements, an absence which, until the labour legislation reforms of 1994 and 1997, was offset by the continuing validity of the body of Labour Regulations and Ordinances dating from the previous regime. The effect of all these factors on collective bargaining is the virtual reduction of the field of application of industry-wide agreements to small and medium-sized enterprises and the frequent limitation of their content to the regulation of basic conditions of employment (pay levels, working hours, etc).

The relative insignificance of the industry-wide level of collective bargaining is also reflected in terms of representative bodies, in that the industrial unions and federations are very much in the background in comparison with the confederations and the enterprise-level representative bodies. A similar phenomenon might have been expected to affect employers' organizations, to parallel this overshadowing of the industry-wide level in trade union organizations. Yet this has not happened, probably because of the importance of the industry-wide level in relations between the employers' associations and the public authorities.

Further Reading

Alcaide Castro, M., González Rendón, M. and Flórez Saborido, I., *Mercado de trabajo, reclutamiento y formación en España*, Madrid, Pirámide, 1996.

Alonso Olea, M., *Introducción al derecho del trabajo*, 5th edition, Madrid, Civitas, 1994.

Alvarez Aledo, C., *El impacto de la contratación temporal sobre el sistema productivo español. Relaciones entre segmentación laboral y productiva*, Madrid, CES, 1996.

Amsden, J., *Collective Bargaining and Class Conflict in Spain*, London, Weidenfeld and Nicolson, 1972.

Barrada Rodríguez, A. and Gonzalo González, B., *La financiación de la protección social en España. A propósito del Pacto de Toledo*, Madrid, CES, 1997.

Cavas Martínez, F., *Las relaciones laborales en el sector agrario*, Madrid, Ministerio de la Agricultura, 1995.

Claver, E., Gascó, J.L., and Llopis, J., *Los recursos humanos en la empresa: un enfoque directivo*, Madrid, Civitas, 1995.

Fernández Steinko, A., *Continuidad y ruptura en la modernización industrial en España*, Madrid, CES, 1997.

Herce, J.A. and Pérez Díaz, V., *La reforma del sistema público de pensiones en España*, Barcelona, La Caixa, 1996.

Monereo Pérez, J.L. (ed.), *La reforma del mercado de trabajo y de la seguridad y salud laboral*, Granada, Universidad de Granada, 1996.

Moreno, G. and Rodríguez, J.M., *La participación laboral feminina y la distribución salarial en España*, Madrid, CES, 1996.

Ojeda Avilés (ed.), *La concertación social tras la crisis*, Barcelona, Ariel, 1990.

Pérez Amorós, F., *Derechos de información sobre empleo y contratación*, Barcelona, Bosch, 1993.

Valdés Dal-Ré, F. (ed.), *Sindicalismo y cambios sociales*, Madrid, CES, 1994.

Appendices

Table 1. *Key employment indicators (1996)*

Total

	Austria	Belgium	Denmark	Finland	France	Germany	Greece	Ireland	Italy	Luxem-bourg	Nether-lands	Portugal	Spain	Sweden	UK	European Union
Total population (000)	8061	10157	5263	5125	58375	81923	10475	3629	57399	416	15528	9928	39270	8841	58784	373173
Population of working-age (15-64) (000)	5314	6695	3512	3384	36968	55042	6796	2324	38978	277	10509	6728	26253	5636	37511	245927
Total employment (000)	3710	3791	2652	2087	22287	34465	3868	1308	20037	219	6846	4443	12396	3963	26177	148249
Annual change in employment (%)	-1.3	-0.1	1.3	1.4	0.0	-1.1	1.2	3.6	0.5	2.6	2.1	0.7	2.9	-0.6	0.9	0.4
Employment rate (% working-age population)	69.8	56.6	75.5	61.7	60.3	62.6	56.9	56.3	51.4	59.6	65.1	66.0	47.2	70.3	69.8	60.3
FTE employment rate* (% working-age population)	65.0	52.5	67.1	58.3	55.9	56.9	55.5	52.6	50.0	57.4	51.5	63.8	45.1	63.2	59.3	55.0
Self-employed (% total employment)	14.4	15.4	8.3	15.1	11.3	9.6	33.7	19.8	24.8	9.1	11.2	26.8	21.5	11.7	12.6	15.0
Employed part-time (% total employment)	14.9	14.0	21.5	11.6	16.0	16.5	5.3	11.6	6.6	7.9	38.1	8.7	8.0	24.5	24.6	16.4
Employed on fixed-term contracts (%)	8.0	5.9	11.2	17.3	12.6	11.1	11.0	9.2	7.5	2.6	12.0	10.6	33.6	11.8	7.1	11.8
Share of employment in agriculture (%)	7.4	2.7	3.9	7.9	4.8	2.9	20.3	11.3	6.7	2.4	3.8	12.7	8.6	3.3	2.0	5.1

Table 1 (continued)

Total

	Austria	Belgium	Denmark	Finland	France	Germany	Greece	Ireland	Italy	Luxembourg	Netherlands	Portugal	Spain	Sweden	UK	European Union
Share of employment in industry (%)	30.3	27.6	26.4	27.1	26.5	35.3	22.9	27.3	32.2	23.0	22.9	32.9	29.4	25.9	27.5	29.8
Share of employment in services (%)	62.3	69.6	69.7	65.0	68.6	61.8	56.8	61.4	61.1	74.5	73.3	54.5	62.0	70.9	70.6	65.1
Activity rate (% working-age population)	72.9	62.8	81.1	72.8	68.8	68.9	63.0	63.8	58.4	61.6	69.6	71.2	60.6	78.1	76.0	67.7
Total unemployed (000)	165.5	410.2	194.6	376.1	3146.3	3465.5	411.8	173.8	2732.6	5.6	467.3	348.1	3523.7	439.3	2346.8	18176
Unemployment rate (%)	4.4	9.8	6.9	15.4	12.4	8.9	9.6	11.8	12.0	3.3	6.3	7.3	22.1	10.0	8.2	10.9
Youth unemployed (% labour force 15-24)	6.0	22.9	10.6	38.2	28.9	9.6	31.0	18.1	33.5	9.1	11.5	16.7	41.9	21.1	15.5	21.8
Long-term unemployment (% unemployed)	25.7	61.2	26.6	35.9	38.3	47.8	56.7	59.6	65.6	na	49.0	53.0	52.9	19.1	39.8	48.2
15-19 year olds in education/training (%)	81.6	93.8	81.5	86.7	92.9	92.0	80.4	82.2	74.9	88.3	81.3	76.2	80.7	76.2	70.9	82.5
20-24 year olds in education/training (%)	32.3	41.4	48.5	49.2	42.4	37.0	30.2	28.0	35.3	34.2	48.4	40.5	44.6	27.7	23.8	37.0

Source: Adapted from *Employment in Europe 1997*,
produced by DG V Unit A.1 in the European Commission
(Luxembourg, Office for Official Publications of the EC) Tables pp. 117-132

* FTE = full-time equivalent

Table 2. Key employment indicators (1996)

Men

	Austria	Belgium	Denmark	Finland	France	Germany	Greece	Ireland	Italy	Luxem-bourg	Nether-lands	Portugal	Spain	Sweden	UK	European Union
Total population (000)	3911	4965	2599	2496	28423	39886	5170	1802	27849	204	7680	4781	19215	4368	28815	182164
Population of working-age (15-64) (000)	2659	3373	1774	1707	18207	27765	3271	1168	19310	140	5331	3247	12977	2864	18886	122679
Total employment (000)	2098	2269	1460	1089	12381	19798	2467	807	12844	139	4035	2461	8062	2051	14423	86384
Annual change in employment (%)	-1.7	-0.2	0.8	2.6	-0.2	-1.7	0.7	2.4	-0.2	1.1	2.0	0.7	2.2	-0.9	0.5	0.0
Employment rate (% working-age population)	78.9	67.3	82.3	63.8	68.0	71.3	75.4	69.1	66.5	75.0	75.7	75.8	62.1	71.6	76.4	70.4
FTE employment rate (% working-age population)	77.3	66.2	76.3	61.4	66.4	69.6	74.4	67.3	65.9	74.8	68.9	74.5	61.0	67.3	72.5	68.3
Self-employed (% total employment)	14.5	18.7	11.7	19.9	15.1	12.3	41.8	27.0	29.2	10.5	13.2	28.9	24.1	16.9	17.1	18.9
Employed part-time (% total employment)	4.2	3.0	10.8	7.9	5.2	3.8	3.3	5.0	3.1	1.9	17.0	5.1	3.1	8.9	8.1	5.5
Employed on fixed-term contracts (%)	8.1	4.5	10.8	14.1	11.5	11.0	10.5	7.1	6.6	1.5	9.1	10.2	31.9	10.1	6.0	11.0
Share of employment in agriculture (%)	6.5	3.1	5.3	9.9	5.9	3.2	18.2	15.9	6.8	2.9	4.8	12.0	9.8	4.7	2.6	5.7

Table 2 (continued)

Men

	Austria	Belgium	Denmark	Finland	France	Germany	Greece	Ireland	Italy	Luxembourg	Netherlands	Portugal	Spain	Sweden	UK	European Union
Share of employment in industry (%)	41.6	37.3	35.6	39.2	36.2	47.1	28.1	34.2	38.1	32.4	32.1	41.6	37.9	38.8	38.5	39.5
Share of employment in services (%)	51.9	59.6	59.1	51.0	57.9	49.7	53.7	49.9	55.1	64.8	63.1	46.4	52.3	56.5	58.9	54.7
Activity rate (% working-age population)	81.8	72.8	87.1	74.9	76.0	77.9	80.3	78.1	73.4	76.9	79.7	81.0	75.3	80.1	84.5	78.0
Total unemployed (000)	77.8	186.6	84.8	189.8	1454.0	1819.2	158.1	105.4	1330.5	2.7	215.0	169.5	1713.6	241.8	1528.6	9277
Unemployment rate (%)	3.7	7.6	5.6	15.0	10.6	8.2	6.0	11.6	9.4	2.5	5.0	6.5	17.5	10.5	9.5	9.6
Youth unemployed (% labour force 15-24)	5.0	19.4	8.8	37.4	26.0	10.3	21.4	18.9	29.2	9.9	10.8	14.3	36.2	21.7	18.0	20.6
Long-term unemployment (% unemployed)	23.5	59.1	28.2	40.4	36.4	44.5	47.1	64.8	64.1	na	53.7	51.3	45.9	21.3	45.9	46.3
15-19 year olds in education/training (%)	83.7	93.1	82.0	87.8	92.2	91.8	81.8	79.6	73.8	89.4	81.1	74.3	78.5	76.6	71.9	82.0
20-24 year olds in education/training (%)	35.3	39.8	48.5	46.5	40.9	38.0	28.7	27.5	32.6	37.5	52.0	35.5	39.1	26.7	24.7	35.7

Source: Adapted from *Employment in Europe 1997,*
produced by DG V Unit A.1 in the European Commission
(Luxembourg, Office for Official Publications of the EC) Tables pp. 117-132

Table 3. *Key employment indicators (1996)*

Women

	Austria	Belgium	Denmark	Finland	France	Germany	Greece	Ireland	Italy	Luxembourg	Netherlands	Portugal	Spain	Sweden	UK	European Union
Total population (000)	4150	5191	2665	2628	29952	42036	5305	1828	29549	212	7848	5147	20055	4473	29969	191008
Population of working-age (15-64) (000)	2656	3325	1738	1677	18763	27277	3527	1156	19668	137	5178	3482	13276	2773	18625	123258
Total employment (000)	1612	1522	1192	998	9906	14667	1401	501	7193	80	2811	1982	4334	1912	11754	61866
Annual change in employment (%)	-0.8	0.2	2.0	0.0	0.3	-0.4	2.2	5.7	1.7	5.4	2.3	0.6	4.4	-0.3	1.5	1.0
Employment rate (% working-age population)	60.7	45.8	68.6	59.5	52.8	53.8	39.7	43.3	36.6	43.8	54.3	56.9	32.6	69.0	63.1	50.2
FTE employment rate (% working-age population)	52.6	39.1	58.1	55.5	46.2	44.1	38.1	38.5	34.7	40.0	34.1	53.8	29.5	56.8	47.0	42.1
Self-employed (% total employment)	14.3	10.4	4.2	9.8	6.6	6.1	19.4	8.2	16.9	6.7	8.2	24.2	16.7	6.1	7.0	9.5
Employed part-time (% total employment)	28.8	30.6	34.6	15.7	29.5	33.6	8.9	22.2	12.7	18.3	68.5	13.1	17.0	41.8	44.8	31.6
Employed on fixed-term contracts (%)	7.9	8.0	11.8	20.5	13.9	11.2	11.9	11.8	8.9	3.1	15.9	11.1	36.7	13.4	8.2	12.7
Share of employment in agriculture (%)	8.6	2.2	2.1	5.7	3.5	2.6	23.9	3.8	6.4	1.7	2.3	13.5	6.4	1.7	1.2	4.2

Table 3 (continued)

Women

	Austria	Belgium	Denmark	Finland	France	Germany	Greece	Ireland	Italy	Luxembourg	Netherlands	Portugal	Spain	Sweden	UK	European Union
Share of employment in industry (%)	15.6	13.3	15.1	13.9	14.4	19.5	13.7	16.2	21.7	6.7	9.6	22.0	13.6	12.1	13.9	16.3
Share of employment in services (%)	75.8	84.6	82.8	80.3	82.0	77.9	62.4	80.0	72.0	91.7	88.1	64.5	79.9	86.2	85.0	79.6
Activity rate (% working-age population)	64.0	52.5	74.9	70.6	61.8	59.8	46.9	49.3	43.7	45.9	59.2	62.1	46.3	76.1	67.5	57.4
Total unemployed (000)	87.7	223.6	109.8	186.3	1692.3	1646.3	253.6	68.5	1402.1	2.9	252.3	178.6	1810.1	197.5	818.2	8930
Unemployment rate (%)	5.3	12.8	8.5	15.8	14.7	9.8	15.3	12.0	16.4	4.7	8.2	8.3	29.5	9.4	6.5	12.5
Youth unemployed (% labour force 15-24)	7.1	27.2	12.6	39.0	32.1	8.8	41.1	17.2	38.9	8.2	12.2	19.9	48.7	20.4	12.5	23.3
Long-term unemployment (% unemployed)	29.1	63.0	25.0	31.0	39.8	51.7	62.6	51.5	67.1	na	45.3	54.7	59.6	16.0	28.1	50.2
15-19 year olds in education/training (%)	79.4	94.6	81.0	85.6	93.6	92.1	79.1	85.0	76.0	87.2	81.5	78.2	83.0	75.8	69.8	83.0
20-24 year olds in education/training (%)	29.3	43.0	48.5	52.1	43.7	36.0	31.4	28.6	37.9	30.8	44.8	45.5	50.2	28.7	22.8	38.2

Source: Adapted from *Employment in Europe 1997*,
produced by DG V Unit A.1 in the European Commission
(Luxembourg, Office for Official Publications of the EC) Tables pp. 117-132

Table 4. *Trade union membership*

	Year	Union membership (thousands)	Year	Union membership (thousands)	Change in membership (%)
Austria	1995	1287	1985	1404	−8.3
Belgium	1995	1585	1985	1499	5.8
Denmark	1994	1808	1985	1730	4.5
Finland	1995	1377	1985	1411	−2.4
France	1995	1758	1985	2555	−31.2
Germany	1995	9300	1991	11676	−20.3
Former Germ. Dem. Rep.	1993	2681	1991	3428	−21.8
Former Germ. Fed. Rep.	1993	7654	1985	8127	−5.8
Greece	1995	500	1985	650	−23.1
Ireland	1993	437	1985	449	−2.6
Italy	1994	6392	1985	6860	−6.8
Luxembourg	1995	85	1987	75	13.3
Netherlands	1995	1540	1985	1290	19.3
Portugal	1995	800	1986	1434	−44.2
Spain	1994	1606	1985	835	92.3
Sweden	1994	3180	1985	3341	−4.8
United Kingdom	1995	7280	1985	9739	−25.2

Source: World Labour Report 1997-98, Geneva, International Labour Organization, 1997.

Table 5. *Trade union density (%)*

	Year	Union membership as a percentage of:		Year	Union membership as a percentage of:	
		Non-agricultural labour force	Wage and salary earners		Non-agricultural labour force	Wage and salary earners
Austria	1995	36.6	41.2	1985	51.7	51.0
Belgium	1995	38.1	51.9	1985	42.0	52.0
Denmark	1994	68.2	80.1	1985	67.4	78.3
Finland	1995	59.7	79.3	1985	61.4	68.3
France	1995	6.1	9.1	1985	11.6	14.5
Germany	1995	29.6	28.9	1991	30.7	35.0
Former German Dem. Rep.	1993	34.1	42.4	1991	41.1	46.2
Former German Fed. Rep.	1993	24.5	29.1	1985	29.5	35.3
Greece	1995	15.4	24.3	1985	23.5	36.7
Ireland	1993	36.0	48.9	1985	41.0	56.0
Italy	1994	30.6	44.1	1985	32.9	47.6
Luxembourg	1995	39.5	43.4	1987	48.0	53.0
Netherlands	1995	21.8	25.6	1985	23.3	28.7
Portugal	1995	18.8	25.6	1986	40.6	51.4
Spain	1994	11.4	18.6	1985	7.3	11.5
Sweden	1994	77.2	91.1	1985	79.3	83.8
United Kingdom	1995	26.2	32.9	1985	36.0	45.5

Source: World Labour Report 1997-98, Geneva, International Labour Organization, 1997.

Table 6. *Change in trade union density (%)*

	Period	Union membership as a percentage of:				Trend[*]
		Non-agricultural labour force		Wage and salary earners		
		Change in density				
		In points	In %	In points	In %	
Austria	85-95	−15.1	−29.2	−9.8	−19.2	-
Belgium	85-95	−3.9	−9.2	−0.1	−0.2	=
Denmark	85-94	0.8	1.2	1.8	2.3	=
Finland	85-95	−1.7	−2.8	11.0	16.1	+
France	85-95	−5.5	−47.4	−5.4	−37.2	--
Germany	91-95	−1.1	−3.5	−6.1	−17.6	--
Former German Dem. Rep.	91-93	−7.1	−17.2	−3.8	−8.3	--
Former German Fed. Rep.	85-93	−4.9	−16.8	−6.2	−17.4	--
Greece	85-95	−8.1	−34.5	−12.4	−33.8	--
Ireland	85-93	−5.0	−12.3	−7.1	−12.6	-
Italy	85-94	−2.3	−7.0	−3.5	−7.4	-
Luxembourg	87-95	−8.5	−17.7	−9.6	−18.1	--
Netherlands	85-95	−1.6	−6.7	−3.2	−11.0	-.
Portugal	86-95	−21.8	−53.7	−25.8	−50.2	--
Spain	85-94	4.1	56.2	7.1	62.1	++
Sweden	85-94	−2.1	−2.7	7.3	8.7	+
United Kingdom	85-95	−9.8	−27.2	−12.6	27.7	--

[*] Trend in union density rate is calculated for wage and salary earners.
Key for trend symbols: ++ Change in union density rate is larger than +20 per cent;
    +   Change in union density rate is larger than +5 per cent, but not larger than +20 per cent;
    -- Change in union density rate is larger than −20 per cent;
    -   Change in union density rate is larger than −5 per cent, but not larger than −20 per cent;
    =   Change in union density rate is not larger than +/−5 per cent. The trend is calculated on the basis of a 10-year period. If the number of years is shorter, trend scores are adjusted accordingly.
Source: World Labour Report 1997-98, Geneva, International Labour Organization, 1997.

Table 7. *Number of strikes and lockouts**

	1980	1985	1990	1991	1992	1993	1994	1995
Austria	9	4	9	9	3	3	0	1
Belgium	–	–	33	62	49	28	30	46
Denmark	225	820	232	203	151	218	240	424
Finland	2182	833	450	270	165	125	171	112
France	2118	1901	1529	1318	1330	1351	1671	
Germany	–	–	–	–	–	–	–	–
Greece	726	453	480	161	824	596	215	110
Ireland	130	116	49	54	38	46	28	34
Italy	2238	1341	1094	791	903	1054	861	545
Luxembourg	–	0	1	0	0	0	–	–
Netherlands	22	45	29	28	23	12	17	14
Portugal	269	476	271	262	409	230	300	–
Spain	2103	1092	1312	1645	1360	1209	908	883
Sweden	212	160	126	23	20	33	–	–
United Kingdom	–	–	–	–	–	–	205	235

* Readers should refer to the source, the *World Labour Report 1997-98* (Geneva, ILO),
  for definitions.

Table 8. *Workers involved in strikes and lockouts (thousands)**

	1980	1985	1990	1991	1992	1993	1994	1995
Austria	24	36	5	93	18	7	0	0
Belgium	–	–	10	11	22	9	6	13
Denmark	62	581	37	38	33	59	37	124
Finland	407	170	207	128	103	23	71	127
France	501	23	19	19	16	20	–	–
Germany	**8451	**781	**257	**208	**598	133	401	183
Greece	1408	786	1304	477	243	182	74	52
Ireland	31	169	10	18	13	13	5	32
Italy	13825	4843	1634	2952	3178	4384	2614	445
Luxembourg	–	0	1	0	– 0	0	–	–
Netherlands	26	23	25	42	52	21	22	55
Portugal	290	199	129	119	132	83	94	–
Spain	2287	1511	977	1984	5192	1077	5437	574
Sweden	747	125	73	3	18	29	22	125
United Kingdom	834	791	298	176	148	385	107	174

* Readers should refer to the source, the *World Labour Report 1997-98* (Geneva, ILO),
  for definitions.
** Refers to former Federal Republic of Germany.

Table 9. *Workdays not worked as a result of strikes and lockouts (thousands)**

	1980	1985	1990	1991	1992	1993	1994	1995
Austria	17	23	9	58	23	13	0	0
Belgium	-	-	103	67	199	55	71	100
Denmark	-	-	98	70	63	114	75	197
Finland	-	-	935	458	76	17	526	869
France	1523	727	528	497	359	511	521	-
Germany	**128	**355	**364	**154	**1545	593	229	247
Greece	2907	1094	23441	5840	2830	1602	666	450
Ireland	412	418	223	86	191	61	26	130
Italy	16457	3831	5181	2985	2737	3411	3374	909
Luxembourg	-	0	0	0	0	0	-	-
Netherlands	57	89	207	96	85	45	47	691
Portugal	533	275	147	124	190	80	97	-
Spain	6178	3224	2613	4537	6333	2141	6277	1457
Sweden	4479	504	770	22	28	190	52	627
United Kingdom	11964	6402	1903	761	528	649	278	415

* Readers should refer to the source, the *World Labour Report 1997-98* (Geneva, ILO), for
definitions.
** Refers to former Federal Republic of Germany.

Table 10. *Collective bargaining structure in selected countries**

	Bargaining levels over past 10 years N/S, C	Dominant levels over past 10 years N/S, C	Trend over past 10 years NS C	
Austria	N/S, C	N/S	s	i
Belgium	N/S, C	N/S	s	i
Denmark	N/S, C	N/S	s	i
Finland	N/S, C	N/S, C	s	i
France	N/S, C	N/S	s	i
Germany	N/S, C	N/S	s	i
Greece	N/S, C	N/S	d	i
Ireland	N/S, C	C	i	s
Italy	N/S, C	N/S	s	i
Netherlands	N/S, C	N/S	s	i
Portugal	N/S, C	N/S	i	i
Spain	N/S, C	N/S	i	i
Sweden	N/S, C	N/S	s	i
United Kingdom	N/S, C	C	d	i

* Readers should refer to the source, the *World Labour Report 1997-98* (Geneva, ILO), for
further details.

N/S	=	National/sectoral level
C	=	Company/plant level
d	=	Decrease
i	=	Increase
s	=	Stable